ATTENTIONAL DEFICIT DISORDER IN CHILDREN AND ADOLESCENTS

ATTENTIONAL DEFICIT DISORDER IN CHILDREN AND ADOLESCENTS

By

JACK L. FADELY, ED.D.

Department of Special Education and Educational Psychology
College of Education
Butler University
Indianapolis, Indiana

and

VIRGINIA N. HOSLER, M.S.

Diagnostic Learning Center
Peoria Public Schools
Peoria, Illinois

CHARLES C THOMAS • PUBLISHER
Springfield • Illinois • U.S.A.

Published and Distributed Throughout the World by

CHARLES C THOMAS • PUBLISHER

2600 South First Street

Springfield, Illinois 62794-9265

© *1992 by* CHARLES C THOMAS • PUBLISHER

ISBN 0-398-05792-3

Library of Congress Catalog Card Number: 92-340

With THOMAS BOOKS *careful attention is given to all details of manufacturing
and design. It is the Publisher's desire to present books that are satisfactory as to
their physical qualities and artistic possibilities and appropriate for their particular
use.* THOMAS BOOKS *will be true to those laws of quality that assure a good
name and good will.*

Printed in the United States of America
SC-R-3

Library of Congress Cataloging-in-Publication Data

Fadely, Jack L., 1934.
  Attentional deficit disorder in children and adolescents / by Jack
L. Fadely and Virginia N. Hosler.
     p.   cm.
  Includes bibliographical references and index.
  ISBN 0-398-05792-3 (cloth)
  1. Attention-deficit hyperactivity disorder. I. Hosler, Virginia
N., 1943–   . II. Title.
  [DNLM: 1. Attention Deficit Disorder with Hyperactivity—in
adolescence. 2. Attention Deficit Disorder with Hyperactivity—in
infancy & childhood. WS 350.6 F144a].
RJ506.H9F33   1992
618.92'8589—dc20
DNLM/DLC
for Library of Congress   92-340
                                                                                    CIP

PREFACE

Historically, learning disabilities in children and adolescents have been recognized more than 25 years in the United States and at this time are still an uncertain and poorly defined phenomenon. Recognized disorders range from obvious language deficits, motoric and spatial difficulties, to learning deficits, and behavioral disorders. Clinical tests, psychological and neurological, can demonstrate specific deficits which account for the learning problem. But often, perhaps usually, such definite and measurable developmental or learning deficits are not evident and thus require school professionals to assume the child has a learning disability. There is little doubt that equal educational opportunity for each child is an important legal and moral belief, but frustrating conflicts have arisen in the definition of the learning disabilities phenomenon.

The current trend in acceptance of theories surrounding the attention deficit disorder (ADD/ADHD) promises to bring additional confusion and controversy to special needs in children. School personnel throughout the country are embracing the concept of medication for such children as a major treatment strategy. In clinical research with ADD children it is evident in repeated studies that there is little more understanding of ADD than there was of learning disabilities in 1965. The ADD movement is of particular concern for special education professionals nationally due to the pressure that ADD become part of services provided in special education.

Surprisingly, little research exists from within the school environment relative to the education and management of the ADD child in the classroom. Most research comes from psychologists, neurologists, and other medical professionals, which is difficult to translate into school services. Our task and concern in this book on ADD is the establishment of a tentative bridge between clinical research and classroom application. To that end we will review recent research in ADD and from this attempt to formulate at least a general definition of ADD for school purposes.

The current controversy regarding the definition in the DSM–III (Diagnostic and Statistical Manual of Mental Disorders) and that in the DSM–IIIR (Revised) centers around the elimination of the term ADD (without hyperactivity) toward a single definition of ADHD (Attention Deficit/Hyperactivity Disorder). ADD research is gaining significant attention and investment throughout the world and the concepts and theories vary from country to country. The United States is leading in the use of medication as a treatment while psychiatric professionals in Europe have less interest in or use of medication as a primary treatment strategy.

A review of current research will demonstrate how tentative agreement is concerning both the definition and treatment of ADD. It is important to approach and understand the differences between ADD and ADHD which have been accepted within many schools as clinical syndromes with two distinct categories. But, as mentioned, clinicians are involved in rapidly changing viewpoints while school personnel accept definitions and criteria which may, within a year or two, no longer have clinical validity.

Specifically, it is imperative that a developmental viewpoint is offered to educators which includes specific differences in how children learn and how impulsivity and attentional difficulties may reflect needs other than ADD. Before accepting a fading concept of ADD, school psychologists, teachers, and other school support personnel need to take an aggressive stance on developing their own theories and definitions. To withdraw from this challenge will assure that, as in the case of learning disabilities, a definition and expectation from clinicians and parents will be imposed on the schools from without.

In the United States where ADD is primarily treated through medication and secondarily through behavioral modification and management strategies, educators are currently accepting both the definition and management approaches without internal conceptualization and strategies within the classroom. Neither medication nor behavioral management strategies are new to educators as both were primary in the treatment of behavioral disorders and hyperactivity during the 1970s and 1980s. They have not, as will be shown through clinical research, been entirely nor, in many cases, even minimally successful.

In recent years there has been an increasingly strong inclination in clinical research to include the more psychiatric parameters of conduct disorders with the ADHD definition. School professionals have long struggled with definitions of programming for emotional disturbance and conduct disorders in children. Combining ADHD with conduct disorders could bring even more difficulties for school personnel. This problem must be addressed quickly before even more difficult programming issues arise.

The major direction in research in ADHD is that of understanding the etiology of the proposed disorder while treatment, other than medication, is secondary. Our stance in this book is that once an acceptable definition is established clinically, it is the professional responsibility of educators to determine skills and management strategies within the classroom. A major problem in the initial development of the learning disabilities field was that of medical and clinical professionals attempting to intervene in the educational and behavioral management of the classroom. It didn't work! The ADHD phenomenon promises to place educators in the same position.

Special education professionals throughout the country are finding increasingly aggressive litigation instigated by parents which attempts to legally determine both the needs and educational practices implemented with children in the area of learning disabilities. One cannot fault the parents for their efforts to assist their children in obtaining equal educational opportunities. Yet school professionals feel a pressure to give in to the demands of individual children which may deteriorate the quality of overall services for all children. There is, in this regard, something of a crisis in special education at a time when all school programming is under attack with available funds shrinking rapidly.

In this climate it is important to look at ADHD and available research from the viewpoint of the classroom teacher and the parent. The family physician, pediatrician, and family practice specialist are in extremely difficult positions. On one hand they are being besieged by anxious and frustrated parents seeking medication for their overly active children, while on the other hand they have the problem of determining both the efficacy of the ADHD diagnosis and obtaining the needed cooperation at school. There is little doubt that monitoring the medication of a child is difficult enough in the hectic world of the physician without the additional expectations that he or she will advise educational institutions on behavioral management. This book will be important for the frontline medical professional as well as parents and educators.

As authors of this review and analysis we recognize the tremendous complexity of issues involved and the impossibility, considering the research, of bringing some sort of final definition to the notion of ADHD. Yet, in light of the need for a voice from within the field of special education, we will offer both data and viewpoints for the consideration of educators. Our own orientation and theory has been gleaned from private practice in developmental and learning psychology, university teacher preparation, and classroom instruction with seriously involved children.

CONTENTS

ATTENTIONAL DEFICIT DISORDER IN CHILDREN AND ADOLESCENTS

Chapter One

HISTORICAL PERSPECTIVES

Estimates of the incidence of ADHD, Attentional Deficit Hyperactivity Disorder, vary significantly from report to report, from agency to agency, from year to year, and are subject to the differences in the data gathering process. The promise, in the coming decade, is that increasing numbers of children and adolescents will be identified as schools now recognize that although ADHD is a category of special needs most do not include it in special education services. While the results of clinical research will hopefully take us toward an understanding of this disorder, at the same time there is a ground swell of interest and grasping of the present notions by educators, psychologists, social workers, and other mental health and educational professionals. There are a number of commonly accepted criteria which appear to define this disorder. But also there are a number of less accepted criteria and concepts which, though accepted in earlier definitions, are no longer part of the emerging theory. There is then a range of perceptions and beliefs about ADHD. Popular myths and beliefs exist in the public mind, others in education, and additional ones in clinical settings. Yet, for those who are working in basic research, concepts are less clear. This is an uncomfortable environment for the mental health of children. In some environments labelling children with the ADHD classification could be less than responsible and used as a means of scapegoating particular children who are unmanageable, or at the very least, to dismiss children with important needs as simply hyperactive and in need of medication.

There is a great distance between the clinical interpretation of the psychological or medical parameters of a particular disorder and the understanding often accepted in the popular literature by parents and teachers. In the early years of the learning disabilities movement there was a significant amount of confusion and misinformation regarding the exact nature of specific learning disabilities. The initial descriptions and criteria used in that field spawned a host of professional disagreements, parental outrage, as well as poorly defined and managed programs. The ADHD phenomenon is already creating the same problems and concerns among many of us working directly with parents and schools. In the last two years, armed with the typical list of eight to fourteen criteria, our clinic is seeing an increasing number of parents who have been referred to their family physician for the purpose of obtaining medication for their children. Unfortunately, the referral is often by a teacher who has diagnosed the child as ADHD. Many teachers, having one child who is receiving medication with excellent results, become advocates of the disorder and refer other children for the same treatment. Often the parents are confused and alarmed as are many physicians.

The purpose of this book, at least partially, is to provide a means of frontline information to both physicians and educators. One thing is certain, research at both a national and international level will continue but translating that information into everyday application must be done with caution and the best available advise at the moment. At the present this is one of our greatest problems. It will be helpful, at the outset, to provide some review of both the history of ADHD and current research.

ADD and ADHD are terms which have grown from research and theories related to hyperkinetic or hyperactive behavioral patterns prevalent in the late 1960s and early 1970s. Consider this forward written by Leon Eisenberg, M.D. of the Harvard Medical School for the book, *Hyperactive Children,* by Safer and Daniel (1976).

> Hyperactivity is in none of these senses a "disease." As it is described in this monograph, it is a collection of signs and symptoms that approaches the status of a "syndrome." That is, it distinguishes a group of children who differ from others, not only at the time when the diagnosis is made but when they are followed up five or ten years later, and who are at increased risk for both present and later academic, social, and behavioral problems. Indeed, it is probable that we are dealing with several syndromes (which we have yet to learn to distinguish reliably) rather than a single condition. The diagnostic problem is made complex by the ability of other known conditions (anxiety, hypoglycemia, etc.) to mimic the clinical features of hyperkinetic disorders. Interesting hypotheses have been put forward about possible underlying derangements (abnormalities in central neurotransmitters, sensitivity to food additives, deviant embryologic development, cerebral anoxia during pregnancy or parturition, and the like) but none have been proved, conversely, each may hold true for some unknown fraction of cases.

If we consider that Dr. Eisenberg wrote this summary of the hyperkinetic disorder in 1976 one must note that his statements are as true today as they were then. Have we traveled far? It may be safe to assume that additional research that has been conducted to determine the definition of ADHD, save research of a medical nature, is much different than that done by Dr. Eisenberg. As we review the latest research in the next chapter it will be important to recall the above discussion. Neither was ADHD discovered in 1980 with the publishing of the DSM–III nor has it been uniquely defined in the present DSM–IIIR. For teachers and mental health professionals working in schools, understanding the greater picture and history of ADHD is important.

Hyperactivity, though it was not commonly diagnosed until the 1960s, was described in medical literature at the beginning of this century in a paper by G. F. Still in 1902 in which children were described by terms closely resembling modern day descriptions. Dr. Still believed that children suffered from "deficits in moral control" and "volitional inhibition" (Still, 1902). Writings beginning in the 1920s and extending into the late 1960s recognized the general syndrome in all parts of the world and it was finally recognized in the second edition of the DSM in 1968 (American Psychiatric Association, 1968).

From the 1920s through the early 1960s the American middle class and upper class collectively developed a greater concern for their children's education and development. Family and group therapies were tried, amphetamine drugs were explored and residential treatment was made more flexible along with increased organization of remedial education (Routh and Roberts, 1972; Waldrop and Halverson, 1971). With the growth of the mental health profession in the 1950s and 1960s, and the subsequent success with medication, use of medication with hyperactive children ensued. By the late 1960s behavioral modification was beginning to take hold and was used with these children. (Childers, 1935)

The key characteristics of these children are and have been overactivity, distractibility, inattention, and poor impulse control with activity, impulsivity, and inattention being the focal points. But in the 1940s and 1950s these were believed to signify brain injury although scant evidence existed to demonstrate this belief (Strauss and Lehtinen, 1947).

In the period from the late 1940s and through the late 1950s many came to believe, following the lead of Strauss and Lehtinen, that hyperactivity was the result of brain-injury (Strauss and Lehtinen 1947). Strauss and Lehtinen's work reached public schools and parents in the late 1950s but only in the form of a list. This list was composed of 10–12 characteristics of such children and included abnormal EEG patterns and soft neurological signs. Very quickly in the early 1960s these children were diagnosed with the condition of "minimal brain injury" which then evolved into "MBD" or "minimal brain dysfunction" (Clements and Peters, 1962).

The term MBD implied an underlying brain impairment despite a lack of evidence that such a condition existed (Rutter, 1977; Taylor, 1983). At this point in the early 1960s the term "learning disability" had not yet been spawned. It is this juncture in history which is critical for special educators to understand relative to much of what has happened with special children in the last twenty years and why the inclusion of the ADHD syndrome at this time is perhaps a mistake.

For a period of five years between 1960 and 1965, during which time one of the authors was actually teaching an experimental class for "minimally brain injured children," a strange twist in the translation of the theory of MBD came into the popular literature. This twist was to cause a split between the movements of hyperactivity and learning disabilities which resulted in the generation of a new field of special education but relegated hyperactivity to a lessor part of that movement. Yet, in clinical environments the theories of MBD and hyperactivity continued to grow. Educators were more concerned with the general theories of perceptual motor and language disabilities. While hyperactivity was a concern in special education, it was not viewed as a primary disability but rather somehow a part of "learning disabilities."

Prior to the early 1960s a list describing the altered characteristics of brain-injured children had emerged as many professionals were uncomfortable with the brain injured notion. Stevens and Birch recommended a "Strauss Syndrome" classification which included the following characteristics (Stevens and Birch, 1957):

1. Erratic and inappropriate behavior on mild provocation.
2. Increased motor activity disproportionate to stimulus.
3. Poor organization of behavior.
4. Distractibility to a more than ordinary degree under ordinary conditions.
5. Persistent hyperactivity.
6. Awkwardness and consistently poor motor performance.

The child had to exhibit several of the characteristics.

During the period between 1960 and 1963 popular interest in the notion that children might have undiagnosed minimal brain injury which could result in inattention, distractibility, impulsivity, and other learning difficulties, caught the attention of thousands of parents across the country. Appropriately, and in turn, Samuel Kirk, in a meeting with concerned parents proposed the term "learning disabilities" in 1963 (Lerner, 1988).

By 1965, in education, the evolution from the clinical concept of MBD to a more general and learning based theory of disabilities was achieved. Many learning disabilities had the flavor of some neurological involvement, but educators and professionals involved in diagnosis in the public schools did not feel comfortable making neurological assessments. By the late 1960s terms like brain-injured, MBD, and neurologically impaired were already well on their way to extinction in the education and the learning disabilities field. However, medical professionals continued to refer to MBD and hyperkinetic theories in their published works. But these works, such as the book by Safer and Daniel in 1976, were very poorly received by uninterested professionals in education.

As special educators moved away from a neurologically-related theory of learning disabilities in the late 1970s toward a more educationally-based definition, so too did the concept of MBD begin to lose luster in the field of psychiatry and other medical specialties (Rie and Rie, 1980). In a series of studies by Douglas and her colleagues, Dr. Douglas (1972) made the case that attentional deficits and impulse control were primary to the hyperactivity syndrome. In the 1968 DSM–II the diagnosis Hyperkinetic Reaction of Childhood was replaced with Attention Deficit Disorder with or without hyperactivity, and the three primary symptoms were now described: inattention, impulsivity, and over-activity. This yielded the cumbersome and wholly unsupported notion of ADHD, Attention Deficit with Hyperactivity, and ADD, Attention Deficit without Hyperactivity (Maurer and Stewart, 1980). Following several studies in the early 1980s this category was eliminated in the DSM–III Revised published in 1987. The one definition of ADHD is now clinically appropriate and use of the term ADD should be discontinued, a task that may take some time in education.

As discussed earlier, the translation of clinical research into the popular and educational literature often involves a significant lag. Subsequently, many school personnel may continue to labor under misconceptions. In the remainder of this book we will refer to ADDH or ADHD to imply this later definition.

A number of commonalities were distilled by Barkley et al. in 1980 to describe and define ADHD from prior efforts including the following:

1. An emphasis on age-inappropriate levels of inattention, impulsivity, and over-activity.
2. The inability of the children to restrict their behavior to situational demands (self-regulation).
3. The emergence of these problems by early childhood.
4. The pervasiveness of these problems across several settings and/or caregivers.
5. The chronicity of the symptoms throughout development.
6. The inability to account for these behavioral deficits on the basis of obvious developmental disabilities. (i.e. mental retardation, severe language delay, neurological diseases, i.e., gross brain damage, epilepsy and severe psychopathology such as autism or schizophrenia.

The criterion listed in the DSM–III Revised (1987) differs from the earlier manual in that they have a single item list rather than three separate listings under each symptom. The cutoff score of 8 out of 14 items has been established in a clinical trial test and the condition of Affective Disorder no longer excludes the use of the diagnosis.

The present criterion for diagnosing ADHD are listed here:

A. A period of six months or more during which at least eight of the following behaviors are present:

1. Has difficulty remaining seated.
2. Fidgets with hands or feet and squirms.
3. Has difficulty playing quietly.
4. Talks excessively.
5. Shifts from one uncompleted activity to another.
6. Has difficulty sustaining attention to tasks or play activities.
7. Has difficulty following through on instructions from others (not due to oppositional behavior or failure of comprehension, e.g., fails to finish chores.)
8. Is easily distracted by extraneous stimuli.
9. Interrupts or intrudes on others, e.g. butts into other children's games.
10. Blurts out answers to questions before they have been completed.
11. Has difficulty taking turns in games and group situations.

12. Engages in physically dangerous activities without considering possible consequences (not for the purpose of thrill seeking) e.g., runs into street without looking.
13. Loses things necessary for tasks or activities at school or at home (e.g., toys, pencils, books, assignments).
14. Doesn't seem to listen to what is being said.

B. Onset before the age of seven years.
C. Does not meet criteria for Pervasive Developmental Disorder.

In 1982 Dr. Barkley proposed more restricted guidelines listed below:

1. Parent and/teacher complaints of inattention, impulsivity, over-activity, and poor rule governed behavior (e.g., sustained compliance, self-control, and problem solving.)
2. A score or scores two standard deviations above the mean for same-age, same-sex, normal children on factors labeled as "Inattention" or "Hyperactivity" in well-standardized child behavior rating scales completed by parents or teachers.
3. Onset of these problems by 6 years of age.
4. Duration of these problems for at least 12 months.
5. An IQ greater than 85 or, if between 70 and 85, comparison to children of the same mental age in using criterion 2 above.
6. The exclusion of significant language delay, sensory handicaps (e.g., deafness, blindness, etc.), or severe psychopathology (e.g., autism, childhood schizophrenia).

Dr. Barkley also proposed a definition which may be of some assistance to special educators as they attempt to develop a classification of the disorder for use in schools. It is as follows (Barkley, 1982):

ADD/H is a developmental disorder of attention span, impulsivity, and/or over-activity as well as rule-governed behavior, in which these deficits are significantly inappropriate for the child's mental age; have an on-set in early childhood; are significantly pervasive or cross-situational in nature; are generally chronic or persistent over time; and are not the direct result of severe language delay, deafness, blindness, autism, or childhood psychosis.

In later chapters we will discuss the problems with this and other definitions of ADHD relative to the school environment. While the clinical understanding of ADHD and research associated with the disorder are troublesome for researchers, its application in the school environment can be devastating to a child, his family, and the overall milieu in which the child participates.

There are a number of assumptions which have appeared in the literature concerning the behavior of ADHD children, but here is a review of the various symptoms Dr. Barkley has postulated:

1. ADHD children are different from normal children on measures of attention span, activity level, and impulse control.

While ADHD children are assumed to be different from unaffected children in these areas, there were substantial disparities in the types of evaluations used to measure these areas, the kinds of settings in which the measures were taken, and the definitions used to select the ADHD children. These factors have led to many failures to replicate findings of others on these constructs (Barkley, 1982).

2. ADHD children have difficulties in rule-governed behavior. Rules are contingency-specifying stimuli (Skinner, 1969) constructed for them by the social community or by the individual, which specify relations (the contingencies) among antecedents, behavior and consequences (Barkley, 1985a).

Dr. Barkley also found that most studies on ADDH children using laboratory tasks of attention and impulsivity are studies of rule-governed behavior, in that instructions (rules) for performing the tasks are given by the examiner. Dr. Barkley felt that this structure resulted in problems related to children sustaining compliance.

3. ADHD children have difficulties in problem solving in academic and social situations (Douglas, 1983).

Problem solving in this case refers to the ability or skill of a child to construct a series of questions which can lead to a solution. A question pertaining to this matter remains, whether ADDH children have difficulties in the skills, motivation, or performance which results in exhibiting rule-governed behavior. Dr. Douglas felt that they are primarily "contingency-shaped" in that they respond to the situational consequences rather than rules (Douglas, 1983).

4. ADHD children do not display their primary problems, or display them to a consistent degree, in all situations (Zentall 1984), under all contingencies and with all care-givers with whom they may have contact (Tallmadge and Barkley, 1983).

The variability of behavior in ADHD children is a significant factor in understanding their response for it may suggest that not only contingencies but also environmental effects have a greater influence than is suspected. This can, as we will see in our own discussions in later chapters, lead to another viewpoint in the etiology of the disorder. Dr. Barkley et al. suggest five major factors which may explain or at least contribute to the variability in the ADHD response:

a. The degree of "structure" in a situation and/or the extent which the setting demands children restrain their behavior and comply with situational cues (Barkley et al., 1985b).
b. The sex of the parent dealing with the child in that fathers have somewhat fewer problems than mothers (Tallmadge and Barkley, 1983).
c. The nature of the tasks that ADHD children are asked to do as well as the frequency with which the instructions for the task are given throughout their performance.
d. The novelty or unfamiliarity of a situation.
e. The contingencies, or schedule of consequences operating during a particular task or setting (Barkley et al., 1980).

Dr. Barkley and his colleagues have been concerned about the heterogeneous nature of ADHD. Efforts have been toward homogeneous grouping of these children with some promising approaches. One approach has been that of the degree of aggressiveness. Aggressive behavior is not described in this instance as overt acts of hostility against others but rather negative temperaments, oppositional and defiant behavior such as refusing to cooperate and quarreling. It has been found that children who are ADHD, and also demonstrate aggression, exhibit more severe problems in academic areas, peer relationships, adolescence, and as studies reveal, have parents possessing a high incidence of pathology. A second approach cited by Dr. Barkley has been that of defining ADHD children as "situational" or "pervasive." The third approach to categorization which has now been disregarded in the DSM–IIIR is that of ADDH with or without hyperactivity.

The prevalence of ADHD is varied from study to study as one might expect in a disorder which is so poorly defined and difficult to establish clear etiology. Prevalence studies range from 1 percent to as much as 20 percent. Generally, though, the 3–5 percent cited in the 1980 DSM–III edition is most common. Boys are generally expected to have a 3:1 to 9:1 ratio in relation to girls for prevalence.

ADHD children are often identified in early childhood and it is felt that by 3 years of age as many as 50 percent of ADHD children have been recognized by their parents. They demonstrate over-activity, short attention, and noncompliant behavior and subsequently parents often have to "childproof" the home. By 6 years of age the behavior of these children has become so obvious that 90 percent of them will have been identified by parents and teachers.

During the elementary years, as described by Dr. Barkley and others, the ADHD child has problems in relationships with peers due to their selfishness, immaturity, heightened emotionality, conduct problems, and relative lack of appropriate social skills. Moreover, with broader involvement in school and social situations, ADHD children can become increasingly difficult for parents to manage. Parents often feel they cannot trust the children to follow rules outside the realm of parental guidance, and parents end up spending more time with their child in order to facilitate organization.

At school ADHD children have difficulties including underachievement, failure to complete assigned tasks, and poor social skills. In adolescence those children who primarily have ADHD without aggression, tend to have problems in school performance. Those having ADHD with aggression fair worse and often become involved in nonexemplary groups. Barkley reports that adolescent ADHD children, while tending to be less active, more attentive, and more compliant than when younger, now may exhibit delinquent behaviors. Difficulties with authority, violation of family rules, traffic violations, and alcohol abuse are potentials for the adolescent. Feelings of low self-esteem and depression may also occur.

Relative to the etiology of the syndrome, there is less theory building than inquiry into symptoms and definition of the characteristics. It has interested us as we have worked with these children over the years that the definition of the disorder has been more important than analysis of the causes for the problem. This may be one of the difficulties in the entire ADHD paradigm. In our own work we have operated from the opposite direction, that specific behaviors of children which tend to form clusters of behavioral and learning deficits may demonstrate developmental differences.

The clinical and research approach operates on the minute, the specific characteristic, and the well-defined detail so important in scientific analysis. It is important to perform the research and to continue the investigation into the clinical nature of ADHD, conversely, for the purposes of successful assistance and management in the classroom,

Rie, H.E., & Rie, E.D. *Handbook of Minimal Brain Dysfunction,* New York: Wiley/ Stevens, 1980.

Routh, D., and Roberts, R. Minimal Brain Dysfunction in Children: Failure to Find Evidence of a Behavioral Syndrome, *Psychological Reports,* 31: 307–314, 1972.

Rutter, M. Brain Damage Syndromes in Childhood: Concepts and Findings, *Journal of Child Psychology and Psychiatry,* 18, 1–21, 1977.

Safer and Daniel, *Hyperactive Child,* Foreword by Eisenberg, M.D., Baltimore: University Park Press, 1976.

Skinner, B. F. *Contingencies of Reinforcement: A Theoretical Analysis,* New York: Appleton-Century-Crofts 1969.

Stevens, G., & Birch, J. A Proposed Clarification of the Terminology to Describe Brain-Injured Children, *Exceptional Children,* 23, 346–349, 1957.

Still, G. F. Some Abnormal Physical Conditions in Children, *Lancet,* 1, 1008–1012, 1163–1168, 1902.

Strauss, A. A., & Lehtinen, L. E. *Psychopathology and Education of the Brain Injured Child,* New York: Gune & Stratton, 1947.

Tallmadge, J., & Barkley, R. A. The Interaction of Hyperactive and Normal Boys With Their Mothers and Fathers, *Journal of Abnormal Child Psychology,* 11, 565–579, 1983.

Taylor, H.G. MBD: Meanings and Misconceptions, *Journals of Clinical Neuropsychology,* 5, 271–287, 1983.

Waldrop, M. and Halverson, C. Minor Physical Anomalies and Hyperactive Behavior in Young Children, in *Exceptional Infant,* J. Hellmuth (Ed.), Vol.II: Studies in Abnormalities, pp. 343–380. New York: Brunner/Mazel, 1971.

Zentall, S. Context Effects in the Behavioral Ratings of Hyperactivity, *Journal of Abnormal Child Psychology,* 12, 345–352 1984.

Chapter Two

REVIEW OF RESEARCH

Research on ADHD has been extensive in the last fifteen to twenty years accelerating in the latter part of the 1980s and into the early 1990s. While clinical research, that done within the context of controlled studies appropriate to detailed analysis of a problem by professionals in the field, is of utmost importance, it is not always practical nor immediately useful to layman or educators. Due to the speed of current media coverage and international communications the accuracy of dispersed information is sometimes questionable. Media professionals stalk the latest information from every corner of the world and in their zest to capture the public's attention they may elaborate or distort knowledge. The ethics of the publishing establishment is not the subject of our discussion, however, it is important for the teacher or medical professional to realize that they have a responsibility to interpret and translate scientific information as accurately as possible. Having stated this need, it is not always possible, even as educators and also as parents, to obtain well-defined information.

Clinicians in every scientific field live and work in an environment where professional methods and ethics guide their work. One of the frustrations which often faces scientists is having their work, or parts of it, published prematurely in the popular literature. The syndrome of ADHD has generated the attention of those in literacy fields due to the pervading controversy about the use of medication with children, the definition of hyperactivity, and, the realization of the male prevalence of the disorder.

Media coverage has created a problem relative to ADHD which needs to be clearly stated and understood. The incidence of educators referring children for medication and the enthusiasm of teachers to label children as "ADD" has become a serious problem. The term ADD has been popularized and even though clinicians are no longer using the term in favor of ADHD, it will be sometime before the popularized perception is changed. To make matters worse, many parents and educators believe

16

that ADHD is a distinct "illness," "disease," or "disorder," consistent with the DSM–IIIR classification.

The use of the term "disorder" brings different images to parents, teachers, and even family physicians than it may to the mental health professional. A disorder implies a serious condition and somehow there is a tendency to see ADHD as a brain disorder or, unfortunately, a subtle and minimal brain dysfunction. Suddenly, it is as if the last fifteen years in neurological, endocrinological, psychological, and other clinical research never happened. On the front line in schools and community mental health clinics we have fought for years in an attempt to avoid the mistakes of the early 1960s when MBD and associated neurological theories of learning difficulties inadvertently spawned the entire movement of learning disabilities.

ADHD is not an exact and homogenous disorder though some clinicians search for the holy grail of a unitary classification for ADHD individuals. Most researchers now recognize that children with ADHD are a heterogenous group who exhibit a range of behaviors that are similar, but which may be caused by a number of conditions and factors. An old saying, "If it walks like a duck, quacks like a duck, and looks like a duck, it is a duck," is not applicable to the ADHD diagnosis and this is one of the thorny problems facing the clinician. Just because a child is distractible, fidgety, and impulsive, does not mean that he is an ADHD child.

In this chapter we want to review, as clearly as we can, current research in the field of ADHD and relate some of our own concerns from the position of educational psychology and implications for interpretation of the disorder within the realm of parents and community.

THE CONCEPT OF ADHD

As we have mentioned earlier, ADHD has its roots in the notions of the 1960s and 1970s about minimal brain dysfunction (MBD). Much of the earlier theory about MBD has been found erroneous (Rutter, 1983). This is not to state that it is impossible that in some cases there is a significant neurological involvement, but the vast majority of ADHD children do not demonstrate specific brain injury or other brain trauma. This is extremely important for, as we make our way through what is known about ADHD, our own conceptualization of the issues involved will affect how we intervene in the behavior of children in the learning environment.

PRESENT CONCEPTUALIZATION IN SCHOOLS

At the present time, when the majority of educators and teachers may not have adequate information or training about ADHD, there appears to be a strong tendency for teachers to see the problem as a "disorder" which is based in psychoneurology. This viewpoint then gives the child not only a social stigma but results in an educational stigma that causes teachers to alter their operational behavior. In most cases, the diagnosis is made on the basis of available teacher-parent checklists which hardly constitute a diagnostic procedure. But given a list of behaviors which describe a known problem there is a tendency by parents and teachers to adopt the label. Thus, these professionals, who have the major responsibility for the education and life of the child, may tend to react to the child unrealistically. Several excerpts demonstrate a frequent problem we face in working with teachers and schools:

> A parent brings their eight year old son for a developmental evaluation because his teacher recommended that the parents see their physician for medication. The teacher has told the parents that she and the school psychologist completed a diagnostic checklist which indicated that the child displayed ADD.
>
> The child demonstrated many learning and behavioral problems but did not truly qualify for the designation of ADHD either by our own psychological assessment or by that of the family practice physician.
>
> The school staff and the teacher were quite disturbed that the child was not diagnosed as ADD and that he would not receive medication. The problem was finally resolved through meetings with the school staff and providing a range of recommendations for the child.

The issue here is not that the teacher is insensitive nor that she is unwilling to help a particular child. The problem is that adequate information and training had not been provided within the school. As a few children successfully demonstrated behavioral change following medication, a little information and dramatic behavioral change in certain children led teachers to recommend the same treatment for other children.

THE EDUCATIONAL CLIMATE AND ADHD

We must also recognize that the climate in schools today throughout the nation is such that a "medical model" for dealing with behavioral disorders is more likely to appeal to teachers. In referring to the "medical model" we mean that parents or teachers view a child as having a problem which is "medical" in nature, that is, something is "wrong" with the child and is based in some sort of neurological or "brain" problem. Layman tend to expect that medical issues require "medical treatment" of medication or some clinical intervention beyond the skill of teachers or parents. The fact that a significant number of nonmedical professionals also tend to imply a "medical problem" exists reinforces this view by parents and teachers that the problem requires "treatment" from outside the school.

Teachers and schools in general are under significant pressure from all sides to do a better job of educating the nation's children. This pressure will continue as increased education and training are required of greater numbers of people to obtain jobs. Literacy is a national problem, educators report a higher incidence of delinquency antisocial behavior, and reading disabilities, while there are increasing problems in funding not only special services for children but regular education as well. If children can be labeled as "ADD" or any other behavioral disorder, the problem becomes one of the medical community and not education. This is exactly what happened in the early days of learning disabilities.

Litigation over special services for children by parents and child advocates is becoming a national problem for schools. The number of lawsuits concerning individual needs and special children are forcing many schools to budget more funds to special services than to general education itself. This, in turn, creates additional pressures on not only teachers but the entire educational program.

There are strong indications that Americans are becoming a nation of drug and technology abusers and in turn increasing their interest in health care. Physicians also are facing significant litigation from patients who expect modern medicine to solve their every problem. The expectations for medicine are perhaps unrealistic but patients armed with the financial support of health and medical organizations are more apt to seek medical care and have higher expectations when they do. The outcome relative to health care is a wider acceptance of medical treatment as a means of resolving problems of both adults and children. In the 1990s there is significantly more acceptance on the part of parents in regards to the use of medication with their children. While there are many parents who are very resistant to the notion of medication for behavioral control, there is much wider acceptance than in the 1970s or even the 1980s.

These factors must be taken into account when one is attempting to work with educators in presenting the concept of ADHD. A central issue is that even with medication and certainly without it, an ADHD child's primary "treatment" is not after all medical. As we will see in coming discussions the primary mode of treatment is in some sort of behavioral management or therapeutical strategy which, as a theory and practice, has been part of education since the early 1970s when behavioral modification was first introduced into schools at a national level.

While both medical and behavioral management strategies are important aspects in dealing with the ADHD child our own experience suggests that there are a number of other strategies that may be even more important to the teacher and parent. These will be discussed in later chapters. A major task for us in this book is to return or place the "control" of ADHD treatment and management primarily in the hands of the teacher and not in the hands of the medical profession. Medical cooperation is important but should be secondary. The most that psychologists and physicians have to offer is the prescribing of medication when needed and, recommendations for general behavioral strategies. The teacher still has primary responsibility to manage the child's behavior, provide educational as well as socialization opportunities, and facilitate achievement, cognitive development, and the development of a positive self-image. Most of this must be done through the teacher's experience and skill in conjunction with the resources of special services. In essence, school personnel MUST take responsibility for management of ADHD children, as with all children, particularly in light of the recent regular education initiative, and play the central role of *CONTROLLERS* for the education of children. Forces from outside the school can play a consultive role, they can provide support services, and cooperative professional analysis, but the primary role and control of the child's program must be that of the school; if not, then psychological and medical professionals should accept full responsibility for the child and his education.

In the early 1960s the notion of learning disabilities was still primarily an invention of the medical community under the concepts of hyperactivity and minimal brain dysfunction. Most schools required a neurological evaluation along with other psychological assessments in order to obtain placement in experimental programs for "neurologically impaired," as the children were then defined. Before the schools finally took control and defined the field as learning disabilities, there were a number of confrontation interactions between various areas of medical and psychological professionals with regard to the exact nature of the so called "MBD" phenomenon. The current rush to embrace the concept of ADHD as a major clinical classification of a specific disorder promises the same sort of problem unless educators become involved in understanding, and interpreting themselves, the notion of ADHD as it relates to the school environment.

HYPERACTIVITY VERSUS ADHD

There is a strong acceptance of the symptoms of inattention, impulsivity, over-activity, and a lack of rule governed behavior as primary to the ADHD disorder. In the 1970s, just as MBD was a major theoretical orientation for children with hyperactivity, so was hyperkinesis viewed as a part of MBD, or, an associated disorder. Each implied a neurological disorder even though in practice the research did not support such theories.

1. ADHD IS CLINICALLY SEEN AS A CLUSTER OF SYMPTOMS OFTEN INCLUDING INATTENTION, IMPULSIVITY, OVER–ACTIVITY AND A LACK OF RULE GOVERNED BEHAVIOR.

Many medical and psychological professionals have used neurodevelopmental immaturities, so-called "neurological soft signs," to imply brain injury or dysfunction (Shaffer et al., 1983). Shaffer and his associates found that so-called neurological soft signs were most strongly associated with anxiety disorders (Shaffer et al., 1985). Rutter (1989) has suggested that all in all the concept of MBD need not preoccupy us any longer due to the fact that validating criterion for the whole of diagnostics and classification fails. Most clinicians now accept the general tenets of the ADHD syndrome as opposed to the earlier concept of MBD. Yet, acceptance of the criteria used to define the syndrome is still strongly debated though most would agree that conceptually there is validity to the notions of hyperactivity and attentional problems.

The relevance of neurological soft signs more often reflect developmental lags in that they sometimes disappear with age (Gittelman and Mannuzza, 1989a). In our own work, the belief of Gittelman and Mannuzza is not a theoretical concept but rather an understandable developmental reality. When one works with children over a long period of time what may appear as some sort of "neurological soft sign" turns out to be related to the peculiar and individual way in which some children develop. Instead of a neurological soft sign it is often specific developmental immaturity expressed when a child is asked to perform tasks for which he is not developmentally ready. One of our most frequent examples of this is the case of a five or six year old who draws a "tail" on a diamond. In clinical research in the 1960s and 1970s this behavior was an example of a so-called soft sign. In reality, when a child has not yet matured in directionality and fine motor skills he cannot predict which way to move his hand in order to produce the complex diagonal lines required in the diamond. To determine the correct direction, the child learns to experiment by moving his hand a short movement in one direction. If the movement results in an opposite direction line, he pauses, then moves the pencil in the correct direction resulting in the ominous tail. In fact, rather than a subtle indication of some sort of neurological difficulty, it is a normal developmental strategy to perform a task for which the child is not developmentally ready.

2. NEURODEVELOPMENTAL IMMATURITIES SUCH AS "NEUROLOGICAL SOFT SIGNS" HAVE OFTEN BEEN USED TO IMPLY UNDERLYING NEUROLOGICAL DYSFUNCTION AS THE BASIS FOR ADHD, BUT THE MBD CONCEPT IS GENERALLY NO LONGER ACCEPTED.

Having finally, after perhaps 30 years, put the concept of MBD to rest, the issues now facing clinicians in regard to ADHD are just as difficult. What is ADHD? The descriptions used in checklists available to parents and teachers, and, the actual guidelines in the DSM–IIIR manual, are extremely heterogenous and diffuse making it difficult to accurately pinpoint a diagnosis. Over-activity for example is seen in anxiety, psychomotor agitation of depression, the excessive energy and talkativeness of mania, and in the hyperkinesis of autism as well as in the definition of ADHD (Weiss & Hechtman, 1986) (Rutter, 1989).

Dissatisfaction with hyperactivity as the central diagnostic feature became less acceptable to most researchers and attention deficits assumed a greater role resulting in renaming the disorder attention deficit by the American Psychiatric Association in 1980. Two years earlier the World Health Organization also made the same move. But, as we have lived with this concept for some years, more and more questions are raised about the concept of attention. Attention is difficult to define for there are varying degrees of attention all dependent on the task, the setting, and the requirements placed on the child.

Inattention is also a feature of psychiatric disturbance in childhood. In Isle of Wright studies, poor concentration was reported by both teachers and parents as characteristic of the majority of children with psychiatric disorders (Rutter, Tizzard & Whitmore, 1970). Attention is not a unitary or singular function for it may be necessary to focus on some stimuli to the exclusion of others (selective attention), while in other situations information from several sources may have to be integrated toward a focal processing, and at times one has to focus attention over frustration and distraction in boring situations (Rutter, 1989). Further, while the actual definition of attention or inattention may be difficult enough, it is also the outcome of complex processes, any of which may be deficits in cognitive function or immaturity.

3. HYPERACTIVITY AS THE CENTRAL CHARACTERISTIC OF ADHD HAS YIELDED TO INATTENTION AS THE MAJOR CHARACTERISTIC BUT ATTENTION ITSELF IS DIFFICULT TO DEFINE.

Measurement of attention, in the classroom or home, is a subjective experience on the part of those involved. The difficulties may lie as much in the synergistic aspects of the environmental and emotional contexts of the situation as in a specific deficit in the child.

Dr. Rutter, summarizing in his research, suggests that, in view of the generality of symptoms of over-activity and inattention, it is not surprising that studies have failed to find either symptom in itself providing any useful diagnostic differentiation (1989). There is also a significant overlap of the symptoms of hyperactivity and inattention with conduct disorders and learning disabilities.

Relative to drug response it has been found that stimulants such as methylphenidate and dextroamphetamine tend to improve attention and reduce activity level in all people, children and adults, irrespective of whether or not they are hyperactive (Rapoport, 1983).

4. STIMULANT DRUGS TEND TO IMPROVE ATTENTION AND REDUCE ACTIVITY LEVEL IN ALL PEOPLE WHETHER OR NOT THEY ARE HYPERACTIVE BUT HYPERACTIVE CHILDREN DISPLAY A MARKED CHANGE.

It may be assumed that a good drug response will be found in children with hyperactivity and inattention. Furthermore, Rapoport and his colleagues (1986) suggested that teachers were good judges of hyperactivity. But in cases of differentiation between situationally hyperactive behavior and pervasive hyperactivity, the case may not so clearly be diagnosed by teachers. In other cases it has been found that hyperactivity at home is a better predictor of drug response than at school since hyperactivity at home may indicate more extensive involvement than when the behavior primarily occurs at school. This would suggest that diagnosis of ADHD should include the presence of pervasive hyperactivity or activity seen in more than one setting. Thus, while teachers may be adept at recognizing an abnormally high activity level in the classroom, this does not always occur at home; if it is in both situations a more clinically significant pattern is seen. The same studies also demonstrated that teacher ratings are often biased by the presence of defiance. Teachers are more apt to refer the hyperactive and defiant child than the less aggressive but active child. This then suggests that many studies involving teacher referrals may consist of highly biased samples. In addition, a good drug response was predicted by the absence of marked anxiety but this is not included in either the American DSM–III or the ICD-9 manual of the World Health Organization. According to Rutter, the presence of disruptive behavior or conduct disturbance does not differentiate responders and nonresponders to stimulants. This suggests that it is not useful to divide the syndrome according to the presence or absence of conduct disturbances. Additional studies have investigated cognitive correlates and developmental delays and their relationship to ADHD. Such studies tend to point out that pervasively hyperactive children tend to have better drug response than situationally hyperactive. In fact, pervasive hyperactivity, onset before the age of 5 years, neurodevelopmental abnormalities, a high frequency of language impairment or other forms of developmental delay, accident prone behavior and marked poor peer relationships along with good drug response, tend to define the disorder.

5. PERVASIVELY HYPERACTIVE CHILDREN RESPOND BETTER TO DRUGS THAN SITUATIONALLY HYPERACTIVE CHILDREN. IN CASES OF PERVASIVE HYPERACTIVITY, DEVELOPMENTAL ABNORMALITIES, LANGUAGE IMPAIRMENT, AND ONSET BEFORE FIVE YEARS OF

AGE AND GOOD DRUG RESPONSE TENDS TO DEFINE
THE DISORDER.

LONG-TERM OUTCOMES FOR ADHD

Relative to long-term outcomes several factors appear evident. The
Isle of Wright data was reanalyzed by Schachar et al. (1981). It was found
that at 14–15 years of age children who had been pervasively hyperactive
at 10 and who had conduct disorders had much poorer outcome than
those who showed situational hyperactivity or no over-activity. Magnusson
(1987), in a Stockholm Longitudinal Study, showed that adult crime was
most strongly predicted by the combination of hyperactivity, inattention,
and aggression in middle childhood.

There have been several studies concerning the relationship between
hyperactivity and inattention. Some have suggested that perhaps inattention is related to an abnormality of cerebral central processing and that
this in turn causes the hyperactivity. But the correlation between
hyperactivity and inattention is not the only factor because included in
the cluster are lower IQ levels, language delays and delayed motor
function. It could also be argued that the generalized delay gives rise to a
range of associated difficulties such as inattention, hyperactivity, language impairment, and lower IQ levels. This means that it is possible
that the attention deficit is part of a more generalized problem in development rather than being the basic deficit itself. We will discuss this
possibility in later chapters, for educationally it can be of crucial importance while it may not be of importance in clinical analysis.

6. IN MANY CASES ADHD BEHAVIORAL SYMPTOMS
MAY BE RELATED TO MORE GENERALIZED DISORDERS
IN COGNITIVE AND LANGUAGE FUNCTION AND NOT
BE THE DEFICIT ITSELF.

Developmental delays appear to be fundamental parts of attention
deficits; however, studies demonstrate that inattention is often associated
with hyperactivity in developmentally normal children. To some researchers this raises questions about the validity of the notion that
inattention and hyperactivity are related to a more basic and generalized
developmental delay. In our own work we have identified several developmental clusters within which it can be shown that hyperactivity and
inattention are related.

An additional area of research has dealt with the inability of delaying gratification or to inhibit responses. Rapport et al. (1986) showed that hyperactive children differed from controls in being less able to delay gratification. Douglas and Peters' (1979) review concluded that a major feature of attention deficit is the inability to sustain attention and to inhibit impulsive responding.

7. IMPULSIVITY AND INABILITY TO DELAY GRATIFI-CATION SEEM TO BE AN IMPORTANT AND CONSIS-TENT FEATURE OF ADHD CHILDREN.

Rutter (1989) suggested that hyperactivity might be an extreme end of a temperament dimension. This area has not been explored by most researchers and is an interesting suggestion though Rutter did not follow up on the notion. As factors in a temperament cluster, over-activity and inattention along with disinhibition may be part of a genetic tempera-ment pattern. If this is true then additional difficulties should be experi-enced by the child including poor peer relationships, compliance, aggression, and other factors commonly ascribed to deficit temperament patterns. Again, with regard to the recent surveys and theories in learn-ing styles and cognitive processing styles there are indications of poten-tially relevant behavioral patterns. In this area, particularly in the educational setting, interpretation of ADHD in relation to a broader concept of learning and cognitive styles may be useful. Certainly we can expect that as research in ADHD continues toward specificity in truly identifying a syndrome, in education there will need to be a readjust-ment and definition of how the disorder can be integrated into curricu-lum strategy.

8. FOR EDUCATORS DEFINITION OF THE ADHD PRO-FILE MUST BE MORE BROADLY DEFINED RELATIVE TO INTERVENTION AND MANAGEMENT STRATEGIES. MUCH OF THE ADHD LITERATURE IS RELEVANT TO RECENT EDUCATIONAL THEORY IN LEARNING STYLES, CEREBRAL STYLES, AND INDIVIDUAL DIFFER-ENCES WHICH REQUIRE CHANGE IN INSTRUCTIONAL CLIMATE.

Educators, psychologists, family practitioners, and others who must deal with the actual lifespace of the ADHD child will need a broad understanding of the various ADHD associations with other learning and behavioral factors. It is one thing to attempt to define and isolate specific factors in a clinical syndrome, but quite another to meet the day by day needs of the child at home and in the school program. For example, if we can identify a child that meets Barkley's more stringent criteria for the disorder (Barkley 1982), diagnosis may be more accurate and differentiating, but that child will still have all of the attendant problems of ADHD which frontline personnel have to manage.

> 9. EVENTUALLY, IF A MORE RESTRICTIVE AND SELEC-
> TIVE CLASSIFICATION OF THE DISORDER IS DEVEL-
> OPED, SCHOOLS WILL HAVE TO INCLUDE ADHD UNDER
> A CURRENT CATEGORY RATHER THAN INTRODUCING
> IT AS A NEW CLASSIFICATION.

INCLUSION OF ADHD IN THE IDEA PARAMETERS

While the research is moving closer to a more acceptable definition of ADHD, at the present time an adequate clinical definition still does not exist. In the educational field the present definition is *not* generally accepted as a separate and distinct category of exceptionality either by the Council for Exceptional Children (CEC), or, other national and state special education services. In a response to the U.S. Department of Education concerning a notice of inquiry, CEC stated several reasons why ADHD should not be included in Part B of the Individuals with Disabilities ACT. (IDEA) These are listed here:

1. Most children displaying inattentiveness, hyperactivity, disorganization, etc. are being served under existing services such as learning disabilities or emotionally disturbed.
2. ADHD children whose educational achievement is not seriously
   impaired, like other children with disabilities who are not impaired
   educationally, should receive assistance within the regular education programs.
3. Evidence suggests that 33% of children with learning disabilities
   also have attention deficit hyperactivity. Other literature suggests
   that 35% of ADD children are currently receiving special education (Barkley, *The Special Educator,* 1990).
4. The National Education Association maintains that children with
   "ADD" can be better served in restructured, more flexible classroom environments where proper behavioral modification techniques are employed.

5. Persons with expertise in the education of children who are members of racial and ethnic minority groups have expressed profound concern that the explicit inclusion of ADD under the IDEA, with its emphasis on common student behaviors like inattention and impulsivity, will increase the over-identification of culturally and linguistically diverse children as requiring special education.
6. ADHD is a condition or conditions which may be among the underlying causes of the established categories of LD or SED presently included in the law. If ADHD were given special status the precedent would be established for dyslexia or schizophrenia.
7. There is no professional consensus regarding an appropriate definition for this disorder, nor are there uniformly agreed-to diagnostic criteria for either a medical or educational diagnosis. (Excerpt from *The Special Educator,* Vol. VI, Issue 16. May 9, 1991.)

Those arguing for the inclusion of ADHD in IDEA as a separate and special category will no doubt continue their efforts but at the present time the weight of evidence clinically for inclusion is nonexistent. Conversely, educators may still find themselves in need of a major effort in reviewing and keeping abreast of the literature concerning ADHD. For while the clinical definition appears to be narrowing, the popular and more generalized definition may be broadening as did the learning disabilities movement in the middle 1960s. If this occurs then the educational community could be in for another round of confrontation between parents and those in the mental health field.

10. CLINICAL RESEARCH IS MOVING AWAY FROM THE CONCEPT OF ADD WITHOUT HYPERACTIVITY AND TOWARD A MUCH MORE RESTRICTIVE ADHD CLASS-IFICATION. BUT LINGERING ADD CONCEPTS COULD CONTINUE TO CONFUSE MANY PARENTS AND TEACHERS FOR YEARS TO COME.

Shaywitz and Shaywitz (1989) upon reviewing the results of their own research in what they call ADD or ADD–Plus have come to the conclusion that a definition should include nonhyperactivity as in the now defunct ADD/ADHD classification. If one reviews their research and avoids other contradictory viewpoints, the broadening concept mentioned above becomes a reality. In the summary of their chapter, Critical Issues in Attention Deficit Disorder, appearing in Sagvolden and Archers' book, *Attention Deficit Disorder: Clinical and Basic Research* (1989) Shaywitz and Shaywitz made a plea to all investigators. They felt that the all too common practice of identification of ADD with hyperactivity tended to overlook the quiet, nonhyperactive and nonaggressive child with ADD or, as they termed the group, ADDnoH. They felt this group, consisting often of high intelligence if not gifted children, was frequently accused of being unmotivated.

Shaywitz and Shaywitz may have compassion for the ADD child but as can be seen above in the CEC response to inclusion of the ADD classification in IDEA, this group of children may soon be relegated to classifications aside from that of ADHD. This is not to say that there are not many gifted children who have difficulties in attention and focusing on their work; however, as we will discuss later, this group most likely falls into another classification. Recognizing and encouraging the viewpoints expressed in this research, particularly in the United States, could have a detrimental effect on the current attempt to change the ADD/ADHD concept, in the perception of teachers and parents, to a single classification system, ADHD.

11. USE OF STIMULANTS MAY NOT ONLY ASSIST MANY CHILDREN IN REDUCING ACTIVITY AND IMPROVING ATTENTION, DRUG RESPONSE MAY BECOME ONE OF THE IDENTIFYING CRITERION.

Additionally, in their research Shaywitz and Shaywitz reported considerable evidence that stimulants such as damphetamine and methylphenidate act via central monoaminergic systems to: (1) inhibit reuptake, (2) increase release of amine, and (3) to some extent inhibit monoamine oxidase activity (MOA), all actions that serve to increase the concentration of catecholamine (both dopamine and norepinephrine) at the synaptic cleft. This suggested that brain catecholaminergic mechanisms could be influential in the genesis of ADHD (Wender, 1971).

Shaywitz and Shaywitz also felt that several studies suggested significant relationships between the symptoms of ADHD and alterations in prolactin concentrations. Additional information on pharmacological studies will be discussed later but considerable research suggests that brain chemicals related to dopamine and other catecholamine reactions may play a critical role in the etiology of the disorder.

ADD AND LEARNING DISABILITIES

Many researchers have been interested in the relationship between ADHD and learning disabilities. For those who advocate nonacceptance of ADHD as part of IDEA this research is of particular interest for it would suggest that ADHD should be and is subsumed within the LD category. One of the problems with the association between learning disabilities and ADHD is the inconsistent criteria used in their identification. Several studies have investigated the number of children diagnosed as LD who also can be defined as ADHD. Rates vary from 33 percent (Shaywitz, 1986) to 41 percent (Holobrow & Berry, 1986) to 80 percent (Safer & Allen, 1976). One would have to question the 80 percent frequency in Safer and Allen's study which was done in 1976 in light of the more recent statistics. With further consideration of the differences in criterion available in 1976 with those in the middle 1980s we would have to accept the more conservative estimates.

If we look at ADHD children regardless of diagnosis, one study found that ADHD children were more than seven times as likely to experience great difficulty in all academic areas (Holobrow & Berry, 1986). In a study by Sandoval & Lambert (1985) it was found that not only reading achievement but hyperactivity and particularly hyperactivity in association with aggression were significantly related to referral for special education. In fact, twice as many hyperactive children as control children who were not LD were receiving special education services.

Shaywitz and Shaywitz concluded that these findings were very important because the implications were that subject selection for learning disabilities is based on children selected by an educational system which carries an inherent bias: criteria for selection employ behavioral criterion, not necessarily those of learning disabilities. They suggested that any data derived from such studies will by necessity be biased and inaccurate as well and will tend to show that hyperactivity and aggression are common in learning disabilities children.

> 12. LEARNING DISABLED CHILDREN HAVE ADHD SYMPTOMS, ADHD CHILDREN MAY HAVE LEARNING DISABILITIES. ARE THEY THE SAME DISORDER? NO! CONFUSION ON BOTH SIDES, THE CLINICAL RESEARCH, AND SPECIAL EDUCATION PROFESSIONALS, HAVE CONTAMINATED MANY STUDIES RENDERING THE RESULTS USELESS.

Water and oil don't mix! One is struck by the peculiar discrepancies which tend to surface in studies concerning ADHD, particularly ADDnoH and learning disabilities and those between learning disabilities and ADHD. A problem we have seen consistently throughout the research on ADHD has been the need for scientific methodology well applied by clinical researchers, and the head-on clash with the problem of defining the syndrome in terms of educational environments and definitions of other syndromes such as learning disabilities. It has been this "clinically messy" problem of specifically defining ADD, ADHD, and other syndromes including learning disabilities, emotional disturbance, conduct disorders, social and cultural effects, and the biological parameters of the ADHD disorder, which contaminates research efforts.

Much of the research recognizes that inattentiveness and impulsivity, difficult as either is to clinically define, are well recognized as part of many behavioral syndromes. Difficulties with rule-governed behavior posed problems as well in that any number of cultural and developmentally appropriate behaviors can account for rule-following difficulties which numbers of children experience. As any teacher in an urban and deprived school environment can attest, impulsivity, inattention, and problems with rule-governed behavior can account for perhaps as much as 80 percent of the school population. Within the same group, even accounting for IQ differences, a deficit of two years in achievement between mental age and expectation is frequent if not the norm for the group. Activity level for such a group is usually much higher than in the other school populations where the same level of activity would be seen as extreme. In many cases aggressive, at least assertive, behavior is survival-oriented and selected from family and community models. In these populations it would be nearly impossible to determine if there were any ADHD children but most could qualify for the now defunct classification of ADDnoH.

We are then, when speaking of bias, in the land of overflowing riches, for most research does not focus so much on the broader issues of cultural deprivation, language delay, or chaotic and impulsive behavior in the urban population. More often research in ADD or ADHD has been in populations where such problems are not addressed in order to focus on a "purer" syndrome of attentional difficulties. If the previous duel classification system were used (ADD versus ADHD) and the ADDnoH criterion applied in these schools it is certain that, as the earlier comments suggested, ethnic, poor, and minority families would be identified disproportionately and discriminated against through greater referrals.

This all suggests that the ADD classification certainly deserved to be eliminated and, as Barkley has suggested, we may be returning to a more stringent definition of ADD which includes only ADHD. The term ADD should be stricken from consciousness for it is almost certain that teachers will more likely select the aggressive and hyperactive child than a child who demonstrates a nonaggressive but more clinically "pure" over-activity. If we accept Barkley's more restrictive criterion and move into the ADHD where hyperactivity becomes a key criterion, particularly when we limit it to "pervasively" hyperactive, then the child with a learning disability, cultural deprivation, or emotional disturbance will become less infused in the ADHD identification.

13. THE NOW DEFUNCT ADD/ADHD DUAL CLASSIFICATION SYSTEM HAS BEEN ELIMINATED, BUT SCHOOLS AND PARENTS MAY MISS THE IMPORTANCE OF THE NEWER AND FUTURE CLASSIFICATION FOR IT WILL NARROW SIGNIFICANTLY BOTH THE NUMBER AND NATURE OF CHILDREN CLASSIFIED AS ADHD.

In our clinic over the past twenty-five years, as more has been learned about dysfunctional families, mental health issues, psychoneurological and temperament differences in child development, and the nature of learning, we have found few children who qualify for a truly "pervasive" hyperactivity syndrome where learning or developmental difficulties are unrelated to the central behavior. Certainly, the notion of early onset and family/genetic history have been critical in identifying differences between what we see as truly ADHD children and those with learning disabilities, emotional difficulties and conduct disorders. The present move toward a more restrictive criterion fits well into the conceptualization which has emerged in our own work with children in schools.

It is our own bias that eventually, if an exact syndrome of ADHD can be established at all, will point to brain chemistry, as in the case of catecholamines, dietary and allergy issues, psychoneurological/genetic syndromes, and to still poorly understood brain differences. All of these in concert with environmental and cultural issues which exacerbate the basic disorder. Such a group is yet to be identified but the research is moving rapidly in that direction. However, many researchers appear less than adequately familiar with developmental issues, with the nature of educational climates and environments, and contemporary difficulties in individualization.

Taylor (1989) has suggested five criterion which he feels are significant in relation to several inherent problems with the DSM–IIIR and ICD-9, which several clinical studies have investigated, and which the epidemiological evidence has supported. His criterion are similar though not as involved as those by Barkley cited earlier (1982/1989).

1. A pattern of markedly inattentive, restless behavior (not just antisocial, impulsive, or disruptive acts) that is excessive for the child's age and IQ, and a handicap to development.
2. Presence of this pattern in two or more situations, such as home, school, and clinic.
3. Evidence of inattention, restlessness, or social disinhibition, from direct observation by the diagnostician (i.e., not solely by unconfirmed ratings from a child's caretakers).
4. Absence of childhood autism, other pervasive developmental disorders, or affective disorders (including depression, anxiety states, and mania).
5. Onset before the age of six years and duration of at least six months.

Taylor and Barkley's views, and the current DSM–IIIR, may all lead toward a new criterion in the coming DSM–IV which will avoid the present trend to include ADD in any special education classification but rather to allow it, as most professionals in special education who understand the syndrome will accept, to be subsumed under the existing classifications in the disability act. As Taylor stated (1989), "We are not examining a fixed neurological condition, but an interaction between brain function and psychological environment."

14. DR. TAYLOR SUGGESTS THAT WE ARE NOT SEEING A FIXED NEUROLOGICAL CONDITION, BUT AN INTERACTION BETWEEN BRAIN FUNCTION AND PSYCHOLOGICAL ENVIRONMENT.

UNDERLYING PROCESSES IN ADHD

Sergeant and van der Meere (1989) have suggested that the evidence supporting an attentional processing dysfunction in ADHD children is seriously open to question. They felt that, unless there is structural damage, the experimental evidence would favor the interpretation that the boisterous difficult-to-manage child is suffering from a disorder in energetical regulation mechanisms. It appeared to these researchers that the accuracy of performance and not the speed of performance has distinguished hyperactives from controls (Hopkins et al., 1979). The research which studies primarily cognitive process may be missing the strategy which the child uses in task performance. Is it possible that "acting before thinking" or "has difficulty taking turns" are indicative of unstable personality traits or some interaction between impulsivity control and the induced strategy evoked by a particular stimulus? It may be that impulsivity and inattention should be studied as a single integrated list rather than separate factors which describe failure of cognitive control.

There are two concepts investigated by Sergeant and van der Meere, the concept of attention relative to controlled information processing, and the energetical aspects or sustained attention. Sanders (1983) developed a model in which task input required cognitive processing toward task output with arousal, effort, and application acting on the process. In this way task processing involves both the cognitive abstract function and the energetical effects of effort. An additional aspect is that of controlled processing, i.e., acute concentration and effort which is laborious and slow, and automatic processing which is rapid and requires little effort.

15. ADHD CHILDREN, ASIDE FROM IMPULSIVITY AND INATTENTION, APPEAR TO HAVE DIFFICULTIES IN DEVELOPMENT OF AUTOMATIC EXPRESSIVE SKILLS IN BOTH VERBAL AND MOTORIC AREAS.

As we will discuss in detail later with case studies, many of the identified ADHD children seen in our clinic reflect very important differences from normal children. In situations requiring sustained concentration (attention and effort) the distractions from external forces (other children, noises, and the teacher's interaction with other students,) often results in a breakdown not only of attention but also a loss of temporal orientation relative to identification of self in relation to previous task orientation and the present. In essence, ADHD children, have difficulty in the maintenance of attention and effort. Once this is lost through intervening and distracting stimuli, they are unable to recall the serial and temporal order as well as specificity of the original task. They are unable to maintain an automatic form of sustained attention to task as other children do. The mechanisms for this failure are clear in our experience. Thus, in later chapters we will discuss this mechanism which we feel differentiates ADHD children from other children and provides an insight, at least in one dimension, into the etiology of the disorder.

Impulsivity in the child who is unable to sustain attention is a nonmediated and nontemporalized behavior resulting from a lack of automatic cognitive microprocessing. This places impulsivity, in our work, as part of a cluster of cognitive and energetic difficulties in these children.

Sternberg (1969) has also proposed a taxonomy of information processing variables shown below. This microstructure suggests a sequence of input (encoding), serial comprehension, decision making, and response (decoding). The decoding could be by motor (writing) or verbal (talking). We will later also return to this model in our case studies. The model, along with Sander's (1983) load and effort model, assists us in seeing at what point the dysfunction in the process occurs.

MICROCOGNITIVE PROCESSES

Encoding—Serial Comprehension—Decision Making —Response-Organization

Studies have emerged which demonstrate that, when controlled processing demands are placed on the ADHD child, he/she can be successfully distinguished from the control child. This would imply that the ADHD child has difficulty in high concentration and effort sustaining attention in task performance. ADHD children have difficulty in strategy, i.e., where they must choose to emphasize speed at the cost of accuracy, as opposed to sustaining work over longer periods of time for the sake of accuracy. This is a critical difference and because ADHD children suffer from the inability to make good choices in strategy we need a model to explain why they have this difficulty.

Sergeant and van der Meere (1989) did not feel that the research in controlled processing identified the specific locus of deficit in ADHD children and decided that the deficiency could be in the transition of controlled to automatic processing. Douglas (1983) suggested that the discriminating characteristic between ADHD and normal children is that the former acquire more slowly the cognitive sets required to gain new information. This is related to our findings. Sergeant and van der

Meere in their own research did not, however, find this to be the case. That is, in a specific clinical study, they did not find that the ADHD child differed from normal children in the degree and rate of acquisition of automatic processing. But our contention will be that the information processing model used in their work, and the microanalysis they made was not comprehensive enough to be understood in this line of research. They are perhaps correct as far as they go but working with children and making an analysis of their learning and attentional patterns in a learning environment reveals very different conclusions.

Sergeant and van der Meere also, in further research, did not find that difficulties in sustained task effort differentiated between ADHD children and normal children. Again, due to the limitations of their model they would not have seen the sort of temporal feedback mechanisms in operation in ADHD children that are apparent in applied learning tasks. In their concluding remarks, however, Sergeant and van der Meere did assert that ADHD children do differ from normal children in the strategy used in information processing and in energetic allocation. Our findings would support this assumption in the classroom.

> 16. MANY ADHD CHILDREN HAVE DIFFICULTIES IN SUSTAINED ATTENTION AND CONCENTRATION. IT MAY BE THAT THERE IS A SPECIFIC MECHANISM IN OPERATION WHICH RELATES TO TEMPORAL ORIENTATION AND ORGANIZATION WHICH LAYS THE BASIS FOR SEQUENTIAL ATTENTION DIFFICULTIES.

CEREBRAL PROCESSES

While many researchers would like, as we have mentioned, to put the MBD constellation of disorders to rest, particularly in relation to ADHD, this is not to say that minimal brain dysfunction does not or cannot play a significant role in the problems of many ADHD children. Cerebral processes, both in the lower and primitive reflex systems, the reticular stimulation function, and finally in the cortex, obviously are the birthplace of both normal and abnormal functioning. We need to reexamine some of the tenets in relation to brain dysfunction without, hopefully, falling into a major paradigm as in the case of MBD. In our own work we have been particularly frustrated by the lack of investigation into a more integrated concept of cerebral processing and development in the case of

ADHD. Much of the research, particularly recently, has been focused toward specificity in syndrome analysis. While this is critical in determining specific elements in the syndrome, it avoids speculation toward a holistic or comprehensive model within which specific results can be understood. In the educational field, where a child represents a complex interactive system of behavioral potentials, teachers and parents must deal with holistic behavior. Thus, while clinical researchers must continue investigation into specific elements, educators must work toward a broader understanding of the syndrome.

Pedagogically, in consideration of deficits in sensory motor, expressive skills, and processing difficulties, it has been logical to attempt intervention in learning via the best channels of function rather than attempting to stimulate the poorer response systems. Professionals in special education and learning styles have, in fact, for the last ten years demonstrated a great deal of sensitivity to this principle and many instructional strategies have been utilized with excellent results. Included in the symptoms of children who were failing and in need of a "best channel" learning style approach, have been inattention, over-activity, and impulsivity. Through structural changes in the classroom, multi-modality instruction, freedom of movement, and cooperative learning groups, many overly active and distractible children have been helped both in special education and in regular classes. The literature in educational psychology and special education is replete with research in this area. It is a well-established area of instructional theory and practice in schools that are responsive to developmental theory and effective teaching practices.

In the early days of the learning disabilities movement, stimulation, i.e., perceptual motor training, language stimulation, cognitive skills training, and other approaches should have resulted in improved development. In general, this was not the case (Hallahan & Cruickshank, 1973). This is not to say that developmental stimulation and training do not have positive effects since learning is a process of change in the central nervous system structure (CNS). But to attempt to alter significant developmental differences may be problematic in a situation where there may be cerebral insult or dysfunction. Most speech therapists and special educators who work with developmentally handicapped would be surprised that cognitive, language, and sensory-motor stimulation do not result in improved function since that is the basis for their profession. In the early years of the learning disability movement the problem was not that stimulation did not effect change but that in cases of known neurological damage stimulation may have had minimal if any effect.

Children with cerebral deficits or operational differences tend to have permanent impairment, even though the effects may vary somewhat with localization, age onset, and severity of the disorder (Woods & Carey, 1979). The existence of reports claiming that children fail to show functional impairment some years after confirmed brain damage may well be expected, and does neither exclude organic cerebral damage in the reported cases, nor weaken the relevance of a neuropsychological approach in observed functional impairment. The damaged area may for instance not be essential for the control of functions examined. Or, the symptoms of brain damage may not be recognized due to poor sensitivity and specificity of the clinical examination (Gillberg, 1982). Diagnosis of specific neurological dysfunction is somewhat straight forward due to observable sensory motor and subcortical dysfunction, but cerebral dysfunction is less available to study or recognize due to the complexity of functions involved. Certainly, when we look at impulsive behavior patterns with features of attentional deficit and over-activity, we cannot rule out cortical dysfunction. Research with various stimulants reinforces that dysfunctional neurochemical factors are at work.

> 17. WHILE "MBD" HAS MORE OR LESS BEEN DISREGARDED AS A FOUNDATION FOR ADHD, MUCH OF THE MORE RESTRICTED DEFINITION OF ADHD OVER ADD/ADHD, SUGGESTS A TREND TOWARD AN ETIOLOGY FAVORING BIOLOGICAL ORIGINS FOR THE DISORDER. THUS, EVENTUALLY A SPECIFIC CLASSIFICATION FOR ADHD MAY INCLUDE GENETIC, DEVELOPMENTAL DIFFERENCES, PHYSIOLOGICAL, BIOCHEMICAL, NEUROLOGICAL, AND OTHER BIOLOGICALLY BASED CRITERION BUT NOT, SIMPLY, MBD.

Hemispheric differences in language and motor processing of children have demonstrated interesting shifts in lateralization relative to speech production however rare. Speech and handedness are genetically determined by polygenic factors (Annett, 1976). Language lateralization is manifested anatomically in the fetus (Chi, Doolling, & Gillis, 1977). Typically, all right-handers (85–90%), two-thirds of the left-handers (7%) and the ambidextrous (0–5%) have speech controlled by the left hemisphere; only one-third of the left-handers (3%) show right hemisphere speech control (Steffen, 1975). Left hemisphere damage will most likely show combined impairment of both the control of speech and the right hand leaving the subject with impaired speech and genetically unexpected left handedness, or, as some have called it "pathological left-handedness." Our own research has given us some interesting theories, to be discussed in the chapters of our own work, concerning the whole question of cerebral dominance, language, and handedness which may make the above assumptions open to additional interpretation. The entire question of cerebral cognitive function and development in relation to sensory motor dominance and attention has not been well researched to this time of potential importance to the ADHD phenomenon.

Speech and articulation require advanced motor coordination particularly in application of these functions in a classroom task. For example, an analysis of reading contains additional insights into the previous discussion concerning controlled and automatic functions as we will see later. All of these functions, however, relate to the frontosagittal area and therefore would tend to be affected by the same damage which might produce an attention deficit. Selective temporary anaesthesia of one hemisphere after the other in the same individual by intracarotid barbiturate injection has demonstrated which functions are conserved and which are lost (Borchgrevink, 1987). This sort of research can demonstrate the sort of deficits which could be expected in brain damage. Review of the recovery sequence of functions in such work has demonstrated that impaired memory span, distal dynamic motor disorder, motor speech disorder, and impaired memory storage ("learning") have been suggested as expected in diffuse cortical brain damage (Borchgrevink, 1989). Borchgrevink further concluded that diffuse prefrontal and frontosagittal cortical damage would most likely lead to impaired attention accompanied by motor program disorder including speech and articulation.

HEMISPHERE SPECIALIZATION

Right	Left
SIMULTANEOUS PATTERN ANALYSIS	SEQUENTIAL PATTERN ANALYSIS
pitch	speech perception
chord	speech production

Right	Left
form	prosody
figure	rhythm
iconic	reading

holistic	logic
intuitive	analytic

(Borchgrevink, 1989)

Borchgrevink, concerned with frontosagittal and diffuse prefrontal cortical damage conducted a study using 56 children (CA) 2–15 years (mean 4.5 years) referred for therapy-resistant communication disorder. They went through a detailed neuropsychological and neuromotor evaluation (TINS, 1987). While details of the study are not reported here, some characteristics are of interest as are Borchgrevink's general summaries. Of the total group, 84 percent of the children were diagnosed as having attention deficit disorder, defined as poor or fluxuating attention for age, considered to require special intervention. This diagnosis was based on both the child's performance during examination and according to anamnestic information. With corresponding criteria, 57 percent showed increased distractibility, 38 percent reduced impulse control, 29 percent hyperkinesis, and 21 percent showed long-term memory impairment. Of the total group five subgroups were distinguished, (1) With ADD without cognitive impairment, (2) Walked before crawled, (3) With cognitive impairment, (4) With ADD, (5) Without ADD.

18. SPECIFIC DIFFERENCES IN HEMISPHERIC ORGANIZATION IN COMBINATION WITH INTERNAL OPPOSITIONAL HAND AND EYE DOMINANCE MAY BE SUGGESTIVE OF A PECULIAR CEREBRAL STRUCTURE WHICH MAY RELATE TO ADHD SYMPTOMOLOGY.

Relative to the total group, the cognitive impairment group showed low memory span, matching their language production level. Attention deficit matched the frequency of impaired memory span. Distractibility and hyperkinesis were increased. Low self-esteem or increased anxiety were infrequent. Of the group, 46 percent were left-handed, and 23 percent showed nonestablished/mixed handedness. Thus more than 69 percent (2/3) of the subjects with cognitive impairment were left-handers or mixed handedness. This group symbolizes for us a cluster of ADHD children who are frequently referred to our office.

Relative to the results of Borchgrevink's total study, we recognize that our intent here is not to detail the specifics of the study but to present his conclusions which speak to the notion of cerebral processes and damage as related to ADHD. To this end we wish to summarize his conclusions.

Dr. Borchgrevink's results indicated that ADHD is an activation deficit caused by prefrontal and/sagittal frontal pathology, probably predominately cortical ("top-down"). Dr. Borchgrevink felt that there is a continuum between ADD and autism, as well as with other cerebral damage. He felt that the continuum spoke to the belief that ADD should be seen as a symptom rather than a syndrome as others have proposed. We support this concept and will include a discussion of theories relating to this notion.

Dr. Borchgrevink spoke directly to the concept of disclaiming MBD as a syndrome which is too vague. On this point, obviously, there are a great many who have worked to attempt to discourage the "brain dysfunction" notion of ADHD. But Borchgrevink feels that MBD should be preserved as a reference for minor encephalopathy in general and lead to increased diagnostic effort in the search for specific organic etiology underlying impaired function or behavior. He further discussed the fact that birth complications, in his study, were most frequent for the ADD group. Hypoxia is the most frequent cause of fetal and neonatal brain damage, and tends to give diffuse cortical pathology when occurring at birth (Towbin, 1981).

> 19. FOLLOWING THE FAILURE OF THE SCIENTIFIC COMMUNITY TO ACCEPT DIETARY FACTORS IN THE ETIOLOGY OF HYPERACTIVITY, THERE APPEARS TO BE RENEWED INTEREST AND POSSIBILITIES IN THE ROLE OF DIETARY FACTORS IN ADHD.

DIETARY ISSUES

Stimulants, rather than dietary management, have more often occupied the attention of the popular literature and parents concerning hyperactivity over the years. But in the 1970s, continuing still but with less attention, dietary management, particularly through the popular Feingold diet, was utilized by a number of parents. The actual number of children who are on some sort of restricted diet today is unknown, but it most likely is substantial. The Feingold diet stressed the presence of food additives, colorings, and preservatives as sources of hyperactive reactions in children (1975). In general the research concerning children who were supposedly affected by additives and colorings has not been substantiated in studies utilizing double blind methodology (Conners et al., 1976) and (Harley et al., 1978). Other studies have shown some positive results but the findings suggest that additives and colorings alone are probably a rare cause of behavioral disturbance (Graham, 1986).

While the focus was on additives and colorings, other less recognized research shows positive effects. Allergies to such items as milk, fish, chocolate, and other foods are well recognized in pediatric practice. Dr. Conners, a participant in the 1976 study listed above, recently stated that while he has always been uncertain about the role food additives and colorings play in hyperactivity, recent research in the United Kingdom has shown otherwise (Soothhill, 1990).

At the Institute of Child Health in London over the past ten years, Soothhill has pioneered a complex and ongoing dietary approach (Graham, 1989). Once diagnosed, children are put on a "few foods" diet consisting of one meat, one vegetable, one starch, water, calcium, and vitamins. If the child responds well, foods are added one by one over the following two to three months (Carter et al, 1985).

Soothhill and his colleagues have been able to demonstrate the effectiveness of this approach in the treatment of eczema and severe childhood migraines. Subsequently, in a study of 76 children with the hyperkinetic syndrome, it was found that 82% responded in the open phase of the trial. Twenty-eight children entered the double blind phase in which the parents and pediatrician found improved response. The results were highly significant statistically (Egger et al., 1985). Interestingly, colorings and additives were the most frequent ingestant incriminated, but 43 naturally occurring foods were also apparently responsible.

Graham (1989) expressed caution about the findings because they were found among an unusual population (institutionalized children) in which allergic disorders and physical symptoms were already known. Immunological mechanisms and possibilities of enzyme deficiency have also been implicated (Brostoff, 1987).

David (1987) has expressed concern about the use of dietary treatment particularly where parents may involve themselves in a process not fully supervised by a physician. He listed six major concerns:

1. There are well recorded instances where children have actually been starved of essential nutrients by the false belief of parents that they were reactive (Warner & Hathaway, 1984).
2. Children subjected to severe environmental stress with parents who attribute the problem to food reaction may be unable to react appropriately.
3. Dietary treatment, when applied appropriately, is very expensive and requires the time of many medical personnel.
4. Restricting the child may be unrealistic and impossible to monitor as he is with peers in local shops and school.
5. The cost of the diet can be high including the expense of tests such as hair, skin testing, and carrying out various provocation tests, when there is no satisfactory proof that they are valid.
6. In some cases children have suffered anaphylactic reactions when they have been restricted and then suddenly returned to certain dietary elements.

There may be potential in dietary management, although at the present the research is difficult to assess and highly questionable. For the classroom teacher it remains experimental and parents pursuing this avenue should be referred to local physicians for consultation before embarking on any specific dietary program.

20. ASIDE FROM MEDICATION, THE MAJOR TREATMENT FOR ADHD INCLUDES BEHAVIORAL MANAGEMENT AND COGNITIVE THERAPIES. YET, RESEARCH DOES NOT SUPPORT THAT THE BEHAVIORAL MANAGEMENT THEORIES ARE SUCCESSFUL.

BEHAVIORAL AND COGNITIVE MANAGEMENT

In the case of ADHD, considering its present conceptualization, methods of assisting children in managing their behavior include a range of strategies including drug therapy, behavioral management techniques, and various cognitive therapies. There are several problems here which have been addressed by a number of researchers and, in some cases, more than one problem has been studied.

Research concerning the treatment of ADHD includes three basic approaches to investigation: drug therapy, particularly methylphenidate, psychosocial therapies, and cognitive therapies. Before discussing the research in each of these areas, it is important to point out that these approaches have been tried alone and in combination yielding a number of conflicting results as well as many positive results. But perhaps most important is the realization that the entire cluster is based on a particular paradigm of diagnosis and treatment, that is, the medical and behavioralist model of conceptualization. The paradigm includes, on one hand, the clinical belief that there is a biological foundation to ADHD for which medication may be utilized, and on the other, that social modification of the child's behavior will, in association with or without medication, change the child's behavior. Further, that these approaches will result in positive changes either through external manipulation of the behavior, e.g., external effects (punishment/reward) on the individual or eliciting moral, logical, or cooperative responses from the child through various forms of reason and encouragement of the child's own control system. The latter, eliciting from the child's encouragement of his own self-limiting and control capabilities, is at the edge of the paradigm for it moves from external intervention in the child's BEHAVIOR through manipulation from without, toward eliciting internal changes in the child himself.

Each of these approaches remains essentially within the medical model, one being almost exclusively medical, i.e., dysfunction within the biological system either neurological, metabolic and endocrinological, or neurotransmitter-based, and the other being psychoneurological, i.e., behavioral management. There are additional paradigms which, as far as can be seen within the research have received little attention, including developmental and integrative functions in relation to environmental effects, cultural/endocrinological, neurosocial and naturally inherent interactive learning systems, and a holistic model of human psychoneurological behavior. Each of these focus on the dynamics of human development within a cultural and social environment which, because of their complexity, are certainly beyond the usual realm of clinical research due to the microsocial limitations of the basic concepts of scientific research. For example, in conducting clinical research, both from limitations of variable management within scientific research parameters, and from control of variables to achieve meaningful results, gross representations of human development and behavior are beyond proof in a scientific environment.

The classroom teacher, the only truly effective agent in relation to management of and teaching toward assisting a child in the control of his own behavior AND learning new ones within the larger purpose of developing productive and adaptive behavioral and cognitive skills, must work constantly within the larger macrosocial environment of the child's lifespace. It is quite impossible for the teacher, parent, or even family practice physician to effectively investigate specific elements scientifically of either the cause or management of the ADHD syndrome. Rather, these frontline agents in assisting the child, must attempt to make value decisions and select one goal over another for the child in relation to multiple agendas proposed by the classroom, the school community, the parents, and the general curriculum of education. Thus, it is impossible for the teacher to know, at any time, whether one child is primarily overactive due to a disorder in dopamine production or utilization, because of food allergies, cultural deprivation, or conduct disorders, or any other of the many proposals for the etiology of ADHD.

While the teacher depends on the medical and psychological community to provide some answers and perhaps medication or behavioral management strategies, she or he must also have greater concepts to utilize in relation to how the child learns, or doesn't, why specific learning and behavioral difficulties may develop and how to alter them, and various paradigms of child developmental theory and learning. So as the clinician provides data, specific information about ADHD, or other microsocial concepts of dysfunction and syndromes, she must have more complex models of instruction and behavior into which she can incorporate the specific research data. I would suggest that today's teacher needs greater training and competence in human development and learning theories in order to do this. Without such a framework, she is left with only the medical concept of dysfunction and must wait until the clinician's behavioral management tools are given to her. This, obviously, is a deficit model of education and is a primary thrust for our later discussions about ADHD in the classroom. As we review the literature one result becomes very clear, while clinical manipulation of behavior through medication or behavioral management is important, the child still has to learn skills, reasoning, problem solving, self-image and social role, goal setting and accomplishment, and individualization. It should be obvious and expected that neither medication nor behavioral therapy will serve to assist the teacher in her assigned role, education of children. Therefore, we must set clearly exactly what can be expected from the study of the ADHD syndrome and subsequent methodology of treatment for the classroom teacher. At best, medication can perhaps allow the child to be more receptive to instruction and socialization but cannot teach nor socialize; the teacher must do that. The goal of behavioral and cognitive management strategies can be no less ambitious and will also result primarily in creating an opportunity for the child to learn but again cannot teach him. Parents and teachers are therefore still responsible and in control of the critical needs of the child, adaptive behavior and learning. If a child does not learn, does not adjust, and does not develop a positive and goal-directed behavioral style, it is primarily the parent and teacher who are the problem. All the medical community can do is make it possible for the professionals to more easily achieve these goals. As educators then we cannot blame nor condemn the clinician or medical practitioner for our ultimate failure.

The role and effectiveness of medication (stimulants) on hyperactive behavior has been well-documented and the various research studies need not be reviewed here. It has been submitted by such research that stimulants, in regard to hyperactive children, seem to normalize the child's behavior so that it no longer differs from other children. The wholesale application of stimulants with active children has been justified by much of the research leading to the above conclusion. But more recently, aided with the experience and work of earlier researchers, it has been found by Abikoff & Gittelman (1985a) that such a level of general expectation does not occur reliably across all deviant behaviors. The most that can be said is the stimulants, particularly methylphenidate, may normalize many but not all aspects of symptomatic behaviors.

Improvement in social behaviors, between child and parents, and other social interactions appear to improve in response to medication. But there has been some concern that stimulants do not improve academic performance and additional concern exists about the long-term effects on scholastic performance. At the present, while medication may not improve academic performance, though some believe it does, medication should be seen as most beneficial in terms of improving readiness to learn and not the learning per se.

In long-term studies of children on stimulants there appears to be little evidence that medication changes deficient learning or social skills and poor academic performance is still present in adolescence and young adulthood. Gittelman suggested, "the positive behavioral changes associated with stimulants are not maintained following termination of medication, necessitating long-term stimulant treatment in many cases" (Gittelman, R., Abikoff, 1989b).

Since stimulant therapy is not and cannot be responsible for the academic aspects of a child's needs, interest in such approaches as behavioral modification, operant conditioning, and contingency-based reinforcement procedures has been high. Gittelman et al. completed a study with 86 children in which behavior therapy included positive and negative reinforcements at home and school. The study included medication alone or behavior therapy alone. The results generally demonstrated that medication was more effective than behavioral therapy (Gittelman et al., 1980). The next obvious step was to combine the two and many studies have taken this approach. In reviewing much of the research Gittelman came to the conclusion that on the majority of measures there seemed to be no difference between medication alone and medication with behavior therapy. The obvious probability is that it is efficient to include both when the case appears to warrant it, but it is not always necessary to combine the two. Rapport (1983) and Sprague (1983) have reviewed much of the literature and concepts according to Gittelman. It has not changed significantly since his earlier research.

Cognitive training (Douglas, 1975) has been suggested as an alternate to drug therapy and has been tried by many researchers. Cognitive training falls within the categories of self-instructional training, cognitive modeling, attention training, social problem solving, and cognitive behavioral modification. The purpose of these approaches is the development of self-control skills and reflective problem-solving strategies. The efficacy of cognitive training has been reviewed by Abikoff (1985, 1987) and has failed. There is no evidence apparently that cognitive training enhances attentional or memory processes.

Again, combining cognitive training and medication would hopefully assist in taking advantage of the improvement in behavior through medication to enhance problem-solving and self-control skills (Horn et al., 1983). Cohen (1981), Brown (1980), and Brown (1986) all conducted studies concerning the use of cognitive training and drug combinations, but their numbers were small and other methodological problems prevented any meaningful conclusions. Abikoff and Gittelman (1985b) with the largest study involving elementary school-aged children evaluated a 4-month program involving cognitive and interpersonal problem-solving skills. A major conclusion of the study was that children who received cognitive training in combination with methylphenidate showed no superiority in multiple and academic measures obtained, when compared to children who remained on methphenidate alone. Similar negative results were obtained on all behavioral ratings tapping adjustment at home and school. Gittelman's conclusions for his own study were the same as for others in that, "none of the research generated results to indicate, or even suggest, that cognitive training is a competitor to stimulants, or that it enhances their beneficial effects."

SUMMARY

This general review of the research brings out many issues which are important to the understanding of the concept of ADHD. Those educators who are currently considering the range of emotions, anxieties, and difficulties related to children who are diagnosed as ADHD must, in light of these findings, reexamine exactly what the role of the school, the teacher, and parent should be in the future. As we have mentioned earlier, there is a strong force toward accepting ADHD as a category within the special education or disabilities field. There are increasing numbers of teachers in our nation's schools who are recommending medication for children. There is and will be an increasing number of parents and parent groups pressuring the schools toward special services and consideration for children diagnosed as ADHD. Finally, as happened in the early years of the learning disabilities movement, a number of well-meaning professionals in counselling and human services will offer a range of services to children. But the question which must be asked, even after reviewing the research, is what is ADHD?

The first issue which exists, one which is central and critical, is that by and large the clinical research both in the United States and Europe, does not strongly support the classification system in the present DSM–IIIR as adequate to accurately identify ADHD children. The elimination of the ADDnoH category is of profound importance in the field where parents, teachers, and even mental health professionals continue to operate on the defunct ADD concept. Helping schools, parents, and teachers readjust their viewpoints and attitudes about ADD toward a more clinical ADHD classification will take much time, and meanwhile many children may be subjected to medication and other interventions while the misdiagnosis moves attention away from other issues and problems which may really exist for the child.

To make matters even more tentative, many clinicians are projecting that the current ADHD classification may also be eliminated in favor of other diagnostic criteria. Barkley and Taylor, cited earlier, are suggesting more restrictive criteria, and if applied as they are now recommended, would likely eliminate most children currently identified through previous ADD criterion and many under the current DSM–IIIR classification. It is possible for the clinician, privy to current research and thinking, to see movement toward an eventual tightening and more clinically professional diagnostic classification. For the teacher, principal, parent, and even frontline medical professional, it is not possible to either understand or incorporate newer concepts as they emerge. Children will be diagnosed, labeled, responded to in many deficit ways, and programs will be initiated before frontline personnel can adapt to newer information and concepts. This is not only detrimental to the educational professional and school programs, it can be disastrous to the family and the child. Thus, while the clinical picture changes in relation to research, the ripple of communication and finally programmatic changes at the frontline level can be three to five years down the road. How do you go back and undo the problems created for many children who, as it finally turns out, did not have ADHD. From this viewpoint it is the school professional's responsibility to take the most conservative profile possible in regard to acceptance or use of the classification of ADHD unless the following precautions are taken.

In cases of suspected ADHD the following steps should be taken by the school professional:

1. Teachers or parents should be informed that problems in impulsivity, inattention, over-activity, and rule-governed behavior should be treated as classroom and parental management issues until such time as a diagnosis of ADHD is completed.

2. If teachers or parents feel there is the possibility that a child has ADHD then a full evaluation should be completed by school special services personnel, the teacher, parents, *and* outside clinical and medical personnel. The completion of a behavioral checklist by either the teacher or parent does not constitute a valid diagnosis but only an initial means for referral. If and until such a diagnosis is completed all possible educational and counseling efforts with the parents and teacher should be initiated at home and in the school.

3. That criterion suggested by Taylor and Barkley should be incorporated by both the school and medical team for the purpose of classification. Summarized here these criterion should be included.

   a. A pattern of markedly inattentive, restless behavior, observed by both parent and teacher through direct observation and interview (not just antisocial, impulsive, or disruptive acts) that is excessive for the child's age and IQ and a handicap to development. Observed in two or more situations (Taylor, 1989) (Barkley, 1982).

b. This pattern to be observed by an outside diagnostician and not solely confirmed by parent and teacher alone (Taylor, 1989).

c. A score or scores two standard deviations above the mean for same-age, same-sex normal children on factors labeled as "inattentive" or "hyperactive" in well-standardized child behavior rating scales completed by two or more members of diagnostic team, parents, or teachers (Barkley, 1982).

d. Onset by age of six years and duration of at least 6 months and optimumly 12 months (Barkley, 1982; Taylor, 1989).

e. An IQ greater than 85 or, if between 70 and 85, comparison to same mental age in using criterion (c) above (Barkley, 1982).

f. Exclusion of significant language delay, sensory handicaps (e.g. deafness, blindness, etc.), or severe psychopathology (e.g. autism, childhood schizophrenia) (Barkley, 1982; Taylor, 1989).

g. If stimulants or other medications are to be recommended that the physician responsible maintain ongoing communication with special services team member and teacher on a biweekly basis to monitor and evaluate efficacy of treatment.

Dr. Barkley composed a narrative definition which may be used in general as a guideline for the school. Reviewed briefly in the first chapter, we present it again in this context.

ADHD is a developmental disorder of attention span impulsivity, and over-activity as well as rule governed behavior, in which these deficits are significantly inappropriate for the child's mental age; have an on-set in early childhood; are significantly pervasive or cross-situational in nature; are generally chronic or persistent over time; and are not the direct result of severe language delay, deafness, blindness, autism, or childhood psychosis.

Relative to the DSM–IIIR list of 14 behavioral criteria in which 8 have to be seen for classification, these should be tempered with the foregoing criteria.

ETIOLOGY IN CLASSIFICATION

With all of these criteria having been satisfied, an additional question still remains and is most often not answered by either the educational or medical diagnostic team. Now that all agree that the child has an ADHD disorder, why and what does he have? The research suggests that the actual cause or etiology of the disorder is still vague and ranges from subtle frontal-sagittal brain dysfunction, to allergies and dietary problems, or biochemical dysfunction in dopamine production. It may be a problem in "top-down" organization or a "middle-out" cognitive processing difficulty. These have all been considered in the research to date and as we have seen in the research summary here, none have proven to be a singular prospect for the cause. We return again to our comment in the first chapter that most researchers accept that ADHD is a disorder with multiple causes and each child may differ.

For educators the matter of etiology would seem to be a mute issue in that neither the skills nor expertise for such assessment exist in the school environment. But educators cannot leave it at that for, as we will see in the coming chapters, there are a number of developmental, cultural, social, and psychological aspects of the disorder that, if not the cause, are highly contributory in the process of the disorder. Educational professionals must realize that ADHD is not like the measles or chicken pox, it does not run its course after which the child survives nicely. The research here has suggested that if a child is truly ADHD then the basic problem is most likely persistent into adolescence and adulthood with the academic problems continuing. It would be symptomatic of the disorder then that many accompanying developmental, social, and educational difficulties will exist which will be open to assessment and treatment within, if not only in the school setting.

In most cases involving a school referral for ADHD, it is interesting to us that in general once the ADHD classification has been applied, there is no further diagnostics in the school concerning underlying developmental and learning disabilities. We find that when one uses the above criterion for diagnosis, that the ADHD child usually has evident learning and developmental difficulties which accompany the disorder. Understanding these difficulties is as important, if not more important, in developing a learning and behavioral management program for the child. This area involves a significant case of negligence on the part of the school, but this is due to the often erroneous conceptualization which centers around the ADHD disorder. This is why the conceptualization of the disorder must be moved from the medically-oriented viewpoint to one which is more developmental and educationally-based, at least, for educational professionals.

In the coming chapters we want to look beyond the restrictive clinical concept and research concerning the classification of ADHD and consider underlying cause and intervention factors which are within the capabilities of school services. The current medication/behavioral management duet of treatment is no longer adequate in assisting the ADHD child in the school environment.

REFERENCES

Abikoff, H. Efficacy of Cognitive Training Interventions in Hyperactive Children, *Clinical Psychology Review*, 5, 479–512, 1985.

Abikoff, H. An Evaluation of Cognitive Behavior Therapy for Hyperactive Children. In B.B. Lahey & A.E. Kazdin (Eds). *Advances in Clinical Child Psychology*, 10, 171–216, New York: Plenum Press 1987.

Abikoff, H., & Gittelman, R. Hyperactive Children Treated With Stimulants: Is Cognitive Training a Useful Adjunct? *Archives of General Psychiatry*, 42, 953–961, 1985b.

Abikoff, H., & Gittelman, R. The Normalizing Effects of Methylphenidate on the Classroom Behavior of ADHD Children. *Journal of Abnormal Psychology*, 13, 33–44, 1985a.

Annett, M. Handedness and the Cerebral Representation of Speech, *Annals of Human Biology*, 3, 317–28, 1976.

Barkley, R. A. Specific Guidelines for Defining Hyperactivity in Children (attention deficit disorder with hyperactivity), In Lahey, B. B., & Kazdin, A. E., (Eds) *Advances in Clinical Child Psychology*, 5, 137–180, 1982.

Borchgrevink, H. M. Cerebral Processes, in *Attention Deficit Disorder: Clinical and Basic Research*, (Ed), Sagvolden and Archer, 1989.

Borchgrevink, H. M. Left Hemisphere: Sequential Analysis, Right Hemisphere: Simultaneous/Instantaneous Analysis? Right (non-speech) Hemisphere Anaesthesia Affects Pitch in Singing While Prosody (pitch in speech) and Musical Rhythm is Preserved, The Second World Congress of Neuroscience (IBRO), *Neuroscience*, 22, (Suppl.), S508, Oxford/New York: Pergamon Press (abstract), 1987.

Brostoff, J. Non-Immunological Food Reactions. Effects of Enzyme Deficiency and Neuropeptides in Food Sensitive Patients, In Dobbing, J. J. (Ed), *Food Intolerance*, 32–55, London: Bailiere Tindall, 1987.

Brown, R. T. Impulsivity and Psychoeducational Intervention in Hyperactive Children, *Journal of Learning Disabilities*, 13, 249–254, 1980.

Brown, R. T., Borden, K. A., Wynne, M. E., Schleser, R., & Clingerman, S. R. Methylphenidate and Cognitive Therapy With ADD Children: A Methodological Reconsideration, *Journal of Abnormal Child Psychology*, 14, 481–497, 1986.

Carter, C. M., Egger, J., & Soothhill, J. F. A Dietary Management of Severe Childhood Migraine, *Human Nutrition: Applied Nutrition*, 39, 294–303, 1985.

Chi, J. G., Doolling, E. C., & Gilles, F. H. Left-Right Asymmetries of the Temporal Speech Areas in Human Fetus, *Archives of Neurology,* 34, 346–348, 1977.

Cohen, N. J., Sullivan, J., Minde, K., Novak, C. & Helwig, C., Evaluation for the Relative Effectiveness of Methylphenidate and Cognitive Behavior Modification in the Treatment of Kindergarten-Aged Hyperactive Children, *Journal of Abnormal Child Psychology,* 9, 43–54, 1981.

Conners, C. K., Goyette, C. H., Southwick, D. A., Lees, J. M., & Andrulonis, P. Food Additives and Hyperkinesis, *Pediatrics,* 58, 154–166, 1976.

David, T. Unhelpful Recent Developments in the Diagnosis and Treatment of Allergy and Food Intolerance in Children, In Dobbing, J., (Ed) *Food Intolerance,* 185–214, London: Bailiere Tindall 1878.

Douglas, V. I. Are Drugs Enough? To Treat or Train the Hyperactive Child, *International Journal of Mental Health,* 4, 199–212, 1975.

Douglas, V. I., and Peter, K. G. Towards a Clearer Definition of the Attention Deficit of Hyperactive Children, In Hale, G. A., & Lewis, M., (Eds.), *Attention and Cognitive Development,* 173–247, New York: Plenum Press, 1979.

Douglas, V. I. Attentional and Cognitive Problems, In M. Rutter (Ed.), *Developmental Neuropsychiatry,* 280–329, New York: Gilford Press, 1983.

Egger, J., Carter, C. M., Graham, P. J., Gumley, D. & Soothhill, J. F. Controlled Trial of Oligoantigenic Treatment in the Hyperkinetic Syndrome, *The Lancet,* i, 540–545, 1985.

Feingold, B. F. Hyperkinesis and Learning Disabilities Linked to Artificial Food Flavors and Colors, *American Journal of Nursing,* 75, 797–803, 1975.

Gillberg, C. Rasmussen, P., Calstrom, G., Stevenson, B., & Waldenstrom, E., Perceptual, Motor, and Attention Deficits in Six Year Old Children, Epidemiology Aspects, *Journal of Child Psychology and Psychiatry,* 23, 11331–144, 1982.

Gittelman, R., Abikoff, H., Pollack, E., Klein, D. F., Katz, S., & Mattes, J. A. A Controlled Trial of Behavior Modification and Methylphenidate in Hyperactive Children, In Whalen, C. K., & Henker, B., (Eds), *Hyperactive Children: The Social Ecology of Identification and Treatment,* 221–243, New York: Academic Press, 1980.

Gittelman, K. and Mannuzza, Long Term Outcomes of the Attentional Deficit Disorder, In *Attentional Deficit Disorder: Clinical And Basic Research,* (Ed), Sagvolden, T., and Archer, T., Hillsdale, NJ: Lawrence Erlbaum Associates, 1989b.

Gittelman, R., & Abikoff, H. The Role of Psychostimulants and Psychosocial Treatments in Hyperkinesis, In *Attention Deficit Disorder: Clinical And Basic Research,* (Ed), Sagvolden, T., and Archer, T., Lawrence Erlbaum Associates, 1989b.

Graham, P. *Child Psychiatry: A Developmental Approach,* London: Oxford University Press, 1986.

Graham, P. Practical Aspects of Dietary Management, In *Attention Deficit Disorder: Clinical and Basic Research,* (Ed), Sagvolden, T., and Archer, T., Hillsdale, NJ: Lawrence Erlbaum Associates, 1989.

Harley, J. P., Ray, R. S., Thomas, L., Eichman, P. L., Matthews, C. G., Chun, R., Cleeland, C. S., & Traisman, E. Hyperkinesis and Food Additives: Testing the Feingold Hypothesis, *Pediatrics,* 61, 818–828, 1978.

Hallahan, D. P., & Cruickshank, W. M. *Psychoeducational Foundations of Learning Disabilities,* Englewood Cliffs, N. J., Prentice Hall, 1973.

Holborow, P., & Berry, P. S., Hyperactivity and Learning Difficulties, *Journal of Learning Disabilities,* 1986.

Hopkins, J., Perlman, T., Hechtman, L., Weiss, G. Cognitive Styles in Adults Originally Diagnosed as Hyperactive, *Journal of Child Psychology and Psychiatry,* 29, 209–216, 1979.

Horn, W. F., Chatoor, I., & Conners, C. K. Additive Effects of Dexedrine and Self Control Training: A Multiple Assessment, *Behavior Modification,* 7, 383–402, 1983.

Magnusson, D. Individual Development in an Interactional Perspective, Vol. 1., Series: *Paths Through Life,* Ed., D. Magnusson, Hillsdale, NJ: Lawrence Erlbaum Associates, 1987.

Rapoport, J. L., Donnelly, M., Sametkin, A., and Carrougher, J. Situational Hyperactivity in a U.S. Clinical Setting, *Journal of Child Psychiatry,* 27, 639–646, 1986.

Rapoport, J. The Use of Drugs: Trends in Research, In Rutter, M., (Ed) *Developmental Neuropsychiatry,* 385–403, New York: Gilford Press, 1983.

Rapport, M. D. Attention Deficit Disorder With Hyperactivity: Critical Treatment Parameters and Their Application in Applied Outcome Research, In Hersen, M., Eisler, R., & Miller, P., (Eds), *Progress in Behavior Modification,* Vol. 14, 219–298, New York: Academic Press, 1983.

Rapport, M. D., Tucker, S. B., DuPaul, G. J., Merlo, M. and Stoner, G. Hyperactivity and Frustration: The Influence of Control Over and Size of Rewards in Delaying Gratification, *Journal of Abnormal Child Psychiatry,* 14, 191–204, 1986.

Rutter, M. Attention Deficit Disorder/Hyperkinetic Syndrome, In *Attention Deficit Disorder/Clinical and Basic Research,* Sagvolden, T., and Archer, T., Hillsdale, NJ: Lawrence Erlbaum Associates, 1989.

Rutter, M. (Ed). *Developmental Neuropsychiatry,* New York: Gilford Press, 1983.

Rutter, M. Tizzard, J. and Whitmore, K. (Eds). *Education, Health and Behavior,* London: Longmans, 1970.

Safer, D. J., & Allen, R. D. *Hyperactive Children: Diagnosis And Management,* Baltimore: University Park Press, 1976.

Sanders, A. F. Toward a Model of Stress and Human Performance, *Acta Psychologica,* 53, 61–97, 1983.

Sandoval, J., & Lambert, N. M. Hyperactive and Learning Disabled Children: Who Gets Help? *The Journal of Special Education,* 18, 495–503, 1984–85.

Schachar, R., Sandberg, S. and Rutter, M. and Smith, A. The Characteristics of Situationally and Pervasively Hyperactive Children: Implications for Syndrome Definition, *Journal of Child Psychology and Psychiatry,* 22, 375–392, 1981.

Sergeant, J. and van der Meere, J. J. *The Diagnostic Significance of Attentional Processing: Its Significance for ADHD,* Hillsdale, NJ: Lawrence Erlbaum Associates, 1989.

Shaffer, D., O'Connor, P. A., Shafer, S. Q., and Prupis, S. Neurological Soft Signs; Their Origins and Significance for Behavior, In Rutter, M. (Ed), *Developmental Neuropsychiatry,* 144–163, New York: Gilford Press, 1983.

Shaffer, D., Schonfeld, I., O'Connor, P. A., Stockman, C., Trautman, P., Shafer, S., and Ng, S. Neurological Soft Signs: Their Relationship to Psychiatric Disorders and Intelligence in Childhood and Adolescence, *Archives of General Psychiatry*, 42, 342–351, 1985.

Shaywitz, S. E., and Shaywitz, B. A. Critical Issues in Attention Deficit Disorder, in Sagvolden, T. & Archer, T., *Attention Deficit Disorder: Clinical and Basic Research*, Hillsdale, NJ: Lawrence Erlbaum Associates, 1989.

Shaywitz, S. E. Prevalence of Attentional Deficits in an Epidemiologic Sample of School Children With Attention Deficit Disorder, *Annals of Neurology*, 20, 416, 1986.

Sprague, R. L. Behavior Modification and Educational Techniques, In Rutter, M., (Ed), *Developmental Neuropsychiatry*, New York: Gilford Press, 1983.

Steffen, H. Cerebral Dominance: The Development of Handedness and Speech, *Acta Paedopsychiatrica*, 41 (6), 223–235, 1975.

Sternberg, S. Discovery of Processing Stages; Extension of Donder's Method, In Koster, W. G., (Ed) *Attention and Performance II*, Noord-Holland, Amsterdam, 1969.

Taylor, E. A. On the Epidemiology of Hyperactivity, In *Attention Deficit Disorder: Clinical and Basic Research*, Sagvolden, T., and Archer, T., Hillsdale, NJ: Lawrence Erlbaum Associates, 1989.

Taylor, E. A. (Ed). The Overactive Child, *Clinics in Developmental Medicine*, 97, London: McKeith Press with Blackwell Scientific, Philadelphia: J.B. Lippincott, 1986.

TINS. The Frontal Lobes-Uncharted Provinces of the Brain, *Trends in Neurosciences*, Special Issue, 7, (11), 1984.

Warner, J. D., & Hathaway, M. J. Allergic Form of Meadow's Syndrome (Munchausen Syndrome by Proxy), *Archives of Diseases in Childhood*, 59, 151–6, 1984.

Weiss, G., and Hechtman, L. T. *Hyperactive Children Grown Up*, New York: Gilford Press, 1986.

Wender, P. H. *Minimal Brain Injury in Children*, New York: Wiley-Interscience, 1971.

Woods, B. T., & Carey, S. Language Deficits After Apparent Clinical Recovery From Childhood Aphasia, *Annals of Neurology*, 6, 405–407, 1979.

Chapter Three

DEVELOPMENTAL ISSUES

The overview of research concerning ADHD brings us to several important generalizations. The first is that while the range of investigations into this disorder are diverse, one is struck by the fact that little has changed, in substance, about the definition of the syndrome since the 1970s. The elimination of the concept of ADDnoH, ADD without hyperactivity, is helpful in that it eliminates many questionable aspects of diagnosis. But even with ADHD we still find ourselves looking to the feature of overactivity or hyperactivity as the truly basic issue. Hyperactivity suggests that a child will have difficulties in attention and organization. Attention problems, difficulties with rules, and distractibility are universal problems not only at various developmental ages, but in certain cultural, economic, and behavioral patterns as well. Without the element of hyperactivity, ADHD becomes less a distinct syndrome. When Douglas suggested in the early 1970s that attention and distractibility were the essential features of the disorder, the change to ADD moved the investigations away from the original foundations of a distinct disorder. Now, in the early 1990s, we are seeing more enthusiasm for the biological foundations of the disorder once again. For all of the resistance and rejection of the MBD concept in the seventies and early eighties, we are moving back toward, if not a subtle or diffuse definition of brain dysfunction, at least a foundation of biochemical, neurological processing, and dietary model.

If, as now appears to be the case, ADHD is the consequence of a number of potential difficulties in central nervous system functions (CNS), it is primarily a medical issue and not an educational one. The research concerning medication and behavioral therapies in the "treatment" of the disorder suggested that medication was the essential factor in improving behavior. The research also seemed to indicate that behavioral modification, cognitive therapies, and self-regulatory training strategies were generally unsuccessful with or without medication. This, too, would imply that the disorder is one founded in CNS dysfunction wherein some sort of pharmacological treatment response is most effective. Where does this leave the teacher?

We submit that the definition of ADHD as a disorder in CNS function which results in pervasive hyperactivity with the consequences of poorly sustained attention and rule governed behavior defines the essential elements of the syndrome. Adding to this the requirement of onset before the age of six years and with a duration of more than six months tightens the definition even more toward a medically-based problem. In our clinical work in the last 25 years this definition fits well the children who we would have agreed are what is now called ADHD. We simply called them, and continue to call them, hyperkinetic!

The important feature of the foregoing definition is the phrase, "pervasively hyperkinetic," for it implies a condition in which the child has no control. He is a victim of forces, dysfunction if you like, and is unable to inhibit or direct behavior. Such a condition takes us into the realm of cerebral palsy, muscular dystrophy, epilepsy, or torets. ADHD should be seen as a disorder in the classification of an involuntary behavioral response as a consequence of CNS dysfunction. Certainly, such children will have difficulties in attention, distractibility, impulsivity, and rule-governed behavior. But their behavior will not be one in which responsibility is a factor, where conduct problems are inherent in the child, or selective inhibition within situational parameters. The child is not capable of personal management and directedness. In this case we have a disorder, not a mere syndrome of symptoms, but characteristics of a disorder.

The early and pervasive onset of the disorder also suggests a problem inherent in the child and not in response to parenting, poor instruction, sociological or psychological processes, or learning disabilities. The fact that it is almost exclusively a male disorder suggests an etiology of genetic and/or endocrinological relationships which again are part of an inherent dysfunction as opposed to simply an attention deficit.

ADHD AS A MEDICAL DISORDER IN CNS FUNCTION

All of this then suggests that ADHD, in its most blatant form represents a medical disorder, should it be founded in endocrinological, neurological, dietary/metabolic, or biochemical, which requires medical intervention. It is a matter of inability in control of attention, impulsivity, and inhibition no less than that of the child with difficulties in control of muscles or reticular excitation. To include, in the same classification, children who have varying degrees of problems in attention or behavioral organization, without pervasive hyperkinesis and the other present ADHD factors, is inappropriate and impossible to classify.

If medical intervention, i.e., stimulants, dietary management, endocrinological management, or other physiological controls, are successful in presenting a child with increased focal ability, then the school has the responsibility for educational management. The ADHD child is, following successful medical intervention, one who falls within the educational environment of the regular school curriculum. Conversely, if medical intervention is unsuccessful, the child may need placement within special education where appropriate behavioral management (seriously emotionally disturbed) or specialized learning strategies (learning disabilities) can be applied consistently. Thus, placement of the child or qualification of the child for special education will depend on the success or failure of medical intervention. Children who do not display the full ADHD syndrome but who are overly active, inattentive, and display problems with rule-governed behavior, are then something else, not ADHD, and the school program must respond to these needs as they would any number of other special individual differences exhibited by other yet different children.

A DEVELOPMENTAL AND BEHAVIORAL MODEL
FOR NON-ADHD SYMPTOMATOLOGY

Children with behavioral characteristics of the ADHD syndrome though not hyperactive, but who may display highly active behavior which is situational, sporadic, and/or are manageable with behavioral management strategies, are children who primarily have an educational and parenting problem. These are the children, previously erroneously included as ADDnoH, who have given researchers such problems in analysis of the ADHD syndrome for they are essentially children with a range of various difficulties but not actual ADHD. If the definitions of Thomas and Barkley, cited in the summary of Chapter Two, are applied, then the previously classified ADDnoH children now become not a classification of a special syndrome but a collection of children with "learning and behavioral" difficulties. It is this group who we feel are within the realm of educational intervention and management and to which our remarks in this and later chapters will be addressed. Our obvious intention here is to suggest also that these are children, dependent on the severity of their condition, with developmental learning and/or behavioral difficulties. These are children who would, if the condition is severe enough, fit squarely into the present learning disabilities and behavioral disorders classifications in special education. For such children who are not seriously enough involved to qualify for special education, we then have a large, perhaps growing, number of children with behavioral and learning problems who are disrupting an increasing number of classrooms.

We have, in this model, a series of groups representing a continuum of severity in symptoms but with significant differences in the foundation of their problem. Some researchers have suggested that ADHD represents a continuum of problems from minor distractibility and impulsivity to autism. We do not see this as simply a continuum of severity but rather of symptoms with different causal foundations.

GROUP A—ADHD CHILDREN
(POSITIVE RESPONSE TO MEDICAL INTERVENTION)

Group A ADHD children represent a medically-based disorder which results in attentional, organizational, and inhibition difficulties. This group responds positively to medical intervention and can be managed in the regular classroom.

GROUP B—ADHD CHILDREN
(POOR RESPONSE TO MEDICAL INTERVENTION)

Group B ADHD children do not respond well to medical intervention and need special placement in order to assist them in learning and adaptation to school and home.

GROUP C—DEVELOPMENTAL ATTENTIONAL DEFICIT
WITH ADHD SYMPTOMS

Group C children display many ADHD symptoms but do not display pervasive hyperactivity and their diagnostic parameters suggest a developmentally responsive causal factor for the difficulties. These children may respond to educational and behavioral management strategies in the regular classroom, but a number of learning disabilities and/or difficulties may also be present and require special attention.

GROUP D—BEHAVIORAL ATTENTION DEFICIT
WITH ADHD SYMPTOMS

Group D children display attentional problems which relate primarily to conduct disorders, parental and sociological problems, language deprivation, and emotional difficulties.

The latter classifications (C&D) are, unlike the basic ADHD syndrome, neither sophisticated nor adequate clinical categories but are rather used here as a means of reference in our later discussions. All of the children in C & D though will display symptoms typical of the ADHD classification and many, on the basis of the behavioral criterion alone, will meet the 8 of 14 requirements on the DSM–IIIR. But none would meet the early onset, pervasive hyperactivity, or other criterion listed earlier in the Barkley/Taylor synthesis adopted in this text as the best classification for ADHD.

We retain the attentional deficit as a primary part of our definitions for, as Douglas stated in the early 1970s, it is true that the essential problem for most children, relative to learning and behavioral organization problems does center around the generalized difficulty in maintaining attention. But much of the research has suggested attention is also the aspect of the attentional deficit disorder which is most difficult to define. The problem in definition of attention lies in the same realm of difficulty as defining consciousness. These are both neurological and philosophical issues which have been the subject of intense and on-going arguments for decades. Little wonder then that attention is impossible to define, let alone diagnose adequately, in a clinical sense. But the difficulty of a child to focus his attention arises from any number of intrinsic and extrinsic factors. We will not accept the challenge here to attempt to define the issue of attention in clinical terms, but we can address the contributing factors in the child's development that give rise to efficiency in attention, inhibition, and focus toward learning and behavioral controls.

In the remainder of this chapter we want to review some general psychoneurological factors and processes typical of children as they learn and develop which can then lay the basis for understanding how things may go wrong. In 1980 William Gaddes authored a book, *Learning*

Disabilities and Brain Function, which he hoped would bridge the gap between neurology and education. His argument was that teachers and school psychologists could benefit from a layman's understanding of underlying psychoneurological processes related to learning. He was, as he described in the Preface, advised by many not to attempt such a synthesis. Our own experience with undergraduate and graduate students in education leans toward the same advice: teachers are not fond of medical terminology nor in-depth discussions about psychoneurological processes.

We are going to make the same optimistic assumption that Gaddes made, that it would be helpful if teachers had at least a general layman's understanding of brain function, because in the 1990s we believe it is time that educational professionals admit that merely learning teaching strategies has little relevance if one does not know when and why they should be used. With the increasingly technological invasion into the classroom, teachers are under more and more pressure to learn about the process of learning, thinking, and development. Further, the inclusion of ever more exceptional children in the classroom, i.e., the "regular education initiative," requires that teachers become more broadly trained in disciplines beyond the teaching of reading, writing, and mathematics. Colleges of education in universities are currently attempting to bring more scientific structure to the management of teacher education curriculum and part of that initiative includes both technology and human development. So today, unlike in the early eighties, it is not so much that teachers are interested in or willing to learn about psychoneurology, as that their profession is increasingly under pressure to do so.

Our approach in the remainder of this chapter is to develop a general psychoneurological foundation of particular systems of CNS function which can provide a conceptual basis for later discussions of inattention, over-activity, disinhibition or impulsivity, and difficulties with rule-governed behavior. Our goal is to develop an overall model of function which can be translated into classroom behavior and learning. Teachers, like most non-clinicians, have different skills, professional interests, and their own knowledge base from which they teach children. We have found that models of CNS which relate and make sense in what teachers see in child behavior, and their own field of knowledge, are effective in helping teachers integrate general CNS concepts into classroom instruction. To this end then we want to relate several general theories about development and learning which can help teachers see how essentially normal children may develop patterns of inattention, disorganization, impulsivity, and problems with rules. Finally, in following chapters we want to illustrate how specific developmental and emotional/social difficulties can result in an "ADHD-like" pattern of behavior and how it can be managed in the classroom. These discussions should also demonstrate why this syndrome of behavior is most aptly managed in the regular classroom.

The following discussions are formulated from work with teachers relative to understanding the development, learning, and behavior of children in the classroom. These general systems have seemed to assist the teacher in a theoretical basis upon which the specific learning and behavioral difficulties of a particular child could be understood. Yet, in many ways, these systems and the explanations are less than accurate within the "clinical realities" of the neurologist or researcher in CNS function. But we mentioned earlier two points: we do not apologize to the clinician for the liberties we take in explanation, and, teachers must operate from viewpoints of holistic behavior and not from specific neurological realities. For those teachers or others who wish to involve themselves in greater detail we will give ample references for further reading. We will utilize these general systems as a foundation for discussions about both developmental and behavioral attention deficits.

SYSTEM I
THE TRIUNE BRAIN

The first global understanding of the brain, emerging only in the last few years, is that in overall functioning of the CNS there appears to be not one brain but at least three. Dysfunction in these areas and inadequate cultural and language learning can present a child that will fit the criterion and symptomatology of ADHD.

In discussing the three brains, Dr. David MacLean, Director of the Laboratory of Brain Evolution and Behavior of the National Institute of Health, states, "the three brains amount to three interconnected biological computers, each having its own intelligence, its own subjectivity, its own sense of time and space, and its own memory and other functions" (MacLean, 1973; Rosenfeld, 1976).

The theory of the triune brain emerging from MacLean's research is critical in a first glance of the brain for two important reasons, it ties together many notions about human behavior into a concrete and CNS-based reality, and it provides a rationale for understanding many significant behaviors seen in the classroom and related to ADHD behavioral symptoms. According to MacLean, and the reason for calling himself a brain archeologist, is that looking at the human brain is like looking back in time to its development from a primitive lizard-like structure to a more mammalian and animal brain, to the present structure of human behavior and thought. The triune brain theory is based on the notion that the brain has evolved and that each of its major phases of gross transition are still part of the whole. In its most basic and lower brain structure (see Fig. 1.) there is a complete brain not unlike that of the reptile! This area of the brain MacLean views as functioning not unlike the present day reptile and hence his name for the portion of the brain, the R–Complex or reptilian brain.

Structures in the middle of our brain operate much like the mammalian brain while the cerebral cortex, the top portions of our brain, he sees as a more recent refinement and development of the mammalian brain. He calls these three "levels" of brain function the Reptilian, the Paleomammalian or limbic, and the Neomammalian. Specific structures in each of these brain levels operate independently of the others, in coordination with one other area or the whole of the brain, or in very special ways in a myriad of associations and interactions with other parts.

Freud spoke of the tripartite self, composed of the id, ego, and superego, but the triune brain gives us a more concrete reality to some of Freud's concepts. We find this very helpful in both understanding the behavior and the process of "thinking" which children exhibit in the classroom. The distinctly human part of the triune brain is, of course, the cortex or cerebrum which is divided into two hemispheres. The neocortex is the seat of all higher functions such as foresight, insight, reason, logic, problem solving, and through vision, hearing, and our bodily sensations we, the cortex, can relate and interact with the world. But this interaction depends upon all of the functions of the subcortical world below. We can be the master of our brain but much of what we assume to be voluntary behavior and actions of our own volitional planning, is in reality created below our cerebrum and in the world of the mammalian and reptilian brains making us less masters than slaves.

The "old mammalian brain" resides in the "limbic system" and is the headquarters of the emotions. The mammalian brain is like the squirrel, the rabbit, or the lion concerned with survival, the preservation of self, and its behavior revolves around eating, fighting, fleeing, and reproducing.

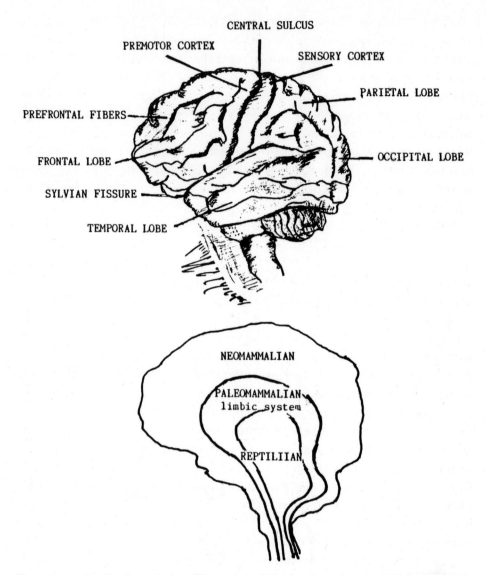

Figure 1. Levels of brain evolution. Illustration of MacLean's evolution of the brain and the general structure of the left hemisphere.

This emotional seat also provides for the sensations of pain and pleasure which are, according to MacLean, either positive or negative, agreeable or disagreeable. How we interpret these sensations in human terms can be more finely tuned to happiness or sadness, joy or sorrow, euphoria or depression, but at the sensation level they simply tend to energize behavior in either a positive or negative way.

The R–Complex is more like the alligator waiting at pools edge where archaic "behavioral programs" operate. The R–Complex, like the lizard, can be rigid, obsessive, compulsive, ritualistic, and even paranoid. The reptilian brain then tends to be more "hardwired" than the mammalian brain and certainly the cortex. The important feature of these brain structures as an overall pattern of brain patterns is their influence on the behavior of children (and, of course, adults). We must realize that these levels of brain structure suggest that in our behavior much of what we may call "genetics," "culturally-learned" or "biologically-based" is really active participation in our lives of the other brains within our head. These brains, as MacLean sees it, are, in the language of the science fiction thriller, "Look it's Alive!" Robert Aubrey, in his many books such as *Territorial Imperative,* has often opened our eyes to the fact that mammalian behavior in ourselves does not make a mockery of humans so much as remind us that for all of our cerebral splendor, we are animals. The key is not to deny our brain but to use it!

MacLean discusses how tetrapods, mammals, birds, and reptiles all use four basic forms of display: signature, challenge, courtship, and submission which are used to communicate to others of the species our needs and intentions. Displays demonstrate an individual's dominance, conversely, his submission, or his love, and territory. Displays are ways of obtaining our animal needs for food, water, a mate, security, and territory. Who hasn't noted the wolf heritage in the family dogs at play when one rolls over and exposes his soft belly to the other in a display of submission. In real battle such a display allows survival and avoids the final terminal event of killing when survival of the species is more important than the individual. In the business and social world our human behavior is replete with endless displays no different than the mammalian brain in our heads.

Rituals abound in our behavior that satisfy the influence of the R–Complex. The size and grandeur of our homes, the powerful automobile, luxurious clothes and instruments of power such as weapons and armies. These are all displays, rituals, and territorial prerogatives no different than those of reptiles and mammals except that we have technology and the intellectual ability to abstract it and write it down.

We must end this brief discussion of the triune brain, but if the reader seeks more indepth inquiry, an excellent layman's book for this study is *The Brain, The Last Frontier,* by Richard Restak, M.D. (1979). The functions of the three levels of brain organization are significant in understanding later discussions, but before leaving this overview, some comments need to be offered which can help guide the reader toward a later synthesis.

In one simple evolution of behavioral response, we can appreciate the connectivity of the triune brain to that of children in the classroom. When faced with a confrontational situation, should it be a peer or an adult, all levels of the triune brain are involved. If a child is threatened, for example by the teacher, his first response (reptilian) may be to act "tough," stare directly into the teacher's eyes in a passive aggressive gaze, or to simply remain very still. At the second level, depending on his age and the situation, he may engage in a physically aggressive way (mammalian) by actually hitting the teacher, he may run out of the room and even the building, or he may, as in an altered wolf submission display, simply drop his eyes, droop his shoulders, and give himself over to what ever the teacher wishes to do to him. Both of these responses, reptilian or mammalian, are frequently seen by the teacher. As the student becomes older and affiliated with support groups (gangs) the teacher's threatening behavior could elicit dangerous aggression from the student.

In the case of cerebral response, a more human one, the child's behavior can now take any of the foregoing strategies or he may now use planning, abstraction, and social language to not only avoid the problem but turn it to his advantage. It is important to realize that impulses from the mammalian or reptile brain flood the child's conscious orientation and the "hard wired" behaviors of the lower brain systems cause the response. But cerebral response can "repress" these impulses, ignore them, or attempt to divert them to other behaviors. Freud spoke of libido energy, an internal force to behavior, and it is logical to assume that the impulses generated by circumstances cause an imperative to act according to the lower brain prerogatives. In this case the child, if he is mature enough and has learned to suppress these impulses, can act in a more rational way. He can respond to the teacher with verbal responses admitting that he is in the wrong and apologizing (even if he doesn't mean it). He may also suggest to the teacher that while he is in the wrong that she is embarrassing and belittling him in front of his friends.

The key to repression and/or management of our impulses is that of language and subsequently "logical or rational" behavior toward reasoning through a situation. It is language and our ability to use it to abstract our behavior, to plan and see alternates, to make comparisons of past and present, and to structure our behaviors that enable us to successfully achieve our goals.

If language and all of the aspects of CNS function which accompany it, to be elaborated later, provide the key to management of impulses from the mammalian and reptilian brain systems, then significant implications exist relative to the ADHD concept of attention and behavior. For example, if a child is inattentive, impulsive, overly active, and has difficulty with rule-governed behavior, one key to his eventual success is that he develop an adequate level of language competency. It is not so difficult to recognize, as we have seen over the years, that children from deprived families where there is not an adequate use of language as a mediator of behavior during the early years, often results in impulse and threat/reward-based behavior. The low language environment displays most of the exact behavioral and learning problems we typically ascribe to the ADHD child. It is so common that we can actually predict that a child who has not been encouraged nor taught to use language in problem solving will be impulsive, inattentive, and have problems with social behavior. It is not that a child is poor, it is the deprivation of language and early social education that leaves the child vulnerable and often controlled by the mammalian and reptilian brain. If the child comes from an abusive home the problem is extended, for now the child must rely on impulse and primitive behaviors merely to survive.

Such children must first be taught in highly structured environments in which both their security and attention can be controlled and focused. They must *learn* to trust, to listen, to consider, and to use verbal cognitive processes to mediate their behavior. This takes time, the five-to six-year-old child entering kindergarten often has already established a personality of "survival" and the use of language will be deferred in favor of fear, caution, distrust and assertiveness, defensiveness and paranoia for survival. To throw this sort of child into the middle class concept of "cooperative education" or progressive "exploratory learning" will create an environment of fear and anxiety for the child. Only after the child learns to organize his behavior and to trust can he begin to engage in cooperative work skills. Unfortunately, schools are not always so sophisticated today to be able to manipulate curriculum environments within one school for a diverse cultural and developmentally different population of children. Those who come able to manage themselves learn; those who don't often are labelled or medicated.

For this sort of child medication only provides facilitation of attention, but impulse control and rational behavior must be learned and medication does not do that, teachers must. One final point here is that this allows us a window into the failure, according to the research, of behavioral management strategies or even cognitive approaches. Learning successful "thinking" skills for personal management cannot be accomplished if the goal of the intervention is that of "management" of behavior. This is also why many teachers are disappointed when medication or behavioral management does not present to them a well-organized and learning child. They do not understand these underlying mechanics of child development and personality nor the concept of ADHD.

SYSTEM II
THE KINESTHETIC/MOTOR SYSTEM

The Kinesthetic/motor system lays the basis for all learning (Ayres, 1972). Attention, mental organization, memory, spatial abilities and even sequential mentation are based on this system along with the foundation for structured language.

In Figure 3 we now relook at this area of the lower brain system for specific functions and integration functions, aside from the behavioral aspects of the whole, i.e., triune brain, and we find a complex of function critical to all that we learn. We also will discover a range of areas in which impulsive, inattention, and unpurposeful behavior can result from dysfunction or a lack of appropriate maturation.

Before we discuss this area some comments must be made concerning the theories of perceptual motor development. Perhaps no other area of development, particularly in relation to learning disabilities, has received so many mixed reviews concerning its importance. The work of Ayres in sensory integration (Ayres, 1975), Kephart and his theories of perceptual motor development (Kephart, 1971), Frostig in movement education (Frostig et al., 1970), and others such as Cratty concerning movement and the intellect (Cratty, 1968) have all seemingly faded into history. During the late 1960s and early 1970s there was much interest in perceptual motor development and learning disabilities. Key aspects of children with perceptual motor learning disabilities included aspects of the Strauss syndrome such as inattention, impulsivity, poor coordination, and spatial organization.

Sadly, for children, research in those and later years did not reinforce the notion that perceptual motor difficulties were significant in learning problems. Study after study rejected the "training" approach used in perceptual motor remediation as neither useful nor valid in resolving so-called perceptual motor disturbances. But there were many problems in the general theory then which recent research has revealed may be resolved. At the time, in the early seventies, when perceptual motor training was popular, it was performed in segmented and specific training activities instead of being an integrated part of a more holistic theory. It was also built on the old "medical model" again. If children had poor sensory motor integration, coordination, or spatial skills, then training (as in treatment) was administered ritualistically. It didn't work, at least not well enough, to offer a solution to the perceptual motor difficulties of most children.

One major difference in thinking today about the brain is, as Dr. Restak pointed out in, *The Brain, The Last Frontier,* "We have tended to look at the brain as a thing when in fact it is a process." This same mistake is part of the problem in the ADD/ADHD controversy when researchers attempt to look at the parts of the brain in order to understand, for example, the complex notion of "attention." The very structure of the scientific process and research, which must be specific, is very difficult to apply to the "process" of attention. We can infer from brain function certain processes but in order to study them scientifically we must break the process into parts. The problem here is a traditional one between those who study behavior and those who study neurons—we can see neurons but only products of processes. In one case we know what a "thing" does but not what many "things" do when engaged in an integrated process. It has been said that if we attempted to build a brain by putting together the parts we do understand that it wouldn't work! The sum of the whole of the brain is greater than its parts. The teacher has to deal with processes and we should not have been surprised when the earlier attempt to repair nonfunctional perceptual motor parts failed.

In our discussions here, we will take what is known about the parts and infer products of the processes for teachers must have some sort of operational concept of how children learn and why they behave in various ways. We will tackle the problem of how to help children with spatial motor and coordination difficulties at several points as we proceed.

In Figure 2 we see an overview of the primary kinesthetic/coordination/balance system. While we are more interested in the general operations or processes involved in this level of CNS function, we will relate some specific functions while leaving out many others. There are

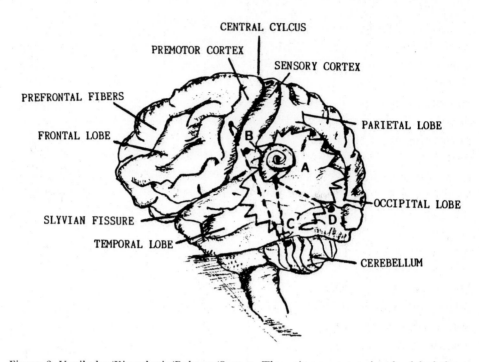

Figure 2. Vestibular/Kinesthetic/Balance/System. The primary system involved in balance and coordination consisted of relationships between the mechanisms in the inner ear complex, the cerebral motor strip, occipital lobes, and the cerebellum. The interaction of this system provides not only balance but basic orientation to space relationships which lay the basis for conceptual abilities such as sequential language function. This system interacts within interfaces between the left and right temporal lobes and the parietal lobe.

two or three gross functions which form a general framework for this second major principle. The first are the reflex mechanisms such as postural reflexes which are "hard wired" into the system. The reflexes, including the plantar, tonic neck, grasping, and righting, all serve as survival motor responses until the CNS matures adequately for volitional behavioral movements. Ayres' work with postural reflexes and vestibular interfaces has done much to propose a theory of how dysfunction in these activities can relate to the development of coordinated movement patterns. The reflexes occur below the cerebral hemispheres and consequently without conscious control. Reflex responses are slowly repressed in normal development as the infant becomes more conscious and volitional. Many neurologists have wondered at the emergence of volitional behavior for it seems to arise in more obvious ways at about three months of age. A famous neurosurgeon, Dr. Penfield, spent much of his professional life attempting to map and discover the specific actions of various parts of the cortex. For all of his knowledge he too was surprised and amazed at this seemingly sudden emergence of self.

As the CNS matures it develops at such a rapid rate and in such complex ways that miracles need not be sought other than the wondrous development of a child. Many neuropsychologists study specific aspects of development in, as we mentioned earlier, very specific and scientific paths. In an effort to maintain scientific objectivity and integrity, the most important aspects of function are often missed. The teacher is more likely to appreciate the global and integrative aspects of development than those which are neurologically correct but seldom inferentially creative. But when we view the development of an individual it is intellectually difficult, if not impossible, to perceive and appreciate the full range of interacting systems and subsystems of the developing person. During the first three months of life the infant, the personality or individual inherent in the system, is more conscious than most adults assume. Until many early neurological functions mature the infant is, in a sense, captured if not bewildered by the biological machine in which he finds himself.

Reflex responses are assumed to consist of nonconscious responses to bodily needs or environmental circumstances. For example, an infant raises his head reflexively to avoid suffocation in a pillow, jerks toward a righting position when held in a precarious position, or extends his foot when it touches the bottom of the crib. While these may be seen merely as neurological responses to sensory data, there is, at another level, an additional response involvement, the R–Complex. MacLean described the R–Complex as a primitive subsystem which is located in the lower areas of the brain, adjacent to, if not part of, the areas also involved in reflex control. Reptiles are habit patterned and ritualistic creatures who, if we consider it so, behave primarily in reflexive patterns and therefore, during the first three months we can assume that much of what exists is a lower level, selfless and basic form of consciousness. This is, though stretching reality a bit, a useful concept as we shall see.

True consciousness, as it is usually defined, is part of higher cortical function and, we may imply that as the CNS develops, the lower brain systems in the form of the R–Complex and reflex system, are less growth-oriented than are other systems such as the cortical hemispheres and sensory integration. Thus, as the other areas of the brain are developing during the first three months, the reflex and lower brain system holds control of the overall responses and behavior of the child. At about three months the other areas of the CNS, particularly those which involve conscious orientation, are now mature enough to begin to control the body in gross ways. At this point a life long struggle begins for the child. From this time on the child will struggle with the lower brain system for control of the body and himself. In a sense, the child must slowly, through language and cultural learning, become capable of suppressing both reptilian and mammalian behavioral tendencies and impulses. These areas of the CNS are critical on one hand for fully functioning sensory integration and many other behaviors including basic attentional and behavioral control. On the other hand they are adversaries of a kind who often propel us into unacceptable behaviors. Understanding this symbiotic relationship within our own brain is important to understanding the sometimes seeming irrational and uncontrolled behavior of both children and adults.

One of the subcortical structures which is important in our understanding of ADHD is the reticular activating system (RAS). This area of the lower brain system is responsible for maintaining an active waking state. Luria (1973) suggested that there are substantial grounds for distinguishing three functional units of the brain, the reticular activating system, the occipital, temporal, and parietal cortices, and the frontal lobes.

Luria felt that the reticular activating system included the midbrain, pons, medulla in the brain stem, and the thalamus as a functional unit. This first functional unit maintains wakefulness and has as a main function that of alerting the various areas of the cortex to incoming information. Dr. William Gaddes suggested that, "this, then, is a physiological center for attention, for screening incoming information, and for activating various cortical areas to maximize attention and mental efficiency. A lesion in this area may result in distractibility and hyperactivity" (1980).

Many sites within the reticular activating system could provide a direct cause for hyperactivity and ADHD in the clinical sense. At a lessor level, another postulate may be advanced, the child who does not LEARN adequate repression of reflexive and R-complex impulses could find it difficult to maintain behavioral control and attention. In such a case, aside from the potential for use of stimulant medication, which therefore may assist in reticular activation, it would seem logical in the educational environment to lower distractions or focus incoming sensory information so that it requires less energy in selective attention, increase the ritualistic structure of the classroom to include daily and unaltered routines, and provide as much supervision and direct contact as possible. In this example we can see how difficult it may be for the child and why his attention is a problem for him.

Luria included the occipital, temporal, and parietal lobes in the "second functional unit." We will discuss these in greater detail but Luria described these as process areas in reception, analysis, and storage. The frontal lobes which Luria called the "third functional unit," were given the responsibility for creating intentions, planning, and managing behavior in relation to an individual's concept of the world.

THE CEREBELLUM

In the lower brain areas, aside from these activating and basic reflex centers, is also the cerebellum which is perhaps one of the most interesting structures in the brain. It looks much like a tiny brain itself, has two hemispheres, and has a variety of functions, some of which have only recently been understood. The traditional understanding of cerebellar function includes the action of a filter for smooth and coordinated muscular activity. Fine motor skills such as writing and dexterity along with the more complex movements of athletic skills are part of the role of the cerebellum. Evidence exists that links the cerebellum to various learning disabilities in motor function.

The cerebellum has other functions and is unique in that it is the only part of the brain where brain-cell multiplication continues long after birth. Dr. James W. Prescott, a developmental neuropsychologist at the National Institute of Child Health and Human Development points out that the rocking behavior of isolation-reared monkeys and institutionalized children may result from insufficient body contact and movement. Dr. Prescott believes that disuse and understimulation of a brain pathway can lead to hyperactive response at a later point (Restak, 1979). He believes that the cerebellum is involved in complex emotional behavior and that it may well serve as a master regulator mechanism for sensory-emotional and motor processes. If the cerebellum of a normal rat is electrically stimulated, within seconds it begins stereotyped circling behavior and compulsive biting. Additional evidence exists that links the emotional centers in the limbic system with the cerebellum. Two-way connections exist between these areas.

THE THALAMUS, MIDBRAIN, AND PONS

The thalamus, part of the reticular formation for attention, is a relay station carrying impulses from the cerebellum, the reticular system, and certain neural ganglia to the cerebral cortex. All sensory information except smell moves through this gate to the cortex. In man it apparently acts as a crude sort of consciousness between the sensory tracts and the cortex. A lesion in this area can result in disturbances in visual, auditory, tactile, and of course, sensory information from the cerebellum. Again, here is a major site in which some degree of disturbance in motor behavior, attention, and impulsivity could occur. The hypothalamus, located near the thalamus, apparently is involved in both cognitive and the autonomic nervous system. Just as interesting is that behavior appears to result from the reflex or spontaneous stimulation of the hypothalamus and related structures and the inhibitory learned processes emanating from the cerebral cortex. Too much hypothalamic stimulation with too little cortical control can result in a child who disregards the rights of others. This is an example of what we have called "behavioral attention deficit." The pons is a bridge for sensory information traveling from the spinal cord to the cortex, for motor pathways from the motor cortex to the cerebellum, and for connections from the cerebellum to the spinal cord. The connections from and to the cerebellum are particularly important for this also involves the "vestibular system" in the auditory complex.

VESTIBULAR FUNCTION

Over a few incidental million years one special organ developed called the otolith in the brain stem of all vertebrates. It is a gravity detector of sorts. It has several canals, known as the semicircular canals, to detect rotation. The vestibular organ gave rise to an outpocketing, which became an organ of hearing. The vestibulospinal system consists of fibers projecting to the muscles of the neck, trunk, and limbs. Connections are also made among the vestibular nucleus, the brain stem, the ocular muscles, and the cerebellum.

The motor strips, located in the middle of the cortex, include incoming sensory information and outgoing motor directions. We can reflect on these subsystems, the lower brain stem and cerebellum, the thalamus, vestibular system, and motor cortex and we have an interrelated neuro-assembly which is primarily responsible for orientation of the body in space, balance, motor coordination, and integration of movement. This we call the primary kinesthetic/coordination/balance system (KCB system). This includes the mammalian and reptilian brains and is more than simply a motor control system.

We have seen in this initial discussion how specific structures, when dysfunctioning, can be primary causes for impulsivity, hyperactivity, inattention, and even rule-governed behavior. But it is most important to realize that difficulties in attention and spatial organization can result from both a lesion (organic basis) in these areas or, because of inappropriate or deprivation in sensory-motor development related to movement. De Quiiros and Schrager (1978) have suggested that hyperactivity results from inadequate motor disinhibition elicited by external stimuli and they felt it was strongly connected to minimal brain dysfunction. Conversely, they felt that restlessness includes poor postural disinhibition by weak internal or proprioceptive stimuli. It is mainly connected to vestibular-proprioceptive dissociation.

MOTOR DOMINANCE

Through the operations and development of the KCB system the child develops early balance and movement skills. Kinesthetic feedback from the two sides of the body merge through the lower brain centers and are perceived within the structures of the motor and sensory strips in the cortex creating within an awareness of laterality, the sides and planes of body concept, up/down, front/back, and sidedness. Between the first few months and the fourth year of life the child defines not only his spatial and external world but himself as well in relation to space and movement (Geschwind and Levitzky, 1968). One finding, though variant from study to study, is a relatively good norm suggesting in general that 65 percent of the population are clearly right-handed, 11 percent left-handed, and 24% mixed. For a detailed analysis of the hemispheric lateralization of dominance one of the best resources is *Hemisphere Function in the Human Brain,* by Dimond and Beaumont (1974).

In our own work we have found an interesting phenomenon which suggests that in children who are left-handed and those who are mixed or ambidextrous, there are some significant predictors relative to behavior and learning. It is our belief that the number of left-handed children is far greater than those studied by most researchers. Functionally, left-handed children are not only organized for oppositional motor preference (working from right to left) but are also cognitively oriented from right to left.

The motor system of the left-handed child may involve not only motor function but cerebral temporal orientation as well. This is to say that the child "thinks" in a reverse pattern as well as desiring to organize motorically in the opposite direction from the right-hander. But this may be ahead of ourselves. First, let's discuss the right-handed child both motorically and cerebrally.

As sensory motor skills and coordination develop the genetic prerogatives of spatial-motor dominance also emerge resulting in a "preferred" directional organization. If the right motor structure is the preferred mode of genetic organization, the left motor strip and all associated functions of the KCB system become "hardwired" into a preferred internal orientation in space, the left-right dominance pattern. Following our cursory review of the underlying structures of sensory motor processing in the preceding paragraphs, we can see that this process is an extremely complex and developmentally-based phenomenon. Children develop eye dominance, hand dominance, and foot dominance from this early pattern of growth. In the right-handed child the right eye and right foot assume dominance along with spatial-temporal effects as well.

In research concerning left and right handedness there have been many conflicting theories presented concerning cerebral differences but one generally consistent finding has been that approximately 65 percent of adults show a larger planum temporal on the left (right-handedness), 11 percent on the right (left-handedness, and equal in 24 percent of the cases in a histological study of 100 adult brains (Geschwind & Levitzky, 1968)). It is assumed that this difference, in this case for speech dominance, also projects probable motor dominance in that speech and motor dominance usually occur in the same hemisphere. Our own work, though, suggests that this is a fairly good breakdown for motor dominance except that we have an additional and perhaps controversial finding which we will come to momentarily.

Studies by Geschwind and Levitzky were somewhat inconsistent with other researchers who found that the number of individuals with left hemisphere preference according to anatomical differences was closer to 90 percent. But when Geschwind's data concerning the equal sizes of the planum temporal (24%) were added to the left dominant group, their data was consistent with others. It is here that we believe Geschwind's data revealed an important uniqueness which was left unnoticed. We would have moved the equal group (24%) not to the left hemisphere group but to the right, at least, for motoric dominance. In essence, our own experience with children over the years has suggested that, regardless of the proof of speech dominance, there are perhaps between 24 and 30 percent of the population who are left-handed or mixed with left-handed mental strategies even though only about 10 percent of the population use their left hands. Neurological research generally assumes that about 10 percent of the population are left-handed. This fits well into the above research concerning speech dominance where usually the planum temporal is larger or equal in 90 percent of the population. Our concern is two-fold, that perhaps the equal group does not behaviorally fit into right-handed mental function, and that regardless of the temporal size relative to speech, that in motor function we see more than 25 percent of children in the normal population as exhibiting a range of right hemisphere/left handed spatial-temporal orientation. Further, an interesting note is that only about 10 percent of the children we see are left-handed but around 25 percent display the right hemisphere/left-handed orientation. Why is this so? We are convinced that of our proposed 25 percent of the population who are genetically left-handed, only 10 percent actually *use* their left hands. They are invisible left-handers that are never included in the studies concerning left-handers because before the age of five to six years they selected the right hand as a result of cultural and family influence. In a word, more than half of left-handed children switch their own hands before the age of six or teachers and parents encourage them to do so without an understanding of the developmental consequences. How then, do we know that these are left-handed children?

The problems associated with dissonance between the internal reference of laterality and cerebral dominance form the basis for a significant number of children who come to our office with problems in attention, impulsivity, and rule-governed behavior.

SYSTEM III
LEFT AND RIGHT FRONTAL/TEMPORAL LOBES

The third major system with which the teacher should be concerned includes the frontal and temporal lobes of the left and right hemispheres. Both in clinical research and in the popular literature these areas of the cortex have been studied and discussed extensively in the last fifteen years. Recently, an undergraduate student, after hearing that we would explore the functions of the left and right hemispheres, explained that another professor had told his class that the "left and right brain" theory had been disproved. Her comment was, I presumed, to let me know that any discussion of this subject would be useless since it was no longer true. In the late 1970s and early 1980s, the "left/right brain" theory became popularized both in the media and in education. As often happens some research by such notable neurologists as Sperry and others reached the popular media and suddenly everyone had right and left brains and was prone to be in fact, "left-brained or right-brained." Cocktail parties soon included discussions by people who were right-brained or left and the characteristics were a relief for those tired of the "what's your astrological sign" group who had bored innumerable people for years. Now, new scientific knowledge had given real proof to differences between the individual brains of people and this provided good popular mythology to replace the concern with astrological signs, though, as it turned out, the brain theory wouldn't last long either. Before long commercials appeared which promised that a particular product would satisfy either your left or right brain. But, as with all misinformation, the public became bored and moved on to another shallow generalization.

In truth there is no such thing as a left-brained or a right-brained person, but clinically the actual research provided and continues to provide valuable insights into cerebral processing. It simply isn't as easily translated into practical application as it appeared at the time. On the other hand, we haven't suddenly given up on the knowledge about this interesting area of the brain either. We want to present a general overview of some of the functions of this third system in our analysis for insights here have significant implications for the overly active and inattentive child as well as other behaviors.

The frontal and temporal lobes (see Fig 3), the two major areas of the cortex, have a distinguishing feature. At birth significant amounts of tissues are "open to programming." It is these areas in which we learn language, plan and foresee events, recall specific information, create ideas and art, develop creative strategies, reason, and explore the universe. This is the most human realm of our brain and where the differences between our mammalian and reptilian subsystems are the greatest. It is where self-concept and consciousness reside though they cannot be placed in a specific neurological tissue. With all of this potential we can assume that it will be impossible to discuss even a small portion of what is known about this area of the brain. That would be a completely correct assumption! We will therefore touch only on major functions and leave additional detail to the coming chapters.

LEFT FRONTAL/TEMPORAL LOBES

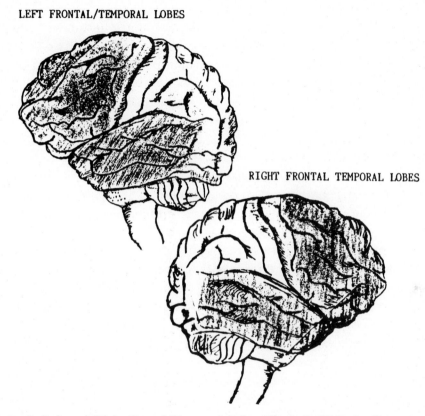

RIGHT FRONTAL TEMPORAL LOBES

Figure 3. Left and Right Frontal/Temporal Lobes (Shaded). With significant areas of unprogrammed tissue at birth, these areas constitute the potential of both language (left hemisphere) and spatial creative (right hemisphere) abilities. While many specific functions are specialized into these areas, the integration of the two hemispheric regions provides the greater potential. However, genetic and prenatal factors can result in significant differences in potential of these two areas resulting in differential abilities.

The left hemisphere of the brain includes much more than the temporal and frontal lobes and before we discuss these areas we need to touch on two other areas, the parietal and occipital lobes. The parietal lobes are located next to the sensory motor strips with an anterior boundary at the fissure of Rolando and its posterior boundary is with the occipital lobes. According to Luria it performs many integrative functions in spatial synthesis, verbal memory, and language. These are very important and will assist us in discussing imagery production. Integration of tactile information and visual perception occurs here. Lesions here can result in such problems as writing and spelling, directional sense, finger localization, poor body image, and integration of space and time. Stereognosis involves the ability to recognize two and three dimensional objects through touch but related problems can also occur. An interesting feature is that when a lesion occurs in the right hemisphere only, there is significant difficulty while left hemisphere involvement is less so. In that the right hemisphere (left hand dominant) is also involved in spatial perception, left-handed problems in stereognosis can be more devastating in regards to spatial-temporal orientation (Semmes, 1965). The parietal lobes relate to perception of objects in space, judging distance between objects, size estimates, serialization, and directional imagery relating to planning out a map and following it, relating spatial events to each other, and personal body space.

The occipital lobes, located at the rear of the brain, are recognized as the visual centers of the brain but, as in the case of the parietal lobes, many other areas of the brain deal with visual perception. Part of the visual lobes deal with direct representation of visual information coming into the brain but much of the lobe deals with processing of visual information into comprehension and recognition which is perception as opposed to mere reception of information. The occipital lobes apparently have a stronger association with the right temporal and frontal lobes than with the same areas in the left hemisphere when the material is nonverbal (Reitan, 1955).

The temporal and frontal lobes (see Fig. 3) are unique in the cortex for they require learning and programming in order to reach their potential. Though they are designed to process information in specific ways, the development of those competencies depends on opportunity and stimulation. The left temporal and portions of the posterior regions of the left frontal lobes are involved in language and speech production. The same regions in the right temporal and frontal lobes appear more oriented to processing spatially related data. The forward portions of the frontal lobes have been implicated in integrative functions such as foresight, planning, and insight.

Both left and right temporal lobes have a major perceptual function in hearing though the left deals more with language and the right deals with nonverbal sounds. The right hemisphere appears more involved in pitch, loudness, rhythm, timbre, and tonal memory (Spellacy, 1969). Left temporal lesions appear to cause difficulties in verbal associative learning (Meyer & Yates, 1955) and right temporal lesions result in disturbances of pictorial comprehension (B. Milner, 1958). Memory is strongly related to left temporal function with some involvement of the hippocampal area.

The frontal lobes appear involved in rapid mental calculation, active imagination, and abstract conceptualizing. There are apparently hundreds of thousands of interconnections between various areas of the opposite hemisphere and the same hemisphere which likely account for these functional characteristics. Further, the limbic system is located underneath the frontal lobes which in some way may relate to the more primitive mammalian input into conscious behavior. Many researchers have related the frontal lobes to serial order behavior (Kimble and Pribram, 1963).

The frontal lobes have been seen as important to higher abstract thought, but much of the research is conflicting. One area of some commonality in various research is that impaired function in the frontal lobes causes a decrease in the individual's ability to synthesize signals from the environment, assign priorities, and make balanced decisions (Restak, 1984). Restak also suggested that physical, electrical, and chemical changes in the brain can lead to significant shifts in behavior. In that the frontal lobes contain such complex interconnections to so many parts of the brain, damage or dysfunction here can result in chemical imbalances even at distant sites in the brain. The interconnectedness of the frontal lobes to the limbic system could have far reaching effects including hyperactivity and inattention. Some of the present research is exploring the possibility of dopamine loss in this area which appears to respond to stimulants.

Frontal lobe seizures render a person unconscious temporarily while not invading the sensory motor and temporal areas of the brain. The most significant difference between other animals and man is the extensive growth precisely in the frontal lobes. Frontal lobe damage appears to result in what neurologists call, "aspontaneity" or a lack of purposeful and directed behavior. At this time pain, emotions and thinking, and a number of complex theories are being researched in regards to the frontal lobes. For our discussion here, suffice it to say that certainly the frontal lobes, the temporal lobes, and the underlying limbic system,

McLean's mammalian brain, are closely interrelated in ways far too complex to explain or apply specificity in clinical research.

Reviewing only the brief discussion here about the temporal and frontal lobes suggests that volitional behavior, motivation, mental organization, creativity, and many other complex psychoneurological functions are operating here. To suppose then that people are left- or right-brained is inappropriate and unlikely in that the whole of the brain operates in complex processes. Yet, one cannot deny that the temporal and frontal lobes of the brain, actually the referential correlates for left and right brain, do specialize in behavior functions along with the myriad of specific functions which particular interconnections perform. While the corpus callosum provides for intercommunication between the hemispheres (when we use hemispheres here we imply the temporal/frontal lobe), each hemisphere apparently can perform without the full awareness of the opposing hemisphere.

At a gross level the following general functions appear specialized in the left or right, frontal/temporal regions of the hemispheres.

Left	*Right*
Verbal comprehension	Nonverbal comprehension
Logic and reason	Gestalt and creative imagery
Sequential processing	Parallel processing
Mathematics	Pattern recognition
Language	Visual (Images/depth)
Linear	Random
Analysis	Synthesis
	Rhythm

By inference	
Social values	Personal/humanistic values
Scientific	Intuitive
	Artistic
	Athletics
Controlled emotionally	Emotionally Expressive
Socialized	Naturalistic

These lists are essentially the sort of thing which set off the popularized notion of left- and right-brained which has become no longer viable in the media. One has to recognize that such lists are overgeneralized stereotypes and yet, integrated processing, as opposed to specific functions, in the two hemispheres is responsible for the unique competencies of the human brain. We must, then, with caution and appropriate reservations, recognize that hemispheric specialization occurs. The foregoing specialized integrated functions represent important operations in psychoneurological competencies. If we accept the above specialties as representations of hemispheric competencies, additional inferences can also be drawn.

In working with children over the years one particular trait has often emerged in some children which has interested us. In general, while language function appears to be localized in the left hemisphere in both left- and right-handed children, differential levels of competencies have been noted. This is to say that, according to many tests related to special skills such as the WISC–R, many children show significantly different levels of competency between major hemispheric functions. Some children for example demonstrate above average verbal abilities while only average or even below average spatial creative abilities typical in the right hemispheric function. In some children the reverse is true yielding significantly higher right hemispheric function than left hemispheric function. Further, as might be expected, in other children specific functions within either dominant cluster also display a variety of higher/lower relationships.

The differential values (level of competency) of various functions and overall hemispheric value often resulted in significantly variant learning and behavioral learning styles between children. Further, when evaluated in relation to overall competencies and personality/social factors, the resultant overview of the child's behavior and learning competencies yielded many insights in his capabilities or learning difficulties. While we will explore some of these insights in coming discussions, we need to continue to review other overall operations in our present discussion.

THE THALAMUS, HYPOTHALAMUS, AUTONOMIC NERVOUS SYSTEM, AND CEREBRAL HEMISPHERES

Next, in relation to hemispheric specialization, let's take an unusual trip into relationships between emotions and behavior which, in later discussions, will reveal some little understood correlates between perhaps ADHD and behavioral difficulties. The autonomic nervous system is composed of two subsystems, the sympathetic nervous system, which is usually activated when high levels of energy use is expected or needed, and, the parasympathetic nervous system which is activated when there is a need to conserve energy. Most of us recognize that when we are in a state of fear, anxiety, hate, or aggression, that all sorts of body reactions occur. Our heart rate increases, adrenalin is released, our muscles become taut and ready, our breathing increases, pupils dilate, and in general the body is ready for action. The sympathetic nerves act by liberating noradrenalin into the space between their endings and the structures on which they work, while the para-sympathetic nerves liberate acetylcholine. Noradrenaline (or norepinephrine) is located principally in the locus coeruleus, a nucleus of the brain stem. Although norepinephrine-producing cells in the locus coeruleus are few in number, branching of these nerve fibers results in amazing complexes of net reaching into almost every part of the brain and spinal cord. Structurally, the synapses of the para-sympathetic system (a synapse is a junction in the nerve) are found in isolated groups of ganglia (masses of nerve bodies) adjacent to the gland or organ controlled, while the synapses of the sympathetic system are organized mainly in chains of ganglia lying along the spinal column. In a sense, the para-sympathetic nervous system's action is piecemeal, while the sympathetic system tends to function as a whole (Gooch, 1974).

It has been shown that if one worries, an explosion of events can culminate in the release of stress-related neurochemicals by the sympathetic nervous system. In such a case increased heart rate is aided by epinephrine (adrenaline) secreted by the adrenal glands. This in turn circulates in the blood stream and activates many of the same synapses as noradrenaline (Restak, 1984). If an individual lives in an environment in which there is constant perceived threat or where that individual feels anxiety, the mammalian flight/fight response can be stimulated resulting in a high level of defensive behaviors and anxiety. As we shall see shortly, many hyperactive children may suffer from a partial or fully responsive behavioral reaction of this sort. The important implication of this is reinforcement of the critical relationship between mind and body or in our current discussion, between the cerebral hemispheres and the mammalian brain and autonomic nervous system.

The hypothalamus is located below the thalamus and apparently is responsible for much of the functioning of the autonomic nervous system. We also recognize this area as part of the mammalian brain cited by MacLean. Research has shown that the posterior of the hypothalamus is the chief regulator of the sympathetic nervous system while the anterior portion is the chief regulator for the parasympathetic nervous system. The parasympathetic nervous system encourages gastric juices for digestion, facilitates salivation, urination, and aspects of sexual readiness. Here also is located the so-called pleasure center. This center is also concerned with regulation of temperature. To some degree the cerebral hemispheres are an activity or doing system while the autonomic may be considered a feeling system and in fact it is here that emotional excitation occurs. In another view the sympathetic system is concerned with arousal, tension and activity while the parasympathetic system is characterized by quiescence, relaxation, and passivity. The autonomic system is highly involved in sleep and dreams.

The autonomic system is at once independent of what we "think" and yet involved with it. The system obviously has to control breathing, heart rate, temperature, sleep, relaxation, feelings, and other ongoing or emerging feelings and physiological responses while we maintain our consciousness. Yet, if we worry, react to someone we have learned to dislike, fear the reaction of a teacher or parent, or love someone, then as a consequence of our conscious or thinking behavior, the autonomic nervous system changes the "state" of bodily function. How the thinking hemispheres, but a few millimeters away interact with the autonomic system, can be fascinating.

Athletes are presently being trained by sports psychologists and physiologists to learn how to maintain a high level of arousal and yet avoid anxiety. Relaxation therapy and concentration training appear to provide stimulation to the areas of the hypothalamus which stimulate the parasympathetic system toward inducing a feeling or relaxation and actual physiological effects.

Now let's return to some interesting research concerning hemisphericity (specialization in one hemisphere) and its relationship to emotions. The work of Dr. Gazzaniga and Roger Sperry, a winner in 1981 of the Nobel Prize in Physiology and Medicine for split-brain research, has contributed much to the theory and application of specialization in hemispheric function. Some of the specializations listed in the foregoing summary of hemispheric function have come from their work. An important finding by Gazzaniga cited by Restak in his book *The Brain* (1984) is that, while there is specialization in the hemispheres, two different individuals may use different cognitive strategies (and therefore different brain areas) to solve the same problem. The particular research cited dealt with the differences in how an experienced and trained musician responded to understanding a particular series of notes or music as opposed to the novice. Rather than suggesting that the two sides of the brain merely respond to either linguistic or spatial/nonverbal imagery, it may be more appropriate to suggest that the left deals with symbolic representation while the right deals more with representations that, "mirror reality," or large chunks of experience and information.

One of the controversial aspects of split-brain research has been the suggestion that an individual may have two personalities, one in the left hemisphere and a different one in the right. Split-brain patients, those who have the two hemispheres separated surgically due to seizures, at times find themselves doing things which "they" have not consciously planned. While teachers don't work with split-brain children and we may question whether or not we have two personalities, there are some practical applications of this principle in the children we have seen.

In the individual with an intact corpus callosum (the connecting link of more than fifty-million-fibers between the two hemispheres) inter-communication between the hemispheres provides a feeling of unitary being. Furthermore without separation of the two hemispheres would one still experience some sort of duality in being? This brings up the "missing keys" syndrome which has plagued us all at one time or another and which can shed some light on this question. We "misplace" items for several reasons but the most common is that we "absent mindedly," as we call it, put the item some place while our "minds" are preoccupied. (Bear with us this will lead to problems children have in the ADHD syndrome.) There are several interesting possibilities and semantic "slips of the tongue here." First, imagine the hemispheres as two complex, though relatively uninteresting, computers which run their programs at random and in some branching paths even though we are not monitoring them. Then imagine yourself as the operator of these computers who relies on them to perform certain tasks for you. This then is somewhat analogous of consciousness and the left and right hemispheres. But suppose you can consciously only utilize one of the computers at a time even though the other continues to run "parallel programs" to what you and the other computer are presently doing. Now we have an analogy of how we may operate. For example, you turn off the ignition of your car after arriving home and come into the house. You are concerned about a meeting you must attend in the early evening and you are somewhat frustrated about having to go. You are thinking about what you must do later at the meeting which brings to "mind" an individual whom you dislike who will be at the meeting. Let's stop here for a moment. What does "bring to mind" mean here and the earlier reference to "absent minded." What do we really mean when we use "mind" in this way? It usually means the conscious act of focusing our attention as opposed to dreamily letting thoughts randomly come to view when we are relaxing or even watching the clouds roll by so-to-speak.

Most of us use such terms as, "get yourself together," "pay attention," "concentrate," or "focus yourself," to mean that we are to attend to a stimuli or situation with organized, logical, and appropriate-to-the-situation attention. This is, in our previous hemispheric list, a verbal or as we now call it, a symbolic conceptual focus. This means that we are using our left hemisphere computer pulling up specific information from memory, planning a sequence of events, and considering appropriate behaviors. This is, interestingly, why we call some professors, "absent minded." We use the term to infer intellectual preoccupation with the common notion of "thinking to ourselves" or mental (conceptual) problem solving.

While we are preoccupied with the verbal left hemispheric computer, what is the right one doing, simply sitting idle? In fact the right hemisphere is actively involved with several functions which support what we are doing, but our attention, our consciousness, is not being focused on that activity. Yet, in the peripheral of our awareness, at the edge of consciousness, we know what is occurring there, we simply are not focused on it. Before stating directly what is happening there, we need to take another diversion for a moment about this right hemisphere computer.

Michael Gazzaniga has concluded that the human brain is organized in terms of a "mental society." He suggests that along side the verbal and in our present case, the left hemisphere, can exist mental units that have memories, values, and emotions and that these can be expressed through a variety of responses. Restak suggested that this whole process may not be in touch with the verbal system at all but have its own existence outside the areas of the brain where logic and language reside. Further, if we consider that the right hemisphere appears to have more relationship to emotions than the left, this adds an additional possibility. Prosody imparts the medolic and stress components of speech. It imparts emotional tone and makes subtle shadings to language. The logical part of the brain, the left, deals little with emotionality for it is illogical and emotions are left, by inference and logic, to that emotional and sensitive brain, the right hemisphere. If someone you don't like compliments you on your dress, often there is sarcasm inferred in the compliment. Without the ability to detect emotional subtlety, we could not effectively comprehend much of our language. Restak speculated, and we affirm in our children, the fact that semantics and prosody are encoded differently in the brain, perhaps in the left and right respectively. In fact, damage to the right hemisphere has demonstrated just this sort of problem, an inability to detect subtlety and prosody to language. Hippocampal monopoly on emotional response though is apparently over. In recent years more and more evidence suggests that the amygdala, a tiny almond-shaped structure buried deep in the temporal lobe (near the hippocampus), actually is the seat of emotional function and response. Thus, while the hippocampus may lend information and have an interactive role of translating information into cognitive input, the amygdala often responds to stress and emotion provoking situations before the individual is actually "conscious of the event."

Further research has suggested that limbic stimulation of the brain, the site where mammalian function occurs, creates intense emotionality. The right hemisphere does not react to inhibit emotional flow so much as the left does. Our rational control of the lower brain system, learned through culture and conditioning, is, in fact, one of the primary causes of stress and anxiety as we mentioned earlier. The right hemisphere is more apt to respond with emotionality due to the lack of social constraints placed on it. The right hemisphere computer then may be more prone to act out and express lower sensations of emotionality. This may be helpful in releasing stress, but it could also create many social problems. Dr. Restak warned though that we should not visualize that "emotions" are localized IN the right or left hemisphere but that "feelings" or emotion are actually created within the hypothalamus and lower brain system via "sensations" which are then interpreted within specialized regions of the hemispheres.

Before leaving this subject of emotionality, an additional study cited by Restak in his book, *The Brain,* concerns a study by Dimond and Farrington in 1977. This study, "Emotional Response to Films Shown to the Right or Left Hemisphere of the Brain Measured by Heart Rate," sought to see if the left hemisphere is responsible for more positive moods (happiness, joy, laughter, etc.) and their expression while the right hemisphere is more responsible for negative emotions (sadness and anxiety). Their study demonstrated that facial muscles of the left half are more active when negative emotions are felt and the right half when positive emotions are felt. Restak felt that it was possible that brain injury to certain areas in the right hemisphere could result in a lack of concern, denial, and difficulties in interpreting emotional or prosodic aspects of language. We will return to this discussion also when we talk about "Behavioral Attention Deficit."

Now, back to the case of the keys. It is possible, as one focuses on the logical problems of the moment, that the keys are placed on a shelf beside the kitchen door. But who placed the keys there? Our consciousness was focused on the problems of the coming meeting and we placed the keys there but the term "we" is used in the best sense of the word. The left hemisphere and our consciousness were engaged while the act of placing the keys, we, was done primarily in nonverbal/motor function. We may say that "subconsciously" we put the keys there but now it may be better to say that the right hemisphere computer, through a subtle and minor conscious intent, encouraged their placement.

Later, still in left hemispheric orientation, we are unable to recollect where the keys are. Our right hemispheric computer, interestingly, KNOWS where they are but they are not stored in language (logical and verbal) memory but in the memory banks of the spatial/visual and nonverbal computer. Thus, we often retrace our steps but cannot "logically" find them. Further, to complicate matters we are repressing anxiety, attempting to "control" our feelings, and denying losing control all of which is increasing our anxiety and releases those nasty neurotransmitters via the sympathetic nervous system. This, in turn, will in fact make it more difficult to relax (the providence of the right hemisphere and the parasympathetic nervous system) so that the right hemisphere can tell us where they are! Now we are back to strategy. If we recognize this sort of problem as a hemispheric and emotional management situation, we can help ourselves relax, let our minds wander a bit, and suddenly, eureka, we know where the keys are.

All of this is to say that when we start to formulate an integrated concept of the interactions between our conscious intent and focus, the left and right hemispheres, and the mammalian system (including the autonomic nervous system), we can begin to make sense of many behaviors we perform and that of children in our classrooms. We can also appreciate that how a child is parented, the environment within which he develops, and the mental strategies he is taught, all interface to create behaviors which can be understood only in the context of the whole reality. To separate the various components and to study only the independent function of one of the parts, results in naming the trees but not recognizing the forest. Yet, understanding the parts is required in order for the whole of behavior to become clear. There are many implications here for impulsive, rule governed behavior, disinhibition, and distractibility in children for a number of reasons. As we put together case studies these speculatory excursions will provide helpful insight in to the problems and behavior of children who are labelled ADHD and others.

BEHAVIORAL AND OPERATIONAL PROGRAMS

We spoke briefly of the lower brain stem's role in reflexes and the fact that this occurred below the cerebral level and therefore was not typically within the control of the higher levels of cognitive function. One major interaction which occurs between System One and Two is a complex and intricate give and take in the development and application of what we will call, *Automatic Behavioral Programs* (ABP). System One includes the lower brain functions, the cerebellum and vestibular system, sensory motor cortex, and other areas, while System Two is typically thought of as the seat of conscious intent (frontal and temporal lobes) and portions of the occipital or parietal lobes. We may consider, for this discussion, that the two systems are being composed of (A) the motor-sensory and movement system, and (B), the conscious intentional system.

As the brain develops we learn many behaviors and actions which become not unlike reflexive behavior but in a more complex manner with important differences. Walking is an example of how these special behaviors and actions occur and develop (ABPs). The lower brain does not have a reflex program for walking because walking involves both learning and practice while reflexes are automatic postural responses. At first the young child struggles and focuses his attention to learn to move his legs while balancing his body in a forward motion. By the time the child is in his fifth year he is able to walk without conscious attention and can, in fact, engage in social communication, listen to the teacher, or even manipulate an object in his hand without any conscious awareness of walking. While not proficient in sophisticated running or even walking movements at this age, the child has developed a basic ABP for walking. Walking has become an automatic operation of the lower brain centers, the sensory motor cortex in the cerebral hemispheres, and portions of the occipital and parietal lobes. Without the development of these somewhat complex programs we could not perform all of the aspects of our general lifestyle. If we had to concentrate on walking, brushing our teeth, or our pencil when we write, then we would be unable to "think" or problem solve. These programs then are a major aspect of our ability to move and think, to concentrate on verbal organization while performing some sort of movement.

As we will see intervention in or the disruption of the development of selected ABPs could have the consequence of laying the basis for impulsive behavior, disinhibition, and distractibility. While certainly brain injury or trauma to any number of sites within the foregoing areas could achieve this end, it is also possible that certain individual brain differences and developmental delays can intervene in development of "automation." To illustrate the significance of these programs, one additional example may be helpful. Dr. William Penfield summarized in his book, *Mysteries of the Mind*, his research with frontal lobe seizures. An individual, upon experiencing a frontal lobe seizure which often did not invade the sensory motor cortex or lower structures, while losing consciousness, would continue to perform the last conscious intention, i.e., getting up from a chair for example, and walking into the kitchen to get a glass of water, and then stop. Upon regaining consciousness, he would be bewildered as to how he got into the kitchen. In this case, an automatic program continued to operate until it was finished.

The importance of automatic programming is extensive and will be a significant aspect of later discussions both of behavioral and developmental attention deficits at home and school.

SYSTEM IV
INTELLIGENCE AND MIND

In Figures 4 and 5 we attempt to demonstrate overall concepts of psychoneurological functioning. Diagrams are mere skeletons of the complex structure of the cortex and yet, these simplified representations may assist in helping us gain some overview of the functions in the operating system. It is hard to present the constructs of System Four for we walk through a well traveled door into the realm of "mind" discussed, in such depth and imagination by significant works. From Julian Jaynes, *The Origin of the Consciousness in the Break-Down of the Bicameral*

Mind, Howard Gardner's *Frames of Mind,* J. Z. Young's *Programs of the Brain,* Bob Samples' *The Metaphoric Mind,* Robert Jatrow's look into the biological/machine interface of the future, *The Enchanted Loop: Mind and the Universe,* and finally the philosophical analysis by Hofstradter and Dennett in *The Mind's I.* With such splendid works abounding we are humbled to spend but a few moments here in the latter part of a brief chapter. We refer the more ambitious "mind" of a teacher or researcher in the musings of the brain and mind to these works with the promise that a little time in these writings will transform their understanding of children.

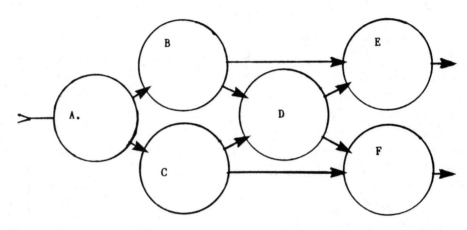

Figure 4. Representation of language portion of cognitive processing. Upon initiation from the frontal lobe (A.) and the reticular system (not shown) incoming sensory information is selected by the right or left frontal and temporal lobes (B & C) for reception and processing. Information is then automatically processed and a response initiated in either motor or verbal function (E & F). If the incoming information requires mediation (cognition), then it is channeled to various points where imagery and integration occur (D) in what is referred to as "central language processing." Then a response is initiated.

We do not suppose, nor do we hope, to present profound insights about the "mind" in this short discussion as these other works suffice for that purpose. We do want to present some notions and speculations which will form at least a basic orientation for the teacher or other professionals concerned with the ADHD child. This is a good example of what we imply when we say that in order to understand the problems of ADHD and their origins, aside from the specific research, we must counter-balance this viewpoint within the whole of mental function.

When a teacher attempts to use a "cognitive approach" to helping ADHD children develop self-monitoring or self-control, strategies what exactly is the goal? The research has already demonstrated, at least within the context of limited samples, that such approaches are not very effective, if at all, without medication. We differ with that research, but a discussion of the range of reasons must wait until we have at least a brief encounter with the notion of "cognitive" and its meaning. We aren't much more comfortable with cognition than we were with "mind" for both are, to some degree, in education and psychology, little more than slang of the modern theorist. Further, we are uncomfortable with many aspects of how educators view learning and learning disabilities as problematic differences in intelligence and accomplishment without any basis for how a child actually learns or "thinks." They are like potters of reality, making empty vases within which no substance resides.

Consciousness resides, in our view, in the processes of the active brain, both the creator and residual of the neurological waves from information processing mechanisms activated by the reticular system rather than in a specific "place" or point in the head. Some theorists and philosophers suggest that there may be a soul or some metaphysical entity which is housed there and which takes its leave at some point during dying, but that is not our concern here. Consciousness implies some sort of internal and centralized control system which shares duties with the other brain systems which exist in the CNS. A child playing in the block corner may be seen as conscious, so too the child reading a book, and also a child dreamily staring out the window at a bee. But in each of these situations the nature of consciousness changes as dramatically as it does when the child is playing with a friend as opposed to when the teacher is reprimanding him for some infraction of classroom rules. In each of these situations the nature of consciousness in the child changes from one which is mostly cerebral, to one more oriented by the mammalian brain, or the reptilian influence. At any moment the teacher or parent must recognize whether they are speaking with a human child, a lion, or an alligator.

What does happen in the child when he is operating primarily within the cerebral cortex, the human brain? Earlier we compared the cerebral cortex to the operation of two computers, one dealing with linguistic structure or conceptual functions, and the other more involved with nonverbal spatial imagery. When the CNS is aroused within the brain stem by sensory SENSATIONS a response comes essentially from spinal reflexes or the lower brain reflecting needs such as when the child feels thirsty, needs to go to the bathroom, or becomes hungry. A fly may land on his nose and he bats it away without conscious intent or awareness at the cerebral level. But while these lower brain responses are being processed by automatic programs (ABP) which do not require higher brain function, he may be engaging in solving a math problem within the cerebral cortex.

Solving a math problem requires information and assistance from several areas of the brain, particularly those in the cortex. Some of the areas include the temporal and frontal lobes, the sensory and motor strips, parietal lobe, occipital lobe, and continuous monitoring and stimulation from the thalamus and perhaps the cerebellum. Here exists one of the most beautiful and sophisticated ballets in mental function. The child sees and interprets the visual symbols on a page (the numbers) which involves both the spatial visual cortex of the right hemisphere and the auditory cortex in the left hemisphere. He sees the relationship of the numbers and makes abstract manipulations of the numbers and what they represent in MENTAL IMAGERY (seeing it in his mind's eye) and resolves the dissonance caused by the problem and then finally writes his answer.

While he was working this problem he was repressing (ignoring) impulses from his muscles for a need to change positions in his seat. This was accomplished with the cooperation of the midbrain and thalamus regions while at the same time the reticular system selectively stimulated the various areas of the brain providing total concentration on the "cognitive task" until the solution was recognized and written down. Once the problem was solved the reticular system, on approval from the thalamus, forwarded the muscle demands and he shifted in his seat before starting the next problem. The teacher moved toward his desk which the mammalian brain recognized from peripheral vision still unnoticed by the boy, and a slight increase in neurotransmitters responsible for "fight or flight" responses ensued. Seemingly at the same time, though actually secondarily to the mammalian alert and readiness response, the boy maintained his pose but consciously now observed her movements without actually looking directly at her. He is no longer truly involved in working the math problem but is posing as if he is. The alert from the lower brain system, followed by consciously switching to right hemispheric data to visualize movements and spatial relationships of the teacher, has inactivated stimulation into the auditory and numerical abstraction areas of the left hemisphere and related centers. He is no longer creating internal imagery, i.e., picturing the numbers, but is directly observing what is going on around him.

All of the foregoing functions, highly simplified, occurred within the space of 30 to 45 seconds! The purpose of this short example is to demonstrate several neurological processing concepts. First, it is important to recognize how complex and interactive the various systems or, if you like, brains, are in the actual "process" of responding, thinking, and integrating information. The following points are made using the forgoing example as a model.

1. Consciousness

For purposes of understanding consciousness, we must realize that consciousness is achieved through stimulation from the reticular activating system. A state of arousal may only penetrate neurological structures within the lower brain centers without interrupting the flow of consciousness in the cerebral hemispheres. Utilizing the cerebellum, the vestibular system, the sensory and motor strips in the cortex, and certain areas of the occipital and even right temporal lobe, the lower brain centers can actually respond to "arousal" from peripheral sensory data, i.e., batting away a fly. Simultaneously, the Reticular Activating System (RAS) can continue to stimulate various areas of the auditory, visual, parietal, and frontal lobes in order to solve a math problem. The difference between the conscious intent activated in the math problem and that of the lower brain activity related to the fly is that in the former case we "perceive" self-awareness or "intentionality" to our behavior which is the locus of awareness or consciousness.

This duel operation, solving a math problem and responding to sensory information, involves different and yet overlapping areas of neurological functioning. But most important to understand is that each of these operations is being controlled by the thalamus and upper brain stem system which can raise the question, "Who is really in charge here?" The upper brain stem is a routing and directing mechanism controlling a highly complex flow of information and can, if needed, alter so-called consciousness. For example, if an individual is concentrating (consciously attending) on a math problem and sees a spider crawling up his sleeve in his peripheral vision, the upper brain stem overrides conscious intention and the individual leaps up and brushes his arm. He "thinks" HE saw the spider and jumped up. In fact, neurologically, the upper brainstem system began response to the spider before it was consciously seen by the individual. Owing to how our system works, through our arrogant "self"-consciousness, we perceive that "WE" were in control. This appropriately provides an integrated self-concept and awareness which allows for an intact wholeness.

This takes us to one of the focal aspects of the ADHD syndrome, attention. What are we actually saying when we state that a child has a "short attention span," or is distractible, and therefore, "inattentive," or, "is unable to concentrate." In one view, consciousness IS attention, when understood as the behavior of focusing on a specific task, over time, to completion. Being unable to focus awareness on a specific task and to sustain that attention until completion has been presented in the research as an integral aspect of problematic behavior in the ADHD syndrome. It can be suggested from the foregoing discussion that there are many points at which attention can be interrupted, or, in a more extreme case, consciousness.

Consciousness is not then simply an isolated action of "being aware" or focused, but rather a dynamic process. As we discuss both developmental and behavioral attentional deficit a cursory understanding of the foregoing processes will be important. To achieve attention to task and to maintain concentration requires many integrative functions. Children LEARN selective attention, increased consciousness if you wish, through processes of suppressing certain forms of information over others. As we can see such suppression requires more than CNS maturation; it requires certain cultural and educational opportunities and cognitive skills which are developed through learning. There is also the probability that differences in temperament, personality, and the actual integrity of various subsystems lays the basis for the "competence" to learn various degrees of attentional capabilities. We will explore how culture and learning can decrease or increase the capabilities of the child to suppress and selectively utilize one subsystem over the other. While a lack of basic genetic integrity in specific subsystems can render the child incapable of learning, i.e., severe retardation or brain injury, in general the teacher and parent can increase, through training and motivation in the child, attentional and conscious intention.

2. Cognitive

From the foregoing example of the child working a math problem we have one description of cognitive. We refer to cognitive or cognition as those "mental functions which involve conscious processing of information toward adaptive behavior." This is clearly a function of the cerebral hemispheres as opposed to the lower brain centers, a distinctive mental operation involving cerebral control. Creativity, abstraction, problem solving, reason, music, art, reading, writing, and philosophy are all examples of cognitive function. In developmental psychology in recent years the so-called "information processing theory" proposes cognition as a mechanistic operation not dissimilar to computer operation. By making an analysis of how the brain processes information (cognitive function) researchers in this view hope to understand how the brain works and perhaps more importantly the nature of consciousness. In many theories today there is a rejection of the notion that there is an "executive mind mechanism." Our earlier discussions have taken the route closely aligned to the information processing model and in later discussions we will use this model to understand attentional and behavioral difficulties. Yet, we also see efficacy to the more philosophical model of a "central executive controller" within the system even though that executive may be influenced and certainly controlled to some degree by the lower brain centers and RAS. There should be some middle ground between a computer model of human consciousness and a biologically-based, if not philosophical, concept of self. In much of our discussion here we will blend assumptions, biological and mechanistic, in order to build mind models for the teacher, parent, or physician to use in attempting to understand the unique processes by which a particular child is operating.

Cognitive refers to those processes which are directed, controlled, and certainly created by a central mechanism or integrating instigator, a useful construct also for the layman in considering this mechanism simply as the "self." It is logical to assume that merely stimulating the cortex by the RAS somehow becomes a mechanistic process whereby we all become conscious and engage in cognition. All of this is central to ADHD, for the issues in this syndrome relate to, as we mentioned, not simply mechanistic attention, but a process of "self-control," awareness, and finally, a level of conscious control over the biological system we know as ourselves. Cognition then becomes a central issue, is the child processing information toward behavioral control and adaptation, or is he responding primarily from the nonconscious and more or less unmediated (a lack of cognition which implies evaluation and environmental reflection in time with elements of self reflection) behavior originating in the lower brain centers?

3. The Process of Imagery

How do we think? How do we involve ourselves in cognition? We are really on weak ground here, but for the purpose of giving teachers and others a sense of cognition which can be visualized, we will present a brief discussion here of imagery. In Figure 4 we see a simplified model of cognition. More will come in later discussions. We have suggested that portions of the left and right temporal and frontal lobes are dedicated to information processing activities. But we also like to visualize the notion that other areas of both the left and right frontal lobes involve an integrative and executive process. We believe, as much research has suggested, that the anterior portions of the frontal lobes involve activities of planning, foresight, and time-space awareness and relationships. We may be wrong, but it assists us in visualization of how a child is "thinking" to believe that reticular arousal of consciousness relies greatly on frontal lobe excitation. It is not that, as in the case of frontal lobe lobotomy patients in the forties and fifties, an individual cannot be "conscious" without anterior portions of the frontal lobes. Conversely, without the anterior portions of this lobe the individual loses initiative, motivation, directedness, and what we usually consider important aspects of consciousness. He may be conscious though in the sense of awareness and certain memory functions but not in the sense of "being directed and in control."

We propose then, for illustrative purposes here, that the anterior portion of the frontal lobes (A/Figure 4) is inherently involved in so-called "consciousness" and assumes a primary role in what we earlier defined as executive functions. With this central focus what then happens? In the case of the child solving the math problems we also suggest that both left and right lateral portions of the frontal and temporal lobes provide verbal and visual spatial information (B & C respectively, Figure 4) to the operations of executive. Further, utilizing information from the left region, i.e., verbal names of numbers, sequential and temporal orientation in the problem-solving process, and, spatial relationships, visual images of written symbols, and visual concepts of objects in space, the executive performs the operations via the process of "internal imagery." Imagery is defined here as an internal awareness of sensory information created from memory and cognition.

Imagery is a central language and cognition process and is central to conventional processing. We say conventional here to suggest that not all individuals utilize nor create imagery with the same degree of sophistication, competence, or, in the more intellectually capable, complexity. But for our purposes we can assume that people typically go through this process in a highly similar though variant way. For example, if we want to change the arrangement of furniture in the living room, we try to "picture" the various arrangements in our "minds eye." We utilize the word, "transformation ability" to define this specific sort of cognitive function. This means that we are able to visualize, internally, variations on a particular theme while maintaining an awareness on the basic mental set as it is. In this case the imagery is primarily visual, as is much of imagery utilized in cognitive function. Imagery can be based on any form of sensory information including smell and taste.

A more complex form of imagery is auditory and involves such activities as talking to one's self, imagining a conversation with your husband or wife, friend or parent. This mental rehearsal involves creating an internal conversation which we define as "auditorization." Many people, when carrying on a conversation, giving a speech, or teaching a lesson in history are able to fluently continue their presentation while also maintaining an internal production of imagery or rehearsal of what they will say as they continue to speak to the audience or pupils. This is a sophisticated form of auditorization, simultaneous verbal expression within the parameters of audience response and climate, and self feedback in order to change what is to be said on the basis of what has and is being said. One would assume that there must be an executive process or consciousness there in order to manage all of these cognitive functions. This being the case, we must also suggest that these complex processes are LEARNED and that to simplistically suggest that a lack of attention or concentration is the result of a vague and sophomore concept of an ATTENTION DEFICIT SYNDROME does not in fact exist as a meaningful construct.

In summary of this brief chapter, we have presented some constructs which can now be utilized to more clearly understand the child. We intend, in the remainder of the book, to illustrate to parents and teachers that, aside from the clinical definition of ADHD, there is no medical syndrome of ADD. Further, the numbers of children in school today who can truly qualify for the designation of ADHD is such a clinically small sample (certainly less than 1%) that their case is seldom the basis for what parents and teachers are currently defining as ADD.

We have suggested two categories, Developmental Attention Deficit and Behavioral Attention Deficit (d/ADD AND b/ADD) which are NOT to be identified as part of the DSM–IIIR ADHD classification but which do include the vast majority of children now inappropriately labelled ADD. Parents and teachers, we hope, will realize that most children today who are inattentive, distractible, overly-active, and who have trouble with rule governed behavior, are primarily children who exhibit behavioral and developmental maladaptation. Further, that this group of children are primarily those who are maladaptive due to a number of developmental differences or difficulties, poor or ineffective parenting and teaching, and most importantly, an inability to mobilize their abilities due to a lack of appropriate regular education interventions and strategies. Finally, the current misguided belief that such children will respond primarily to medication and/or behavioral modification strategies, is to ignore the vast potential of educational strategies available to help such children "learn" successful adaptive behaviors.

If educators and frontline medical personnel are unable to correctly interpret this knowledge to parents, then we are in for another fiasco like learning disabilities in the 1960s. Responsibility for the inappropriate and poorly managed behavior and learning of today's children can only be given to we educators and to parents. It will not be solved with behavioral modification nor labels. In the final analysis, the only hope for the child rests in changes in today's school curriculum and climate to meet the needs of a modern, competitive, and changing urban and international world.

REFERENCES

Ayres, A. J. Improving Academic Scores Through Sensory Integration, *Journal of Learning Disabilities*, 6, 338–343 1972.

Ayres, A. J. Sensorimotor Foundations of Academic Ability, In Cruickshank, W. M., & Hallahan, D. P. (Eds), *Perceptual and Learning Disabilities in Children*, Vol. 2, Syracuse: Syracuse University Press, 300–358, 1975.

Cratty, B. J. Movement and the Intellect, In Hellmuth, J. (Eds) *Learning Disorders*, Vol. 3, Seattle: Special Child Publications, 524–536, 1968.

De Quiros, J. B., & Schrager, O. L. *Neuropsychological Fundamentals of Learning Disabilities*, San Rafael: Academic Therapy Publications, 1978.

Dimond, S. J., & Beaumont, J. G. *Hemisphere Function in the Human Brain* (Eds), Halsted Press: Wiley and Sons, 1974.

Frostig, M. The Role of Perception in the Integration of Psychological Functions, In Cruickshank, W. M., & Hallahan, D. P., (Eds), *Perceptual and Learning Disabilities in Children*, Vol. 1, Syracuse: Syracuse University Press, 115–146, 1970.

Gaddes, W. H. *Learning Disabilities and Brain Function*, Springer-Verlag: New York, 1980.

Geschwind, N., & Levitzky, W. Human Brain: Left-Right Asymmetries in Temporal Speech Region, *Science*, 161, 186–187, 1968.

Gooch, S. *Total Man,* 80–84, Ballantine Books, New York, 1974.

Kephart, N. C. *The Slow Learner in the Classroom,* Columbus, Ohio: Merrill, 1971.

Kimble, D. P., & Pribram, K. H. Hippocampectomy and Behavior Sequences, *Science,* 139, 824–825 1963.

Luria, A. R. *The Working Brain,* Harmondsworth: Penguin Books, 1973.

MacLean, P. A Triune Concept of the Brain and Behavior, University of Toronto; *Zygon/Journal of Religion and Science,* Vol. VIII, No. 2., June 1973.

Meyer, V., & Yates, H. J. Intellectual Changes Following Temporal Lobectomy for Psychomotor Epilepsy. *Journal of Neurosurgery and Psychiatry,* 18, 44–52 1955.

Milner, B. Psychological Defects Produced By Temporal Lobe Excision, *The Brain and Behavior,* Vol. 36, Proceedings of the Association of Research in Nervous and Mental Disease, Baltimore: The Johns Hopkins University Press, 177–195, 1962.

Reitan, R. M. "Certain Differential Effects of Left and Right Cerebral Lesions in Human Adults," *Journal of Comparative and Physiological Psychology,* 174–477, 1955.

Restak, R. M. *The Brain The Last Frontier,* Doubleday and Company, Garden City, New York, 1979.

Restak, R. M. *The Brain,* 164–165, 252, Bantam Books, New York, 1984.

Rosenfenld, A. H. Archeology of Affect, National Institute of Mental Health, NIMH Program Report, 1976.

Semmes, J. A Non-Tactual Factor in Astereognosis, *Neuropsychologia,* 3, 295–315, 1965.

Spellacy, F. J. Ear Preference in the Dichotic Presentation of Patterned Nonverbal Stimuli, Unpublished Ph.D. Dissertation, University of Victoria, Victoria, B.C., Canada, 1969.

Chapter Four

DEVELOPMENTAL ATTENTION DEFICIT
DISORDER (d/ADD)

In 1976 Safer and Allen in their book, *Hyperactive Children: Diagnosis and Management*, listed a number of features which were significantly associated with (or positively correlated with) hyperactivity (cited in Chapter One). At that time, before the concept of Attention Deficit Disorder, and, of course, the Attention Deficit Disorder without Hyperactivity (ADDnoH) or the present ADHD, hyperactivity was seen as a single disorder which included not only clinical aspects of the hyperactive (HA) behavioral pattern, but also elements and features of learning disabilities. Yet, in that early period it is important to recognize that these two professionals already acknowledged the existence of children who demonstrated major features of the HA syndrome without actual hyperactivity.

The major features of the HA syndrome reported by Safer and Allen included the following:

1. Inattentiveness
2. A learning or perceptual-cognitive disability
3. A conduct problem
4. Immaturity

This pattern or specific features could occur with or without HA. They also listed several historical and developmental features that were significantly associated with the HA pattern:

1. HA children tend to have a family history of learning problems.
2. Approximately 20–35% of fathers of HA children have a history of hyperactivity or repetitive behavioral difficulties in childhood.
3. HA children are usually described by parents as extremely restless, temperamental, meddlesome, and disruptive.
4. They often shift from one activity to another.
5. They often destroy toys by tinkering repeatedly with them or taking them apart.

6. In preschool years and mid-childhood they forget academic material that has been memorized.
7. They have difficulty learning to tell time and putting their shoes on the right feet.
8. They have more spelling errors than expected of children their age.
9. Not uncommonly, they continue to have reversals in writing and in reading words after the age of 6–7.
10. They have difficulty grasping number concepts and have many problems with fine motor skills.

THE MEETING OF HISTORY AND THE FUTURE

In 1976 researchers were only beginning to shift from the generalized concept of MBD and hyperactivity. Safer and Allen had obviously begun work on their book prior to 1976 and their research much earlier so that the final publishing date represents theories primarily developed in the period of the late 1960s to the early 1970s. In a real sense, while they had some essential concepts, their book was written too late. The time had past for the notion of MBD and hyperactivity as a major syndrome as Douglas (see Chapter Three) and others were already describing the same syndrome as an "attention deficit disorder." In the new concept which fully emerged in the 1980 DSM–III, MBD and hyperactivity were no longer seen as primary features. Yet, most of what Safer and Allen reported was valid and foretold much that is now occurring though they could not have known it then. We have singled out their book from many others for they were developing a line of inquiry that today can be clarified which, at the time, was not possible.

In this chapter, among other concepts, we will also touch on one aspect of Safer and Allen's theory, that of the ten characteristics listed above, while recognizing that the hyperactivity theory will be subsumed within the ADHD concept. ADHD has been reviewed in the previous chapters and we have made clear that this syndrome is acceptable to us and that it represents a small clinical group which should receive the attention primarily of the medical profession and secondarily that of educational establishment.

The first and broader concept of Safer and Allen's work we want to now revisit in the early nineties and demonstrate that they were actually describing, at least in part, what we now see as a major "Developmental

Attention Deficit disorder (d/ADD) which is inappropriately being called ADD but which is a developmentally- and genetically-based pattern with significant implications. Further, we see this, and the "Behavioral Attention Deficit Disorder" to be presented in Chapter Six as an important concept which must finally be understood by educators and psychologists.

The advantage in using the term, "Developmental Attention Deficit Disorder (d/ADD)," is that it may be possible to change the orientation of parent groups and many professionals now advocating, inappropriately, the ADD concept. In that we can ethically continue the concept of ADD it will not be necessary to attempt to convince these many groups that what they believe is an incomplete theory, so much as to help them to a more sophisticated, and for the children, productive and beneficial paradigm. In essence, we do not have to change boats in the middle of the stream but essentially clarify and supplement what is presently believed about ADD. Also, significant implications for educational programming will come from this discussion and should demonstrate that (a) the d/ADD child is primarily a child for whom regular educational services are an appropriate placement, and (b), that the needs of this child provide the impetus for dramatic changes in the concept of special and regular education.

Beyond the foregoing expectations, in the following discussions we also believe it can be demonstrated that d/ADD children are appropriately placed in the regular education program but that the particular needs of this child, if extreme, fall within the area of learning disabilities. One of the troublesome aspects of the old ADD concept was the problem of separating so-called ADD children from those with learning disabilities. In our definition presented here, this is not a problem for, as we will see, the d/ADD child has difficulties which are similar and appropriate to those of learning disabled children. There is no need with the d/ADD concept to attempt to separate these two areas.

Before proceeding further let's formulate a tentative description and list of criterion for the d/ADD classification to guide our discussion and case studies analysis of various deviations in the category. The overall description may be stated in the following way:

> d/ADD is a syndrome of developmental learning and behavioral difficulties represented by an inability to organize spatial/temporal skills. Inattention, impulsivity, difficulties in rule governed behavior, poor academic skills particularly in reading, math, spelling, and writing, along with preoccupation with fantasy, imaginative and affective atti-

tudes, provide signal characteristics of the syndrome. Over-activity may be present but ADHD and hyperactivity or aggression are not represented in this syndrome.

The foregoing general description provides also that the syndrome is most often observed within the primary years and, though present earlier, most often does not present a problem to teachers and parents prior to entrance into kindergarten or later. In preschool, though the behaviors are present, their features do not usually present a problem unless the child is required to enter into formal educational and social environments related to learning. The following behavioral descriptions are symptomatic of the difficulties experienced by these children:

1. A history of learning and developmental difficulties in the family structure. Fathers most frequently report similar patterns, though not always, in their early school experience.
2. Difficulties in maintaining attention to academic tasks and following through to their completion.
3. Early difficulties in cerebral dominance particularly with cross dominance in visual/hand profiles and early uncertainty of hand selection.
4. Many of the children demonstrate early speech and language difficulties including linguistic reversals (reversal of syntactic order), articulation deficits, and expressive inability.
5. Impulsivity and difficulties delaying gratification or tolerance for directions and rules.
6. Poor fine motor skills in writing though some may be highly artistic and skilled in mechanical or motor skills outside of formal academic requirements.
7. Continued difficulties in reversals of letters and letter sequences into late first and second grades. This is also seen in spelling and math. They tend to continue dependence on finger counting or mnemonic aides longer than most children.
8. Difficulties learning time and adapting behavior within time limits for academic tasks or play situations.
9. Tendency toward catastrophic reactions in situations of conflict, overstimulation, extreme threat or fear, and where a high level of personal control is required.
10. Preoccupation with fantasy, imagination, and creative activities, i.e., building, drawing, playing "superheros," television, electronic games, and other active visual/spatial activities. May also tend to take personal risks while involved in fantasy play.

11. Difficulties taking turns and engaging in give and take with peers. Appears to need friends to play with and then may dominate or even ignore playmates.
12. Appears to need affection and can be highly affectionate with family.
13. Often displays intuitiveness about acceptance from peers and adults and need a high level of reassurance and acceptance from authority.
14. Tendency to have feelings of failure and uncertainty and in many cases feels incompetent in academics. They often display feelings of unworthiness.
15. A high level of chaos exists in their room at home, their desk at school, and they display a constant inability to locate and remember school assignments, articles of clothing, chores, and other daily routine responsibilities.

Most importantly it must be remembered that many of the foregoing characteristics are typical of many children at various developmental stages or during adjustment periods in family and school life. At least ten of these characteristics should be observed within both the school and home environment consistently over an extended period. Yet, in that this syndrome can be represented by a number of "normal developmental" phases, care should be taken to review underlying problems which lay a basis for the difficulties as opposed to perhaps temporary problems in family life, at school, or transitional problems which all children may experience. Finally, these problems must interrupt successful adaptive and learning skills in school and at home.

In that many of these criteria were part of the now disregarded ADD syndrome, it can be seen why the label was dropped. This is not a clinical or medical syndrome in the sense that the child exhibits differentiated characteristics which imply a medical or behavioral disorder. The foregoing characteristics are developmental-behavioral "clusters," that is, while any specific characteristic may be seen in all children at a particular time, when several are seen in one child over a period of time they suggest an underlying difference or difficulty in development. At this point the child needs special assistance and understanding in order to compensate, overcome, or work through the difficulties.

THE IMPORTANCE OF THE d/ADD
AND b/ADD CLASSIFICATIONS

For parents and teachers the distinction and the need to differentiate between ADHD, a clinical syndrome defined in the medical literature (DSM–IIIR), and a nonclinical syndrome or classification for other, though similar children, is of utmost importance. In the clinical syndrome of ADHD, as the research has demonstrated, medication and certain behavioral management strategies are the primary modes of intervention. Yet, for ADHD children and particularly, for those who do not meet the more stringent criteria of ADHD but who display such problems as inattention, impulsivity, and rule-governed behavior, there must be additional and more extensive interventions. At the present, parents are seeking special assistance for the non-ADHD children under the defunct label of ADD which carries with it the same interventions as ADHD, medication and behavioral management strategies. Yet, the research with ADHD has demonstrated that the behavioral management approaches are by and large ineffective without medication. The general consensus in professional education is that the so-called "ADD" child's needs should be met within the regular classroom. With the designation of d/ADD and b/ADD we have a very different picture and one for which this book was written. We can now look into various intervention strategies that go far beyond the notion of medication and behavioral management strategies.

Suppose d/ADD and b/ADD children display particular developmental differences which require unique educational approaches, different strategies in teaching reading and writing, or cognitive approaches in altering their strategies in dealing with academic and behavioral expectations. To merely attempt to modify their behavior will fail for they need much more extensive assistance. In one example a nine-year-old boy, because of developmentally different cognitive competencies, could learn to read but not under conventional teaching strategies. Behavioral modification approaches were tried in order to control his attention and motivate him to apply himself. But the underlying developmental difference had to be understood in order to determine how he should best be taught. Mistakenly, the school staff assumed that he was ADD and asked for medication, which the physician refused to prescribe, and many attempts to control his attention failed. The school staff did not understand his special developmental needs and the child as well as the school staff were frustrated. He ended up in psychiatric care which also did little to assist him because his basic differences were still not accounted for nor understood.

Before we assume that children can have a generalized attentional deficit without some sort of discernable underlying difficulty, we should look more critically at how children develop and how this has relevance for understanding their learning needs. In order to understand the many possibilities for difficulties in attention and organization of learning behavior, we must look more practically at the general psychoneurological framework we discussed in the proceeding chapter. Our discussions may meet the needs of parents and teachers but our particular concern is that physicians and school psychologists recognize these concepts so that they can aide in interpretation and remediation of the problems. First, we will highlight some overall developmental strategies and a model for this process, and then we will illustrate these processes through case studies.

AN INTEGRATED MODEL OF THE LEARNING/DEVELOPMENTAL PROCESS

In Figure 5 we elaborate somewhat on Figure 4 presented earlier. The processes we are attempting to demonstrate are difficult to illustrate in an integrated visual model, yet, once this model is understood, it is helpful in looking at the needs of many children with attentional problems.

A. *The brain stem and medulla*

Section A represents the lower brain centers and particularly the reflex and spinal response system. We also include in this section the reticular activating system (RAS) responsible for cerebral arousal. Its major projection, relationship to another area, in this model is within the second circle, i.e., the cerebellum.

B. *The cerebellum*

Section B or the second circle represents primarily the cerebellum (part of the R–Complex) and particularly its relationship as part of the vestibular system resulting in both fine motor control and balance.

C. *The midbrain, thalamus, hypothalamus, and routing functions of the upper brain stem.*

Section C or the third circle represents the routing system for sensory data, the mammalian responses, and all of the projections into the various systems of the cerebral hemispheres.

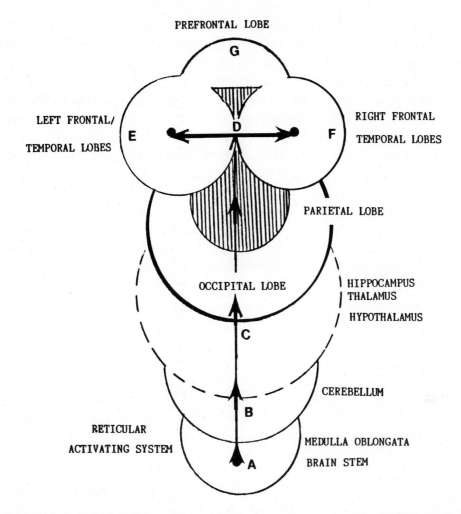

Figure 5. Representation of interactions within major cerebral systems. The CNS is composed of levels of cerebral processes between subsystems. The foundation system (A) involves the reticular stimulation processes for alertness or orientation while the cerebellar system (B) provides many functions beyond that of motor and spatial coordination. The upper brain stem system (C) involves the function of master control of neurological routing along with many hormonal, endocrinological, and emotional operations. The cerebral hemispheres (D)(E)(F) are the seat of all higher mental function. The anterior portion of the frontal lobes (G) apparently provides the role of directedness and volition with portions of the parietal lobes acting as a mechanism of sensory integration and imagery production.

D. *The cerebral hemispheres*

Section D represents the cerebral hemispheres including the temporal, frontal, parietal, occipital, and sensory motor cortex.

E/F. *The left right temporal lobes including portions of the frontal lobes.*

Sections E & F represent those large areas in the temporal and frontal lobes which are unprogrammed at birth and which are often thought of as the "left and right" brain.

G. *The anterior portion of the frontal lobes*

Section G represents that forward portion of the left and right frontal lobes commonly ascribed the responsibility for integration of concentration and purposeful behavior.

The darkened portion in the center of circle D represents the cerebral processes of attention and information processing particularly that of imagery production and higher cognitive abilities. It represents the use and integration of left and right hemispheric processes.

The perpendicular line drawn from Circle A through all other circles and into circle D represents both the RAS system's effects on higher structures and the central mediation of balance and control of the body. The horizontal line within circle D represents the spatial-temporal organization of the system and cerebral dominance. The positive and negative signs within this circle represent a dominant and nondominant cerebral function.

We will refer to these various levels of CNS function in our coming discussions and while the visual model is not absolutely necessary to understanding the discussions, visual representations will help many of the readers. We will return to his model later but at this point we need to introduce what may be called a "ecological" concept of child development and responsiveness.

DEVELOPMENTAL ECOLOGICAL SYSTEMS

A developing child is a dynamic and fluid phenomenon ever changing, responding, acting upon, and integrating individual who is difficult to shape in whole, but responsive to internal and external processes resulting in a transient and stable personality. As parents and teachers we ever risk disappointment as we try, usually with only partial success, to mold and control the child. We perceive the child as an individual with definite characteristics and yet, in all normal instances, we seldom comprehend nor understand the changing child before us.

The child we perceive, teach, evaluate, and parent is less a stable individual than a fluid process having changed to some degree even as we attempt in a moment to describe him. One of the hallmarks of the human mind is its ability to classify, to categorize, and to seek uniformity and certainty in the external world. This ability has led to the development of an ordered, purposeful, and mostly predictable culture and civilization even with all of the turmoil in the world. This tendency to categorize and classify, as important as it is to the development of a society, also often makes us unable to see the flexibility and fluidity of the changing child. We have difficulty perceiving a dynamic process for we attempt to stabilize it in order to understand it. Piaget has come the closest in an attempt to understand the PROCESS of cognitive development and, predictably, psychologists and the lay public have found his theories of child development difficult to grasp if not obscure.

Parents are also fond of believing, as all of us in the behavioral sciences once thought, that their influence is the most profound in the developing child. This led not only to the notion of the "proud parents" when the child was successful, but also to the neurosis of the parent who found themselves with a child whom they could not be proud. Just as we once felt a successful child suggested effective parenting, so did we blame the failing child on poor parenting. But now, as important as parenting is, we also realize that parenting is only one, but perhaps the most important, of the influences which shape the child's development and seldom can we, as parents, totally take responsibility for either the success or failure of our child.

We use the term "ecological" to suggest an interaction between complex internal and external mental environments which provide input and feedback to the developing child. Imbalance, poor timing, personal or family crisis, improper or effective parenting or education, threats and hostile activities, and basic physiological needs can all cause difficulties in the developing child. As the child meets such antagonistic insults from the environment or within, the internal growth of the CNS attempts to adjust personal competencies to meet the challenges for well-being and stability.

We propose at least seven interacting systems to which the child must respond and manage in order to adapt to his environment. In fact, the child himself is part of an overall system of personal consciousness and movement toward a central role of control and management. The concepts of "system" and "process" are often strange to the parent or teacher in describing the developing child. They sound mechanistic, cybernetic, or nonbiological and therefore impersonal and unfeeling. We do not wish to take away the compassion of human relationships, the joy of individual creativity, or the sanctity of the self, but in order to objectify, at least through example, the concept of CNS growth, we do have to utilize a model which provides more substance than the notion of "a problem child" or a "learning disability" and, of course, an attentional deficit. In order to do so, at least as a means of looking at processes, we must take a less subjective view of the inner workings of the developing child.

The notion of a "system" implies a complex grouping of entities, i.e., various aspects of the central nervous system, or the emotional and supportive climate of the family, which interact to produce some sort of specific outcome or product. For example, the child's mammalian brain is a CNS "system" with certain integrities and entities which act as an independent and coherent system. There is the "blood system" with which we are familiar, the autonomic nervous system, the R–Complex system, and the so-called, "personality system." External to the child, are the full range of parental behaviors, culture, and supportive authority adults which can be seen as a "guiding system" acting on the child.

Processes are the activity of "systems" in their own internal operations or, interaction with other systems. For example, in consciousness the child utilizes the visual/spatial system, the hemispheric systems, reticular activating system, and others in "processing" sensory information toward some personal goal. A child does not merely "think" for this cognitive activity will utilize a number of alternate systems in order to "process" information for some special purpose. Thus, "thinking" is a process which involves interactive internal CNS systems in order to reach a mental goal.

It is important for the teacher or parent to think in terms of systems and processes for only then can we begin to gain even a marginal understanding of behavior or development in a child. This should tell us then that the brain, attention, and learning are complex systems of interaction with intricate processes which must all be stabilized in order for the child to successfully manage his behavior. To suggest that medication or behavioral modification are adequate to somehow cause all of this processing to occur is an unfortunate naiveness on the part of adults.

The seven ecological systems include the following classifications:

1. *Genetic/temperament system* — This involves the basic genetic factors which compose the initial foundation of the child's differentiation as an individual.

2. *Environmental system* —The environmental system includes the family, the general sociocultural climate, educational and recreational organizations, and the physical environment.
3. *Sensory-motor system* —This system includes the basic sensory and movement processes by which the child interprets, defines, and interacts with his environment.
4. *Spatial-temporal system* —This system involves the processes of organization in sequential and logical patterns within a temporal order and logic.
5. *Linguistic system* —This system involves the acquisition, use, interpretation, and application of language by the child.
6. *Psychoneurological competencies system* —This system involves the so-called, intelligences inherent and developed within the child.
7. *Ego-conscious executive system* —This system embodies those areas of self direction, consciousness, and ego definition.

We want to touch on these seven interactive systems, in what we call an ecological mental climate, which we believe can provide insight into the development of the child. With these in mind, our discussions of d/ADD will be much more fruitful. Once we can see how various difficulties in a particular system can influence the child positively or negatively, then we no longer have to work with the vagueness of a general concept such as d/ADD.

1. THE GENETIC/TEMPERAMENT SYSTEM

Before the child becomes an individual the foundations of his emergence are programmed and active in the life we see before us on the day of his birth and even earlier in his movements and responses in neonatal life. Mothers know this but they don't write research projects or apply for grants to do so. Every child comes, at the moment of birth, different from all others and yet, owing to the arrogance of culture, we expect that he will at once become "like all others" and somehow different. What do we really want, a "sameness child" or one who is different? We are given difference and struggle to sameness often unhappy when he becomes undistinguished in life. Parents are often victims of their own selfishness.

In 1968 Thomas, Chess, and Birch presented a book to the professional community, *Temperament and Behavioral Disorders in Children* (Chess et al., 1968). Recently, a psychologist, in his review of work and description of ADD included references to the "temperament" of children which contributed to their ADD characteristics. His point was that in describing their child, ADD parents had to take into account that early temperament differences could account for some of the child's difficulties. We are seeing more and more softening of the "clinical" analysis of ADD by many professionals as they explore in more detail the nature of childhood and their own growing awareness that there is more to a child than attention, impulsivity, or rule-governed behavior.

Chess and his colleagues proposed, from their research, that early temperament arose from genetic and prenatal development and, present at birth, provided a general range of individualized behavioral responses. They isolated nine temperament factors including:

1. Activity level
2. Rhythmicity
3. Approach or withdrawal
4. Adaptability
5. Intensity of reaction
6. Threshold of responsiveness
7. Quality of mood
8. Distractibility
9. Attention span and persistence

In a sense this cluster of temperament characteristics formulates for the child a unique "birth personality" which has influence over the child during his initial months and into the first two years. The foundations of the temperament cluster come from the various levels of integrity and genetic prerogatives within the child. We are perhaps seeing the "raw" stuff, if not the "right stuff," of which he is made.

Activity level refers to the actual motor component of the child, how much does he move, how motorically responsive is he to the environment, and how much does he squirm.

Rhythmicity refers to the child's pattern of sleep-wake cycles, rest and activity periods, eating and appetite behavior, bowel functions, and overall cycle of alertness and interaction as opposed to a lack of consistent physiological schedules.

Approach/withdrawal refers to his initial reaction to new stimuli should it be food, people, places, or toys. Does he attempt to interact or withdraw from various stimuli?

Adaptability refers to the ease with which he can adapt to differences in people, situations, and personal management of his own behavior.

Threshold of responsiveness refers to how easily he responds to stimuli or how difficult it is to obtain a response. It is a measure to some degree of alertness.

Quality of mood refers to the amount of positive, joyful, and friendly behavior that exists in contrast to crying, unfriendly, or unpleasant behavior.

Distractibility refers to how easily the child is interrupted in his behavior by external stimuli. How easily is he distracted from goals he may have?

Attention span and persistence refer to his ability to maintain attention and behavior to a specific goal or task.

An overall pattern of early temperament, in our experience, can be joyfully fulfilling to a young mother or it can be a devastating problem which grows with the child. The child who is highly active, persistent, negative and fussy, difficult to stimulate into paying attention, and who does not adapt to new situations or events, can be frustrating to the quiet, nurturing, uncertain, and highly sensitive young mother. The child can react to her frustration, she to his, and a difficult cycle of interaction can result in poor bonding, threatening responses, and insecurity. Yet, the same child with an experienced and active mother who is secure and supportive within her own personality, can provide the limits and structure to assist the child in early adjustment.

Temperament, as with reflexes, comes with the child, and though we know of few who have done so, we like to compare temperament to a birth personality, a set of interacting responses generated by the totality of genetic and biologic integrity. This means that the potentials inherent in the infant's overall biological structure, provide at this moment in the early days of life, the most fundamental cluster of the child's future self. This set of temperament characteristics, to the researcher, involves levels of activity, approach or withdrawal tendencies, persistence, and so forth. One can measure and contrast such differences between children and estimate that one child is more active, less attentive, or equally alert than another. But, for the mother, the same child is seen in a more holistic way for she sees a unique personality. In one case the view is the forest and tree analogy, the researcher sees the trees and the mother the forest.

Temperament, in our view, forms a general response system from which later personality and behavioral tendencies will grow. This makes sense to the mother of several children for she can relate how a specific child behaved early in life and how, in many ways, his adult personality still displays many of those characteristics. But this is not an example of genetic determinism, rather, it is to state that the earliest pattern of CNS integrity must provide us with the general structure from which personality and behavior will arise. For example, the alert, active, assertive, and curious infant does not usually develop into a quiet, shy, withdrawing, and distractible child or adult. Environment then, a collection of several external systems, can influence a child's personality and behavioral development but only within certain early determined parameters. This influence can enhance the child's potential or limit it and the positive or negative value of these parameters can only be determined by the values of parents, teachers, the community, or, eventually the child himself.

Temperament as a Feature of ADHD

Temperament is much more than the mere cluster of general characteristics of early personality. Unfortunately, only in the last fifteen to twenty years has the field of developmental pediatrics begun to fathom the tremendous implications of this early work by Chess and others. The infant, as a total biological entity, is growing at tremendous speed during the first few months. The goal of all of this growth is independence. As we mentioned earlier, much of the cerebral cortex is "unprogrammed" at birth. While tissue in much of the visual cortex, the parietal lobes, the motor and sensory cortex and most of the lower brain systems are programmed for survival and development at birth, much of the temporal and frontal lobes are not. These areas await early development in coordination, sensory processing, integration of movement, and a host of other early patterns of maturity, before the child can begin serious integrative "learning" in order to adapt to the environment and eventual independence.

The whole of the child must await early learning in order to adapt and to organize him or herself toward eventual "volitional behavior." Volitional behavior, that is, being able to orient and direct oneself is rudimentary by the end of the first three months but highly refined even by 24 months, depending on a functional and continuously evolving and integrating complex of systems development. But there is an ever higher level of cortical control as each of the subsystems matures and is made operational. Eventually, within the first two years, the first major accomplishment of independence is seen in the young child. But suppose there are problems in one of the subsystems. Temperament can be the early signs of the nature of a child but it can also be the early warning signs of troubles in one system or another. Even now, few pediatricians are well trained in understanding these signs. The research on infant crying, for example, is only now beginning to yield data which illustrates that the baby's crying patterns and responses can tell much about the infants needs or. . . . difficulties.

Each of the nine characteristics, if we think of the central nervous system as a fan with lower CNS function at the bottom and higher function at the top, may have roots in the lower or more primitive parts of the brain. An activity level which is incessant and which appears beyond the control of the infant, can indicate problems in the RAS, in the thalamus, or in sensory motor function. Conversely, such problems can exist, as earlier discussions of research suggested, in the frontal lobes in energetical factors in volitional attention caused by dopamine dysfunction. Here we have the truly hyperkinetic child who may become the ADHD child. We may see such signs early in life then which, due to our lack of understanding of development and normal levels of activity, are not understood by either the parent or pediatrician. This would suggest that there is much research to be done in pediatrics within this area.

As the birth rate of infants born to teenage mothers and to "crack" or drug involved mothers increases, how will they be able to effectively monitor, understand, and intervene in their infants needs or seek medical attention? Too often in the climate of a teenage mother without adequate prenatal care, there is also conflict, frustration, deprivation, and neglect which in themselves may enhance the distractibility level of a normally active infant. If such a child is placed in an inadequate daycare environment and is denied the opportunities that regular pediatric care can provide, will this not exacerbate the problems of the infant and totally ignore many of his early distress signals resulting in ever increasing dysfunctional growth and personal control? Toward this negative end then, if these sorts of parenting situations increase, the numbers of eventual ADHD children should also increase.

The most disastrous consequence of this sort of maternal environment is that the infant, during these first critical months and years, will continue to "program" the frontal and temporal lobes, but do so with a high level of mammalian and reptilian control for behaviors will be learned primarily for survival and not independence. Once programmed for survival, it becomes more and more difficult to "reorganize or program" the child for the neurostructure is permanent. To change deficit neuro-programming takes far longer than the establishment of original patterns.

This then is a good example of how "ecological climates" can produce children with attentional and organizational deficits. These become, due to their early patterning in the CNS, lifelong tendencies and subneurological sets. One does not "erase" these sets. One has to work for years, successfully, to develop higher level programs which can repress and override these early patterned response potentials.

All of this leads us to realize that, at least in this potential etiology for ADHD, much of the future work and research must be in infancy and prenatal analysis rather than in elementary school. This also shows the reasons that medication can have the most impact while behavioral modification is, in the long run, doomed to failure. It is here that the early programs for exceptional children throughout the country are so important and yet, in terms of the earlier discussion of climate in education today, so unlikely a priority.

With this in mind, one can see the importance of prenatal, birth, early family history, and early developmental patterns and why they are so important in the diagnosis of ADHD. When we see parents in the clinic and generate our assumptions concerning the developmental abilities and structure of the child, it is this early family history which gives us the most important insights into the child's needs. In most public school programs analysis of the child is done by and large with little or no family history taken by school personnel. This is why clinical involvement in the diagnosis of ADHD as opposed to other potential factors is critical and most often beyond the usual diagnostic routine of the school. BEFORE any school makes the diagnosis of ADHD, a clinical assessment must be made of the child and his family to broaden the ecological involvement of diagnosis. The school may identify potential ADHD children, but the actual diagnosis and case analysis must be made by a multidisciplinary team including both in-school and external professionals.

If the diagnosis is more likely that of d/ADD then the school should include the parents in the internal assessment. In that our thesis is that most such children will not be ADHD children but d/ADD then the school is quite capable of making an analysis and instigating intervention. If that is ineffective, then the broader community diagnosis is appropriate.

If temperament can be seen as a representation of overall function of the CNS in its earliest development, then the temperament cluster is to the whole of the CNS as reflexes are to the lower brain centers. Temperament then represents the earliest manifestations of the emerging child's integrated responses. As the CNS matures there is a purposeful development toward eventual cerebral organization which will provide effective management of the individual's needs. The CNS in toto, as with the reflexes, has a momentum toward integration of its overall function in order to facilitate adaptivity which in turn assures security, nurturance, control, and independence. As control is moved from the lower brain systems to the cerebral cortex during the first few months of life, the early temperament patterns become dominant and development proceeds through the elaboration of basic genetic/temperament clusters. As the child now grows, interacts, and adapts to his environment, the early temperament patterns and overall CNS integrity become subsumed into the new patterns of dynamic change.

It is during these first few months and years of life that the emerging energies of the child's "will to be" meets with the other ecological influences and is left from the confrontation with the fundamental behavioral patterns which will, in our opinion, set the parameters for later development throughout a lifetime. In this way the basic genetic prerogatives may be slightly or significantly altered as the child attempts to assert his will. For the more passive, receptive, and submissive child these influences can have a significant impact while for the assertive, curious, and risk-taking infant less impact may be realized.

It is probable that the early genetic temperament patterns of certain children will require that more conscious, consistent, and limiting controls be exerted through other ecological systems in order to direct the energies of the child. Other children will require less monitoring and control in order to achieve effective social adaptation. Critical, however, is the realization that this difference between children requires significant variation in parenting and social shaping conditions. In the main, throughout the population gene pool, most children, assuming an artificial percentage of 50–60 percent, will respond successfully to general social conditions and opportunities, resulting in at least minimally to highly adjusted children.

But there are a significant number of children, perhaps as many as 30 to 40 percent, who require what may be called, "special environments" and conditions to assist them in successful adjustment. Of this smaller group of 30 to 40 percent, some will be at-risk and vulnerable children, those who are withdrawal, high threshold, low activity, and accommodating children. Another group within the minority of poorly adapting children, will be the assertive, willful, and low threshold children who do not respond to the typical social conditioning processes. It is this group of children from which one type of d/ADD children will come. These will be children with high intensity behavior; curious and directed, assertive and aggressive, independent and difficult to manage, and they may not adhere to social expectations so much as challenge them.

Temperament and Culture

There is a feeling, reported by child care workers and preschool teachers, that in recent years the levels of activity, distractibility, impulsiveness, and difficulties with rule-governed behavior are increasing in children. In our own preschool and among teachers in other preschools, we find this problem a topic of conversation. Teachers in daycare facilities also report that the seeming increase in activity level is perhaps due to more cases where both parents are working and the increasing number of single parents. Certainly, with the increased awareness of ADD symptoms many elementary teachers are now reporting increased numbers of children identified in their classes as ADD. But we will submit that these are not ADHD children but rather d/ADD and b/ADD children.

Dr. Eric Erickson long ago proposed eight stages of human development in which the first three stages symbolized phases of development for the preschool- and elementary-aged child. The first three stages are summarized here:

STAGE ONE—Trust versus Mistrust

This stage suggests that during the first eighteen months a child develops internal feelings of trust for his environment and caregivers through the interaction and security provided. Erickson felt this was the most important stage for it lays the basis for and quality of all subsequent phases. The child who is nurtured in a secure and supportive environment, in this view, establishes an attitude of trusting those about him and is able to move into an exploratory and expanding environment based on this internal feeling of trust. Yet, if there is conflict, a lack of security and nurturance, and even abuse, the child develops an underlying structure of uncertainty, mistrust, and defensive orientation to the world.

If we return to our discussions of the development or CNS cerebral structure and the mammalian and reptilian responses of flight or fight, defensiveness, and survival skills, this first stage then ends in a CNS structure designed for survival, one that is typical of the animal who must develop defensive strategies to protect himself and to fight for the goals of his needs, i.e., food, water, security, and stability.

Considering that this period of CNS growth is designed to program higher cerebral functions into the system which will allow for adaptation to the environment, then in the negative case the child remains more mammalian-controlled than cerebrally-directed. This, in turn, delays, if not prevents, the eventual movement into a cerebrally and more rational management of one's behavior and maintains the cerebral functions, i.e., cognition and cognitive strategies as a servant of the mammalian system rather than the opposite.

This is one developmental difficulty which can result in a d/ADD or b/ADD behavioral syndrome. This can result in a maladaptive child who is assertive and aggressive, and who is unable to focus on more linguistic and rational behavioral patterns. He simply cannot trust his environment and therefore, higher cognitive function is more tied to survival than to the development of successful social patterns.

Certainly, this sort of d/ADD child can be the result of a deprived, hostile and abusive, and threatening environment. This is perhaps a conclusion that most child care workers and teachers would accept as probable in a preschool environment where economic and cultural deprivation are typical. But it is not only in a deprived environment that the mistrusting child can be found, difficulties in parenting, abuse, and a lack of adequate nurturance can be found in middle and upper class homes as well. Children will learn survival skills in any environment in which one has to deal with hostile and degrading adult responses.

STAGE TWO — Autonomy versus Shame

This phase involves children eighteen months to three years of age. When a child feels wanted and nurtured, and explores his environment and feels safe in doing so, he moves into feelings of independence and competence. He grows less dependent and more independent. But in environments where there is not support or encouragement the child can arrive at this stage filled with mistrust. Where the parents cannot give adequate time and nurturance to the child to assist him in learning independence, he may develop feelings of incompetence and worse, shame, for his failure. This then results in continued defensiveness and rejection of authority and power struggles can develop. When parents are both working and the child is in a daycare situation where there are not enough well-trained workers he may find it difficult to obtain the needed support there also. If the child is one who is active and aggressive, who has developed feelings of mistrust, and finds the day care environment one where he has to struggle for attention, serious d/ADD behaviors can result.

The child who feels trust and who is receiving good parental support at home arrives at this stage with increasing feelings of competence and independence and is willing to accept rules and social expectations in stride.

STAGE THREE—Initiative versus Guilt

According to Erickson the child who is healthy and successful in the first two stages enters the period from three to six years with feelings of accomplishment and competence. He learns to fit into the social and learning world of preschool and kindergarten. But, conversely, when the child arrives at this stage with mistrust, aggression and defensiveness, and feelings of shame, he may become physically abusive and hostile toward authority and rules. He is an angry child who has difficulty meeting the expectations of adults and having learned primarily survival skills, is poorly equipped to enter into cooperative and structured learning experiences. We now have the b/ADD aggressive child who will need much help in learning new skills. His success will be dependent on the teacher and parents helping him learn to trust, to take risks, and to develop adequate social skills. This can take not only a few months but perhaps years and the simple use of medication or behavioral management will not serve to solve these complex problems.

Additional discussion of these problems and others which relate more to the b/ADD (Behavioral Attention Deficit) child will be discussed in the Chapter Six. Now we want to look at the third developmental system, Sensory-Motor Development.

2. THE ENVIRONMENTAL SYSTEM

We will bypass the second system, the Environmental System, until Chapter Six.

3. THE SENSORY-MOTOR SYSTEM

The sensory-motor system includes, as we have discussed, the cerebellum, upper brain stem and thalamus, the vestibular system, portions of the parietal and occipital lobes, and the sensory and motor strips in the cortex. As we have reviewed the functions of this system in general, now we want to discuss it in terms of functional or operational outcomes and processes which lay the basis for the child's movement skills. This system particularly is a good example of how the sum of the parts is greater than the individual functions of specific parts. Much of the CNS displays this characteristic. If individual processes are assessed in the functioning CNS, one is always surprised that the outcomes of interactions within systems are greater than the mere sum of the functions.

In the sensory motor and movement systems of the body the human animal differs greatly from other animals and it is surprising how little attention is paid to the holistic implications of these differences. The kinesthetic and tactile senses are fundamental to the development of balance and flowing integrated movement patterns. Most significantly though, are implications for relationships between cognition and the sensory motor system. We have learned from the children in our clinic how important this relationship is and yet, there is a tendency to view "thinking" as separate from physical activities. Professionals often are unaware of the significance of sensory motor function. We will first discuss some general characteristics of sensory motor function in relation to development and then, in the coming discussion we will look more critically at how such function relates to cognitive abilities.

The infant, during the first few months of life, must gain control of the sensory motor system through maturation in cerebral organization. We must conceptualize here the notion that during the first three months, when the sensory motor system is primarily controlled by the mammalian system, the infant slowly becomes more conscious and sensorially aware resulting in a slow but volitional ability to respond to tactile and kinesthetic information which has been flowing into the cerebral sensory cortex. This information eventually will cause a response in the cerebral motor strip which has the capacity to initiate movement. Through trial and error and kinesthetic feedback, the infant begins to learn motor responses. From the first three months forward the infant exerts his will more and more resulting in the control of gross limb movements, head movements, and gravity-resistant muscle responses.

Through the integration of sensory information from the vestibular/cerebellum system the infant will soon sit-up, crawl, and by four months begin the basic locomotor movements of scooting and creeping. During this period the infant becomes not only aware of tactile-kinesthetic capabilities in locomotion but also there are residual competencies now being assimilated which are far more significant. In the animal kingdom locomotion skill is critical to survival and most are able to walk and run in minutes to days following birth. But here lies the significant difference between humans and other animals, the human is developing a higher capacity of self awareness and cognition.

As the infant learns to slowly move his limbs, unlike other animals, he is also becoming self-aware of his body, of its existence, and subsequently his own existence. Even in the famous case of training chimpanzees to use symbols to communicate elementary needs and to see themselves in a mirror, these animals are not in possession of man's significant frontal and temporal lobes. Within the temporal and frontal lobes human infants have the potential to symbolize, abstract, and to communicate but this capacity must first be organized within a real, concrete, and tactile, sensory world. Without the existence of a physical self, one does not "think" for we have yet to evolve into a nonparticle energy capable of immediate cognition. Without the presence we do not exist! Here, in the first few months of life, as the infant becomes aware of HIS ability to control movement of this physical entity, he comes to know a rudimentary self and he forever transcends other animals.

From the middle of the first year many programs begin to develop within the cortex through the ACTIONS of the infant ON the environment. But not only is the infant learning through manipulation about his environment, he is also exercising his increasing capacity to abstract his environment. As he plays with the hanging mobiles in his crib he marvels at the feel, their movements, the shadings of color and texture, and their predictability. And when he sees them tomorrow he will remember, from basic programming in the visual, tactile, and auditory cortex centers what occurred yesterday. The experience can be called to "mind" in order to predict the present and future from the experience of yesterday. By repetitive actions on the same object or material he will endlessly repeat experience until it has become an "automatic" system program.

An automatic program in cerebral function is very different from a mammalian or reptilian reflexive response. For example, toward the end of the first year when the infant learns to roll a ball back across the floor to his brother, HE does not have to experiment, HE predicts what will happen and performs a motion without conscious experimentation. Eventually, in his second and third years he will elaborate this simple motor movement into early throwing and kicking skills. The automatic programming in such movements are learned; performed repeatedly until the lower brain systems will perform them simply when he thinks of them. Walking will become, by the months 10 to 14, the same sort of programmed movement. He will intentionally attempt to walk at first, fall down, repeat the attempt, and finally make short awkward movements resulting in a few unsteady steps. As he continues to practice from the end of the first year through the fourth year his walking skills will elaborate into not only automatic walking movements but hopping, jumping, climbing, and eventually skipping as well. At each level of elaboration and sophistication motor skills in locomotion, balance, gross and fine motor movements, and integrated cooperative play movements will all become automatic programs carried out by the movement system simply at the slightest request from his cerebral system.

It is significant to understand this concept of cerebral programming of motor functions through the actions of the lower brain systems. This cooperative interaction between cerebral and cerebellar (lower system), as we will see, becomes critical for eventual ability to conceptualize, think, and perform complex cognitive functions. An additional discussion must ensue here before we proceed with the cognitive foundations laid by these processes. Interestingly, adequate control and automation of this cerebral/cerebellar system (we will use cerebellar here to imply the entire vestibular-cerebellar system) is also responsible for an additional feature, relaxation and attention. For eventual cognitive control, the child must develop an intimate relationship between the ability to be free of physical distraction and yet perform physical functions. To walk down a hallway in conversation and yet avoid running into other people, the individual must be able to converse ("thinking"), while the lower system automatically engages in avoidance maneuvers peripherally dictated by subconscious commands.

This intimate relationship and coordination between cerebral desires and lower brain system function not only allows us to write our thoughts, read a page in a book, or type commands into a computer, but it also allows us to relax the physical system as we engage in cognitive function. This is the "mind/body" synthesis, the development of "oneness of self" and in part, the "ying/yang" melding created in eastern philosophy and the martial arts. Thus, is created the ability to "focus" oneself on inner thoughts and on intense awareness of self in relation to the environment. When these systems are not in consonant interaction and balance, there is a confrontational flow created between cerebral function and mammalian or reptilian agendas, one aspect of a d/ADD syndrome is created. There are other confrontations as we will see.

Laterality, Directionality, Spatial Orientation

There are many processes which arise during the early years but returning to our essential focus here, that of the sensory motor system, we want to focus on the development of relationships in sensory motor function and cognition. As the kinesthetic aspects of development proceed, balance, kinesthetic feedback, and lateralization become templates for cognitive awareness. The infant uses lateral awareness to fabricate an orientation to space about him, i.e., up/down, side/side, front/back. The extension of this growing internal orientation of physical self and its dimensions, allows the child, now in the third and fourth year, to conceptualize space about him and to use that orientation mentally.

Sensory motor responses, such as turning the head in the direction of a sound, dodging a snowball, catching one's self from falling in a particular direction, or swatting a fly on the right side of the head, are all reflexive actions taken by the mammalian or lower brain systems. They are actions in which the cerebellar system "overrides" the now dominant cerebral structure, interrupts present consciousness preoccupations, and responds to a serious or immediate need for response. Such situations demonstrate, again, this intricate interaction between cerebellar and cerebral relationships. But it also demonstrates where the primary system exists, the upper brain stem and the RAS along with the cerebellum, much like our family dog, allows itself to be dominated until such moments when only it can react adequately.

While the cerebellar system can react to basic environmental situations, learn basic motor programs, and perform complex movements through learned special "programs," it does not think or reason. Its lateralized and differentiated physical structure does, however, lay the basis for organization of many cognitive functions, and in this way, becomes an essential part of the "process" of cognition.

Interestingly, in order to imagine, visualize, or conjure images in our heads, we are dependent upon the sensory programs and images which are stored in our memories. Imagery, as we will discuss later, is a primary cognitive process and requires a relatively well-organized and intact sensory motor system. Also, as interesting perhaps is that much of so-called "thinking" occurs within a serial or sequential pattern of images, i.e., the first thought, leading to the second, and to the final thought, all of which proceed in a sequential pattern. But this is a bit ahead of ourselves and we will return to the sequential patterning momentarily.

First, we must realize that the cerebellar system provides a "centering" in mental function. The awareness of sides, of up and down, and front and back, places our general cognitive awareness into a position we call, "centrality," or, a feeling of being in the center of our physical self. This, relative to cognition, is a major concept of human thought, unlike anything possible in the general animal kingdom. This not only provides reality to our sense of self and being, but localizes that awareness within the center of our head. We now have established a central point for consciousness though it is achieved not so much by an actual physical reality as in mentation.

This is why excellent function in kinesthetic and tactile information, in the flow of information in the vestibular system where placement of awareness is juxtaposed and superimposed with the feelings of self in relation to gravity, and the responses of the sensory and motor cortex, are so important to attention and focused awareness. Children who have poor kinesthetic function, who have dysfunction in vestibular control and balance, or poor physical coordination, often also have difficulties in focusing attention, in orientation to a central awareness, or in managing the physical system in automatic programming. Their bodies and their kinesthetic/tactile informational flow disrupt their ability to attend, to focus, and to integrate "mind and body."

In the past researchers have struggled with the importance, or lack of it, of early physical coordination, perceptual-motor interfaces, and general gross and fine motor coordination. They were looking at the individual parts and attempting to measure their importance to academic subjects, over-activity, or other perceptual motor functions, with higher thought processes such as academic skills. They were disappointed for they often found no relationship when in fact the relationship is too complex to be measured by assuming that a particular action was important. They did not account for nor understand the underlying and unifying PROCESS, for they were measuring individual actions rather than the process.

Children with d/ADD often exhibit a number of sensory motor deficits and while good coordination does not predict eventual excellence in school, intelligence, or attentional proficiency, they are an inherent part of the processes of attention, focal and nonactive concentration, and the ability to relax and maintain attention to task. This fundamental basis for eventual mental organization, as we will now see, is but one part of an ever more complex organization.

4. THE SPATIAL-TEMPORAL SYSTEM

At this point we have an operational physical, sensory-motor, and self-awareness system but we are not yet capable of real thought and cognitive organization. Here is the foundation of the physical presence, or self-existence, or awareness of directedness. Now we have to use this underlying system, and the cerebral consciousness, in an integrated way. As the cerebellar system has been developing movement proficiency, so have the cerebral hemispheres been developing early language and spatial imagery toward the potential for higher levels of intellectual competency. Yet, the integration, the link, between these two systems is incomplete. There is a BRIDGE between the physical system and all that it provides, and the language and thinking system, we call it the "spatial bridge."

Spatial refers here to the awareness and application of basic underlying physical organization. For example, feelings of physical awareness on one side of the body now become, "left or right," "up and down," and "front or back." We now use language and consciousness to "name" points in space of which our physical and sensory system have provided an awareness.

Orientation and "physical awareness" of these points in space outward in all directions can be named and therefore abstracted. Thus, at the highest level of awareness or "thinking" we have an intersection with our lowest and most basic awareness, the physical system. This intersection is provided by our "projection" of internal physical awareness outward into space and this we call, "directionality," or the projection outward from our bodies of these internal physical awarenesses. The act of projection into space from our mental physical awareness we call, "spatial abilities" or spatial relationships.

It is very important to understand this intersection between the physical system and the cognitive or conscious system. The conceptual notion that there are a number of abilities (processes) which provide an intermediary point between these two systems is highly significant. Further, we realize that in our attempt to provide a conceptual model for the development of cognition, attention, and general mental organization, we are taking giant leaps across infinitely intricate psychoneurological specifics. But, while there are exceptions at each level of our model, this sort of paradigm seems to assist teachers in understanding the reasons for various instructional strategies which we will further illuminate.

The spatial bridge involves utilizing the underlying cerebellar system as a template for organization of linguistic function. In Figure 5 there is a perpendicular line drawn from the lower brain system into the areas of the frontal and temporal lobes with an additional line drawn horizontally at the top of this line. This "T" structure symbolizes the internalization of a lateralized awareness for the child of his spatial world. The spatial structure of the child extends in all directions from his central ideation of space about him. Most important for thought and cognition though, is that of recognizing the lateral plane.

The child's awareness is focused in the central portion of his cerebral hemispheres. Here he conceptualizes a sidedness which is eventually known as left and right but more importantly is, due to hand and cerebral dominance, given a priority in thinking of space. The right-handed child, left hemisphere dominant, has a dominant spatial/directional orientation not only of left and right but LEFT TO RIGHT. That is, in that his right hand is dominant (see Fig. 6), neurologically there is a predominant "internal orientation" or "feeling" that "things" should be constructed from left to right. When the child extends his hands in front of him, the right hand naturally, and physiologically, extends to the right. His left hand extends to the left. These are natural movement patterns for the right and left hand. If the right hand is dominant, as it is in perhaps 60 to 70 percent of the population, he conceptualizes space and movement as best expressed in working left to right. For the left-handed child, conversely, his natural spatial/directional orientation is from right to left.

This cerebral orientation of left to right, or, right to left is provided by the cerebral hemispheres. This is an integration of cerebellar and physiological structure with hemispheric conceptualization. In essence, the lower brain system with its creation of motor function, connected to the cerebral hemisphere through this internalization of space as the intermediary, combines with cerebral dominance to create a preferred pattern of movement. This spatial bridge then provides the mechanism for integration of upper and lower brain function.

With this underlying mechanism the child begins an intense and significant growth in mental function. He can imagine TIME and temporal orientation, and with this he can conceptualize the past in relation to the future and each in relation to the present. Without space and some means of conceptualizing it, time remains a sensory reality but a mental vagueness. Thus, there is a left and right, a center between the two, and a series of points in between. The tip of the left hand extended far to the left, the tip of the right hand extended far to the right, provides for the child a concept of points in space. His centered self-awareness provides a central point in front of him. The spatial concepts of centering and, far left and right in combination can now be used to organize the passing or movement of time. Things begin at the far left and move to the far right in a natural sequence of movement for the right-handed child. Moving an object or even his hand across this spatial continuum at a definite rate can now be related to the movement of the sun, to a beginning and an end, to the first position and the last, and finally from yesterday to the present directly in front and to tomorrow far to the right.

The cognitive significance of this developmental milestone, occurring between the fourth and sixth year, cannot be underestimated for this interaction between the physiological structure of the body and the language structure of the hemispheres, in a large measure, makes organized attention and thought possible. Now the child can make sense of numbers, or serialization, of Piaget's "reversibility in cognition" and in a myriad of academic skills ranging from scanning words, to spelling, and planning a sequence of events. To some degree it is part of Bruner's theory of the scaffolding of the mind, and Kephart's "perceptual-motor match."

The organization of spatial structure into left-right patterns of directional conceptualization gives language meaning, or, in truth, gives communication meaning. Our language is dependent, at least in early years, on perceptual words and words that describe actions. Until the age of approximately six years, a child's language is primarily used to communicate a rich world of increasing sensory sophistication. How big or small are things, how long, how sharp or furry, what color, taste, or smell, how light or heavy, how deep or tall, wide or narrow, and how do they behave, are they scary, "feel good" or "fun?" These are all words which describe a spatial and sensory world.

But sensory language, with integration of higher cerebral function and space/time relationships, becomes rapidly more complex and abstract after the spatial bridge with higher function develops. As this developmental level is reached children talk about similarities and differences, groups and categories, classifications, and future or past relationships. Children can integrate the sensory words of "fun" or "scary" with past experience or the future, they can plan ahead and prepare, reflect and avoid, or suddenly gain an insight into their own behavior. They no

Visual motor coordination and match. Visual dominance is much different than the concept of motor dominance. In motor dominance one particular hemisphere of the brain usually assumes the responsibility for motor behavior. The motor dominance provides a frame of reference to position in space which is an expressive neurological function. In visual dominance we assume one eye leads the visual direction while the other eye then "follows" to the spot selected by the "sighting" or dominant eye. Naturally, both eyes receive light images simultaneously in most cases. Each eye sends the information to the hemispheres of the brain. As is shown in Figure 3, light entering the eyes from the right visual field is sent from each eye primarily to the left hemisphere. Light entering both eyes from the left visual field is sent primarily to the right hemisphere. Light entering the eyes from the right visual field is forwarded most to the left hemisphere which controls motor movements on the right side of the body. Light entering from either side of the visual field is apparently sent to the hemisphere of motor control for the side of the body in that visual area. It is suggested that a right handed child will tend to write with his paper in the right visual field since he gains the most information to the hemisphere involved in motor movements on that side of the body.

Visual-motor match involves a continual feedback of visual information about the exercise of motor movements. Motor behaviors occurring on the right side of the body and in the right visual field are relayed to the left hemisphere where responsibility for controlling motor movements takes place and a continual feedback of motor movement through the visual system accomplished the so-called "visual motor match" which is the coordination of motor movements with visual feedback.

Additional feedback is also provided through kinesthetic feedback. Again, kinesthetic feedback on the right side of the body is returned to the left hemisphere providing both visual and kinesthetic feedback to the left hemisphere which assists in more accurate control of motor movements and the development of efficient motor coordination.

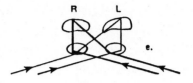

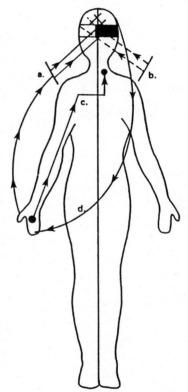

Figure 6. Visual-motor relationships.

longer, by the age of seven, are so impulsive, emotionally explosive, or unable to follow rules, for now they have a more sophisticated awareness of not only themselves but their behavior and that of others in relation to rules, timing, and expectations. They can, with these cognitive/spatial integrities, objectify themselves and their behavior. Interrupt, delay, or avoid the development and reinforcement of any of the above systems, and the child now becomes less or totally incapable of managing his attention, his orientation to time, and his tendency toward impulsivity. Here then is a d/ADD child. Interventions in the home, in preschool, kindergarten, and first grade can assist the child in compensation. But does the teacher, the physician, or school psychologist understand these concepts? If not, the child may simply be medicated and attempts made to modify his behavior. It will fail!

5. THE LINGUISTIC SYSTEM

By seven years of age, as we see above, we now move away from the sensory- and movement-based world of the young child and in the direction of developing many early areas of the sophisticated communication and value-oriented patterns of adult behavior. The language areas of the CNS now become dominant and provide the basis on which the child organizes his world. But the processes of language are in every moment, for the seven year old, dependent on the sensory, spatial, and motor systems. Eventually, the separation will become more distant, but for the elementary child it is still often difficult to separate a thought from a feeling, a tear from a smile, or a touch from flight.

It is easy to see how immaturity, delays, and disruptions in these developmental patterns can create at least transitionally a d/ADD child. Depending on the conditions, the family, temporary crisis, or a hostile and unsupportive environment, a child can become unable to control or integrate all of these systems. In such settings the mammalian brain takes control and what little may have been gained in integration is temporally lost. To simply attempt to medicate or behaviorally modify such a child is to miss entirely the issues. This is why we are so concerned with parents and teachers who simply look at impulsive or overly active behavior and call it ADD. We have only touched the surface!

Cerebral Dominance and Language

Language, as a spoken symbol system for sensory reality, provides a basic communication between people. It is primarily a means of serving each other's personal and cultural needs. We do not intend, however, to attempt a detailed discussion of psycholinguistics or even of basic cultural/language relationships that is best done by professionals in those fields. But we have to involve ourselves at least in some speculative and cursory discussion of language in relation to our topic of cerebral processes. Before further discussion of language processes, however, we need to continue our exploration of the notion of how cerebral dominance and spatial organization relate to the function and process of language.

What we must attempt to discuss now makes us slightly uncomfortable, for while it will have relevance to teachers and school psychologists, it is neurologically speculative but functionally relevant. This is to say that the foundations of our presentation are based in applied study with many children but has not been committed to basic research procedures. We will welcome those in psychoneurology to consider these considerations for basic research, but for our purposes here we want to present our applied conclusions which appear important in working with children instead of "studying" them in a scientific procedure. These conclusions then are of value, in our experience, for teachers but are not clinically defined for researchers though they may want to pursue these directions. We will offer some general references for the researcher such as Beaumont and Dimond's book, *Hemispheric Function in the Human Brain,* in which there is an extensive body of research on the subject of cerebral dominance. Also we would direct the researcher to William Gaddes' book, *Learning Disabilities and Brain Function,* in which there is a chapter on cerebral dominance.

The difference between what we are about to present and that of researchers in psychoneurology is that here we are dealing with "processes" and outcomes as opposed to specific neurological research focused on a specific neuropathway or complex. We have gleaned the following information from empirical data in our case studies where we were concerned with analysis of learning and behavioral problems. Processes are difficult if not impossible to study in the laboratory sense for there are too many variables, difficulties in subjective and objective judgments, and the impossibility of either measuring or controlling the entirety of the process.

As we have discussed, lateral dominance in motor function provides both a spatial orientation of organization for temporal function, i.e., right-left, up-down, etc., and a preferred directional schemata for organization of mental function. In the right-handed child this results in the conventional schemata of left-to-right planning and organization. The relationship to language, in our work, has been interesting in regards to spatial-directional orientation. The right-handed, right-eyed, and right-footed child is usually also "right-ear dominant," being more competent in processing language through the right rather than the left ear. This is established in research in the general references cited above. It has also been established clinically that the pattern of right-eye, right-hand, and right-ear, etc., along with the opposite for the left-handed child are typical for the right- and left-handed child. Further, it is relatively easy to obtain some degree of assuredness of the operational dominance which a child displays.

The interesting aspect of cerebral dominance, in relation to language, is that, aside from the established dominance of the left hemisphere (temporal-frontal lobe) for language, internal conceptualization of language is also tied to the spatial-motor dominance of the individual. The additional realization that in perhaps 90–95 percent of the general population, whether they are right- or left-handed, the left hemisphere is still the dominant hemisphere for language is also very important. This too appears to have been well researched. But, and this is critical to understand, while language is usually within the left hemisphere and therefore that hemisphere is dominant for language, the same hemisphere is not always dominant for spatial-motor function.

In the right-handed, cerebrally left hemispheric dominant child, the underlying conceptualization of language content is naturally organized in a left-right pattern. In essence, when the child "thinks" about what he is planning to speak, he naturally organizes those thoughts and internal "IMAGERY" in a left-to-right pattern. Thus, when the child thinks of a situation in which, for example, he was playing with some friends and there was an incident which he wants to report, he thinks of that SEQUENCE of behavior in a left-right pattern of imagery. When he begins to report this verbally, he utilizes visual imagery in a sequential pattern and speaks the syntax and phraseology in a left-right pattern. Therefore, he states, "Yesterday when Bob and I were playing, Tom hit

Bob and we both were caught by the teacher." All of this makes sense both to the child and to the adult to whom he was reporting. When the child thinks "back" to yesterday and the incident, internal imagery searches and finds that information (yesterday) in a left-scanning pattern. He is reporting it in the present which is NOW and conceptually is represented by in "front of us."

The left-handed child, interestingly, all areas of development being equal, may have more trouble reporting the same incident, particularly if he is younger than seven years. The left-handed child could say, "Tomorrow morning when Tom and. . . . I mean Bob and I were playing, Tom. . . . hit Bob and both . . . we both were caught by the teacher." What is happening here? The internal reference in imagery is reversed, this child has difficulties in conceptualizing before and after, yesterday and tomorrow in combination with language. He thinks of what happened but as he is saying the words, the opposite word is selected from the lexicon rather than the appropriate one. Further, in the case of the placement of the word "both," there is a sequential reversal little different from the b-d reversal in writing.

This is one of those, "almost true" conceptualizations we mentioned earlier, the process of sequential memory does not always seem to function in this way and not with all children, but the left-right patterning of visual imagery gives us a model which allows us to understand differences in children. This notion will be particularly useful momentarily as we discuss additional children with differences.

One of the important concepts here is that kinesthetic and spatial orientation provide the basis for organizing temporal abilities. The cerebellar and vestibular systems provide, along with the dominant motor strip in the cortex, a template for organizing the temporal structure. This, in turn, provides an underlying imagery "grid" against which language organization can be developed.

CEREBRAL AND LATERAL DOMINANCE MODELS

Group A—Model (1)
>Right-eyed, right-handed, lateral dominance
>Left hemisphere cerebral dominance

Model (2)
>Left-eyed, left-handed, lateral dominance
>Left hemisphere cerebral dominance

(Model 2a)
        Same as 2 except right hemispheric cerebral dominance.
Group B—Model (3)
        Left-eyed, right-handed, lateral dominance
        Left hemispheric cerebral dominance
    Model (4)
        Left-eyed, right-handed, lateral dominance
        Right hemispheric cerebral dominance
Group C—Model (5)
        Right-eyed, left-handed, lateral dominance
        Left hemispheric cerebral dominance

The typical right-handed child (One) and the left-handed child (Two) provide two basic models of "temporal-spatial/motor-cerebral dominance" templates for language and cognitive function. There appear to be two more which are of great significance. William Gaddes in his book, *Learning Disabilities and Brain Function,* mentioned five lateral dominance models, right-handed, left-handed, mixed right-handed, pathological left and pathological right-handed. Our models are similar with some differences in interpretation.

Mixed right- and left-handed children (Three) compose a significant number of individuals and pose a particularly difficult diagnostic problem. For the clinical researcher, determination of handedness can involve specific neurological procedures and, though tenuous at best, such diagnosis could form the basis for some of the tenets we propose here. For the teacher and school psychologist, however, a less arduous but functionally more practical series of indicators is available.

Considering the typical right- and left-handed child, a certain range of indicators of dominance are listed here:

Group A—(1) Right dominant
        (2) Left Dominant child

1.   Right eye dominance (Opposite for left)
        Indicators: Child holds hands in front forming a circle with the
                thumbs and fore fingers. Hands out stretched the child
                is instructed to look WITH BOTH EYES through
                the hole (about the size of a quarter) at a target such
                as the examiner's nose. The dominant eye is used
                though the child believes he is looking with both eyes.
                Other strategies can be used. (Sighting a gun)

2. Right hand dominance (Opposite for left)
   Indicators: Strength of hand grip, preferred hand for fine motor activities, holding both hands forward at shoulder level with eyes closed seeing which hand maintains upper position. Have child stand in front of you and tell him to be ready to do something quickly when asked. Hold your forefinger and thumb together making a circle. Hold out in front of you and ask the child to put his finger through the hole. Child will use dominant finger and hand.

3. Right foot dominance (Opposite for left)
   Indicators: Have child stand on one foot. Usually will use dominant foot but this is variable. Have child kick a ball.

4. Right ear dominance (Opposite for Left)
   Indicators: Have child put a play phone to his ear to pretend to make a call. Observe child in class to see which ear he tends to present in order to hear more clearly. (Audiology exam may be available.)

5. Reading skills—Left-right sequencing—(Left can do)
   Indicators: Is able to scan easily across page of print, does not lose his place easily. Does not reverse letter sequences or individual letters, does not display auditory reversals in spelling.

6. Writing skills—Left-right sequencing (Left adapts)
   Indicators: Does not display unusual reversals in making letters. Does not switch hands.

7. Sports and gross motor—(Left may excel)
   Indicators: Performs sports and activities well without confusion and switching hands.

8. Speech and language—(No problem for left by 7 Yr)
   Indicators: Displays good syntax and no confusion in expression.

9. Temporal organization—(Left adapts and does O.K.)
   Indicators: Learns to tell time adequately without confusion. Knows east and west without confusion. Can relate sequence of events without confusion.

10. Behavioral organization—(Left adapts)
    Indicators: Can remember sequence of behavioral events. Can place

self in sequence of events. Is able to maintain control of behavior without impulsivity.

These criterion, applied in the school setting as opposed to a diagnostic setting, are relatively reliable in determining handedness. There may be some minor differences but when these criterion are applied in both testing and classroom observation, it is illustrative of the child's cerebral dominance. For the left-handed child, age seven or above, the foregoing criterion are much the same as for the right-handed child except that, of course, the child is left-eyed, handed, footed and dominant in left ear function. For left-handed children younger than seven years, some of the criteria, other than eye, hand, and foot dominance, may display differences. Young left-handed children must work harder to learn good temporal organization and prior to the age of seven years many problems are typical.

In Chapter Three we presented data concerning the hemispheric differences by Geschwind and Levizky in which it appeared that in 100 brains studied histologically, approximately 65 percent displayed larger planum temporate on the left, 11 percent on the right, and 24 percent displayed equal sizes. This suggested dominance in the left hemisphere which also suggested motor dominance will follow this pattern. This neurological analysis of brain structure is highly debatable and most other researchers found 90 percent larger on the left.

Over the years we have seen several thousand children, especially boys, with various learning disabilities. Through the 1970s it became apparent, in studying the characteristics of these children that certain lateral dominance factors were highly frequent. This data led us to write several early books relating to cerebral and lateral dominance difficulties in overly active, distractible, and impulsive children which appeared to formulate a general syndrome of developmental differences. When speaking of cerebral dominance we usually refer to hemispheric differences in specialization while in lateral dominance we are usually referring to motoric and spatial factors. These differences, listed in the early part of this chapter, were very similar to those reported by Safer and Allen's book on hyperactive children. The major difference between our syndrome and that of Safer and Allen is the severity of "hyperactivity." While many of our children had overly active and distractible behavior

patterns, most though not all, did not display what we considered pervasive hyperkinesis. Briefly, these characteristics were as follows:

1. A history of learning and developmental difficulties in family
   structure, i.e., fathers early experience.
2. Attentional difficulties
3. Difficulties in cerebral dominance
4. Early speech and language problems
5. Impulsivity
6. Poor fine motor skills
7. Reversals
8. Difficulties in temporal order and time
9. Catastrophic emotional reactions
10. Preoccupation with fantasy
11. Difficulties in social rule-governed behavior
12. Need for support and affection
13. High nonverbal sensitivity to behavior
14. Feelings of failure
15. A lack of order in home and school

This d/ADD pattern including most if not all of these characteristics
were common in these children and they were often diagnosed by others
as ADD, dyslexic, hyperactive, depressed, or simply learning disabled.
We contend that a large majority of children now being presented as
ADD children by parents and teachers are these children. It can be
suspected from our presentation here then that, if these assumptions
and our work are valid, that these children should not be considered
ADD but are part of the general pattern of difficulties typical of
the classification of learning disabilities. It is obviously also true that
many children viewed as ADD or learning disabilities are not children
who fit into this pattern. But the pattern is so significant relative to
its prevalence in the general so-called ADD or learning disabilities
classification, that we hope that teachers and school psychologists will
begin to understand its dynamics. One important aspect of this paradigm is that it also, once understood, provides direct intervention strategies for its resolution.

Now let's look at the CNS dynamics of these children. These are the
mixed dominance children along with the final group in our classification,
pathological left- and right-handers. In our own work we suspect and
have come to expect that as many as 25 to 30 percent of all children

who display overly active behavior and difficulties in learning and adjustment will display all or many of the characteristics of this pattern. These are children with cognitive difficulties in organization and learning in school. Borchevich's study of cognitively-impaired children presented 40–60 percent of impaired children as having left or mixed dominance. Such statistics would suggest that we are seeing an important syndrome.

Mixed Dominance Syndrome
Group B—Models (3) and (4)

If we look at the general school population, while the number of mixed dominant children does not approach 40–50 percent levels as in the impaired population group, it is significantly high. We suspect that as many as 20–25 percent of the population exhibit identifiable characteristics of poor cerebral dominance or lateral dominance. In surveys conducted with undergraduate and graduate students over a five-year period we found a consistent 25 percent displaying cross lateral dominance in visual-hand and other indicators.

Mixed dominance is a somewhat vague and difficult classification. In our work children display lateral dominance problems and this is more typically related to the learning and behavioral difficulties than the notion of mixed dominance. Thus, in this case we are really referring to cross eye-hand dominance, difficulties in kinesthetic skills, AND what we refer to as "cerebral style" preference. We find the following characteristics in this group of children:

(3) Right-handed, left-eyed, left cerebral style.

The right-handed, left-eyed, and left cerebral style child is one who is basically a left-handed child relative to genetic determinants. This is a very common syndrome in our work with children who have behavioral and learning difficulties. This child is essentially one who, most often for cultural reasons, has switched from left-to-right-handedness at an early age if not prior to four years of age. Annett (1964) proposed that handedness is genetically determined and, without regressing into a discussion of handedness, basically demonstrated that 64 percent of the population would be expected to be pure right-handers, 32 percent would be mixed, and 4 percent pure left-handers.

This is interesting in that the predictions are closely related to the work of Geschwind and Levizky in which the left hemisphere appears dominant in 65 percent of cases, 32 percent mixed, and 11 percent right. While the two sets of data were related to language on one hand and hand dominance on the other, it may be that there is a significant factor inherent in the statistic. Again, our experience suggests, from an educational and learning disabilities point of view, that 20–25 percent of the general population will display some characteristics of mixed cerebral or lateral dominance. The importance of this is that if such a CNS organizational pattern creates developmental differences which result in learning and behavioral problems, could not teachers and school psychologists identify children with potential problems in preschool and kindergarten and develop compensations or outright successful patterns of visual-motor and language skills? The answer is yes, this can be done!

We see the mixed or cross lateral dominance as an issue in child development and learning. The following discussion along with some case studies later will assist us in seeing the nature of this problem. The left-eyed, right-handed, left hemispheric cerebral style child then is a child who has learned to use the right hand, but what does the left eye suggest? The brain usually will select the dominant eye relative to ITS preferred cerebral style. This means that, relative to spatial-temporal organization, the brain is programmed for a left-handed or right hemisphere motoric style. Yet, the child appears to be typical in language and is dominant for this function in the left hemisphere.

Characteristics of this third model, the left eyed, right handed, and left hemisphere cerebral style child exhibits the following characteristics on our ten point profile:

1. LEFT EYE DOMINANCE—Motorically this implies a right-to-left motoric orientation as with the left-handed child. We find that when a child is left-eyed, barring any significant visual difficulty or injury to the right eye, that this is a significant indicator of spatial-temporal orientation.
2. RIGHT HAND DOMINANCE—From all indications this child appears right-handed.
3. FOOT DOMINANCE—is often mixed but there is frequently a left foot preference again suggesting the left-handed spatial temporal system.

4. LEFT EAR DOMINANCE — Again, an indicator that here is truly a left-handed child.

5. READING SKILLS — Poor left-to-right sequencing, loses place and unable to find it. Tendency to read and view books from back to front, interest in looking at words from both left-right and right-left patterns. May be seen as having some form of dyslexia.

6. WRITING SKILLS — Difficulty in writing, many reversals past typical period, reversals in sequence as well as structure, poor formation of letters, unwillingness to give up printing for writing, much frustration with writing assignments, often draws letters well but actually writes very poorly. In some cases actually uses left hand for writing and eating while all other activities are right-handed.

7. SPORTS AND GROSS MOTOR — May be clumsy, have poor general coordination, a lack of good balance and kinesthetic skills. Conversely, some of these children are excellent athletes but usually in sports that are not dependent on rapid-eye hand coordination such as hockey, soccer, swimming, wrestling, golf, and track.

8. SPEECH AND LANGUAGE — Often displays some speech and articulation difficulties. Tendency to have problems in syntax and tense. May display linguistic reversals.

9. TEMPORAL ORIENTATION — The child has difficulties in remembering and organizing left-right patterns, difficulties in telling time, in remembering sequence of events, inhibiting behavior, and maintaining attention.

10. BEHAVIORAL ORGANIZATION — Difficulties in controlling impulsive behavior, overly active and wanders both physically and mentally.

The key to the left-eyed, right-handed child is to recognize that essentially he is a left-handed child. He has simply switched hands or he has been coerced to do so. This means that his language is basically typical and organized in the left hemisphere. The child who is basically left-handed but uses his right hand does have, however, significantly different problems than the left-handed child using his left hand. The left hemisphere motor strip controls the right hand and the opposite for the left hand. When there is a genetic prerogative for left hand dominance, the right hemisphere motor strip is also dominant. Consequently, when the child makes motor movements, the right motor strip attempts to initiate and control them. In that the right hand is being used, there is some competition and eventually cooperation between the two motor strips to operate the right hand. We call this "ipsilateral control." This form of control is difficult and often the child ends up using the right hand as a left hand even hooking the hand like a left-hander does. Thus, while the left-handed child using his left hand can eventually learn to work in reverse in order to write left to right, the left-handed child using the right hand has difficulties in "feeling" directionality.

Geschwind and Benson concluded in their research that "the demonstration of a larger pyramidal track in the right cord suggests that hand preference may depend upon the increased innervation available to one side of the cord, which leads to finer digital control on that side." If this is true, the child who switches hands for whatever reason ends up like the driver of a car in which every move of the steering wheel results in the reverse direction moment. The hard wiring which is genetically determined, provides a physiological and neurological foundation for not only handedness but, as we have suggested, also determines the temporal organization tendencies. This results in a "left-handed" mind set in a child who is using his right hand, which complicates not only fine motor skills but visual and cognitive scanning prerogatives as well.

These children, if understood early, can be given more time in learning to write, additional practice in reading, and constant assistance in reorganization in their work. But the additional issue of cerebral dominance or style can complicate things even more for the next model (4) is the same child except he also has a right hemispheric cerebral dominance style. The child who is left-eyed, right-handed, and who has a left hemispheric cerebral dominance style is able to effectively use language to monitor his motor system. But, as we will see, if such a child also happens to be right hemispheric cerebral style-oriented, even more difficulties compound the problem.

The type 4 child is left-eyed, right-handed, and right cerebral dominant, that is information processing competencies are higher in nonverbal function than in auditory sequential learning. The child tends to be the daydreamer, creative fantasizer, and imaginative learner. Nearly always a male, he tends to lose his orientation to time and place resulting in great difficulties in maintaining attention to task if the task is verbally-based. For example, reading comprehension is difficult while drawing or art may be quite interesting. In many cases, we have seen such children with normal verbal abilities but gifted nonverbal competencies. Such a child is pulled into visual spatial analysis of his environment and often ignores verbal information though he can learn as well as the average child. These children have a tendency to watch what the teacher says instead of listening. In that they don't listen and have a tendency to become involved in nonverbal mental orientation, they are unaware and have difficulties in time and sequence.

The high spatial cross dominant child is further confused by the utilization of his right hand when internally he is actually left-handed. With the combination of high spatial intelligence and mixed lateral dominance, it is difficult for this child to deal with structure and sequence. They often appear hyperactive and distractible and though they are active, their problem is not ADHD but rather developmental differences which must be altered through effective learning and development. To end this discussion we need to mention the model of lateral dominance style.

The Pathological Left-Hander (5)

One group of children who are fairly rare but who do appear from time to time is the pathological left-handed child. In this case the child has sustained cerebral damage in the left or both hemispheres and though genetically right-handed, due to the organic difficulty, learned to use the left hand. There is some research on this model including that of Luria: 1966, Subirana: 1964, Zangwill; 1960, and Milner; 1966. While these children have difficulties in fine motor skills, directional orientation, and spatial skills, they also, as might be guessed from earlier discussions, display problems in cognitive organization. They frequently display early speech and language problems.

There is also the possibility of pathological right-handed children, but we have not seen this difficulty in practice suggesting to us that it is more rare than the pathological left-handed child.

6. THE PSYCHONEUROLOGICAL COMPETENCIES SYSTEM

Howard Gardner in his 1983 book, *Frames of Mind,* presented a theory of multiple intelligences. We have found this book and others by Dr. Gardner very helpful in the practice of educational psychology, for the theory of multiple intelligence has many attractive features in understanding individual children and their differences. It is surprising to us, in fact, that all educators have not embraced many of his concepts in order to understand and assist children with developmental differences. In our own work, we too have found that one must consider the possibility that the child before us differs not only in the usual ways of physical differences and temperament, but that surely genetics and culture have also had their influence on shaping the processes of intelligence.

Intelligence, by and large, in our experience with adults and college students, is seen by the general population as a "thing" which a person has or does not have. Once intelligence tests became popular in the fifties and sixties the concept has grown until it has taken on a life of its own. Further, there are a number of common notions or beliefs which people appear to hold concerning intelligence. We list a few here as a prelude to our discussion:

1. Intelligence means one is "smart." Smart usually is seen as being clever in either verbal ability or the ability to think and reason.
2. One is usually born intelligent.
3. Average intelligence, especially among educational professionals is seen as an I.Q. of 90–110 and any score below this range implies the person is less intelligent just as someone with an I.Q. above 110 is more intelligent than most people. But this somewhat primitive bias is seen in astute professionals as well. In many studies concerning ADHD, researchers note that intelligence below 70–80 infers an inferiority which precludes application of the ADHD syndrome in that the inferior intelligence is usually the problem and not attentional deficit. We assume that this means someone with such a low I.Q. could not attend well in any case!
4. I.Q. is fixed and though education and opportunity may mediate the level somewhat, the level of attainable intelligence is fixed at birth. Many professionals hold this same belief about the intractability of intelligence.
5. People may be talented but that is not the same as being intelligent. For example, intelligent is seldom used as a descriptive term for athletic skills, musical skills, or artistic skills. These are usually described as talents and not intellectual competence.
6. Perhaps one of the most insidious beliefs held by more people than can be accepted, is that certain cultural and economic groups are usually less intelligent. This may sound more ominous than it is. The stereotyped "hillbilly," "farmer," "poor," or "dumb jock" are all popular examples of common beliefs about intelligence.

We do not need a long discussion here about the nature of intelligence for most of the readers are quite versed in such concepts. Yet interestingly, we must assure that we have a common language in referring to this area. Further, aside from specialists in psychoneurology and psychology, both teachers and even parents will perhaps review this work. Therefore, we must assure that all agree at least on the basic tenets concerning intelligence.

There are many theories about intelligence including those of such professionals as Sternberg, Piaget, Bruner, Kaufman, and Gardner. There have been "g" factors or a search for the central intelligence, information processing theories, genetic and environment theories, and so forth. Our particular orientation toward intelligence is an eclectic approach held between genetic and environmental factors. If confronted for a brief and relative concise statement about intelligence, then the following statement is representative of our thoughts:

> Intelligence refers to one or all of a number of psychoneurological competencies which form the basis for adaptive behavior within a specific set of cultural requirements. Intelligence is the efficiency and effectiveness of the psychoneurological processes in their response to the external requirements.

So, there it is, nothing is perfect and even a "tongue-in-cheek definition is perhaps adequate. This is not intended, obviously, as a new or astute description of intelligence but simply to lay the basis for later discussions. It does give a definite orientation which, if considered carefully, implies a theory and philosophy about intelligence. We are firmly committed to the belief that by and large personal competencies are an inherent part of the developing CNS and that these are primarily in the providence of our genes. Expression of one's genetic potentials is dependent on environment, opportunity, and action but the first prerogatives are in our biology. Conversely, we believe that while there may be limits to an individual's potentials, these are more often underestimated than overestimated.

Intelligence in this view, one of inherent potentials, varies from individual to individual and in a number of areas. We accept the general classifications of Gardner for the various intelligences which are, linguistic, musical, logical-mathematical, spatial, bodily-kinesthetic, and personal. While there may be other views, these will suffice for our purposes here.

There are several basic beliefs which, in part, are supported by much research and which we accept in our work with children:

1. Children do not, usually, display a specific potential without opportunities and experience in order to develop that potential.

We hold that most children will express the various potentials they have when given at least a minimal opportunity and encouragement to do so. Unfortunately, without such opportunities many children never develop much of the general potential they have. Many individuals finally express a specific potential which, though latent much of their life, comes to fruition later. Given an adequate early environment and a capable teacher and educational opportunity, most children would express a greater diversity and level of competency than is now typically the case in a homogeneous and often limited school climate and curriculum.

2. All children, including mildly mentally handicapped individuals, have potentials which can be developed under the proper circumstances and therefore, all children have potentials beyond what ever level they currently function.
3. Children who display maladaptive behaviors are complex individuals and given the opportunity will exercise positive growth. We have found few children whom we felt did not WANT to be capable. We operate on the principle that every child would like to be successful.
4. In every case where a child is displaying incompetence in various potentials, one cannot separate his inability from unsuccessful parents or teachers who provide the life space milieu within which he operates. In essence, the child, the family, and the school provide an inseparable "system" in which no part is maladaptive without inconsistencies and failure in other parts of the system.
5. In the case of d/ADD the child's difficulties in developmental competence must be identified and interventions given in order for the child to express his ability in personal control and general learning which are positive and omnipresent in all of his interactions.

The idea of various forms of potentials, we prefer the word potentials to intelligence because the word, "IQ" no longer has relevance in modern child development, is an important concept for the teacher and clinician. It implies a "system" of human development rather than an entity or "thing" such as intelligence. The human brain and certainly the "mind" must be seen, as we have suggested, as an interactive and interdependent collection of subsystems. This requires us as professionals or even parents to marvel at the development of a child and to see him, from the moment of birth, as a complex individual constantly evolving, always becoming as Gordon Allport liked to suggest. The child of yesterday is always changed tomorrow and in a moment we can but glance at a dynamic process and not a static individual. In this case we must always be inferring where a child has been, where he is heading, and what barriers or opportunities are presently encumbering or freeing him.

The most obvious competencies of the child are the sensory motor and spatial functions we have been discussing. How these develop and what potentials are there must be a concern in the case of the ADHD or d/ADD child for these are central to the notion of over or hyperactivity. How a child moves, his balance, spatial abilities and general fine motor skills are but specific aspects which must be recognized and understood.

The language system, linguistic capabilities in speech, in syntax, communication, and personal expressiveness are a critical area of expertise which varies greatly in children. With language the child can conceptualize his world, abstract it, and create internal imagery through which he can manipulate information into new ideas and solutions. For the ADHD child language can become a means of understanding himself and initiating ways in which he can manage his own problems.

Musical competencies are not reserved for those who are highly capable; music is part of every child and is intrinsic to spatial motor abilities. Rhythm and movement are a foundation upon which not only personal feelings and emotions are expressed, but they are critical in reading, speaking, athletics, and nonverbal communication.

Logical-mathematical competencies allow the child to reason, to work with serialization and sequences, and to see relationships in abstract sets. Such competencies also allow the child to make deductions and formulate probabilities.

Spatial intelligence allows for conceptualization of visual and dimensional relationships which are important not only in mathematical reasoning but more importantly in areas such as artistic skills, design, and construction.

Bodily-kinesthetic competencies allow for movement skills, athletics, and performance in dance and interactions of the self with the physical environment.

Personal intelligence involves an inner awareness not only of self but of the needs and feelings of others. This sensitivity is fused with a number of cultural and political factors toward understanding how groups relate to each other, to philosophy and religion, and to the simple interactions of interpersonal relationships.

We may agree or disagree with these constructs proposed by Gardner but the general concept is one that serves well to help us escape the bounds of intelligence and recognize that intelligence is no longer the issue. We must look at processes, or interactive systems in CNS function, at genetic probabilities, and the outcomes of complex social and educational influences in order to understand the "child" and his behavior.

7. EGO-CONSCIOUSNESS/THE EXECUTIVE SYSTEM

Our final concern in this chapter is the "ghost in the machine," the centralizing force, the self. We tread lightly here for there are ancient philosophical issues being restructured by the trindle of modern theories in quantum physics and mechanics which surround our thoughts when we dare speak of consciousness. Such thoughts are certainly not within the limits of this particular book. Thus, though we are suggesting the inadvisability of engaging in a description of consciousness here, we do want to use illustrative examples in this overview of notions to discuss consciousness.

We do want to begin with one brief thought which, though bothersome to even the physicist in the study of quantum physics, is critical to the understanding of children. When we attempt to study the mind (personality) expressed by the child, we are constructing the child from our own consciousness. We do not so much see a child as the child created by our observation and interaction. He is, therefore, not "the" child, but "our" child!

One of the most astute comments we have heard a teacher make is one which occurred as a passing comment in the hallway. On reflecting on the behavior of a particular child a teacher said, "Joey is not finding it possible to attend well today, I wonder what I am doing wrong?". This is a critical insight for all of us to experience, for the behavior of a child, under normal circumstances, is as much a consequence of our behavior as teachers as it is of the child himself. This also leads us to the problem of understanding the "mind," "ego," or "consciousness" of the child. When is the child himself aware and planfully attending and when is he merely responding to a set of circumstances that surround him? When is the child's behavior wholly his own and when is it more the mammalian or reptilian brain that is reacting?

This issue is central to the notion of behavioral modification, of cognitive shaping, or contingency management, for these approaches also carry with them in their execution a theory of child behavior and consciousness. These are, in the main, behavioralist notions at worst, and cognitive theories at best. In the first case we are acting "on" the child and in the second we are attempting to "elicit" a particular compliance through logic from the child. In neither case, however, may we really be in contact with the child's conscious and organized response. In the ideal situation the child himself is recognizing and choosing to respond in a certain way following his own and self-created adaptive choice.

In the truly conscious response of a child he is monitoring the life space climate and making a decision to respond in a certain way, to volitionally attend, to choose one response over another. Behavioral modification and all such approaches attempt to "shape" a child's behavior toward certain ends which serve our needs, though we hope such behavior will result in his eventually choosing the same response. In order for a child to attend, to focus on a specific task or choice, HE has to initiate the action. It is this inability to choose, to focus his own consciousness, which is the issue in much of the ADD and ADHD phenomenon. To date, clinicians and teachers have chosen to act "on" him rather than helping him learn to create the action. We see this not only as detrimental to the development of the child, but also negating the very ends we seek, his developing ability to focus himself.

When adults talk to children, particularly in a classroom or clinical setting, we certainly are seldom speaking with the "real child" who exists. Yet, the effective teacher or any professional who works with children, must attempt to foster in the child a feeling of trust so that he can respond as honestly as possible.

Consciousness, in general terms, can only be defined as that state in which the child is focusing his attention, monitoring feedback, and adapting behavior in response to the demands of the situation. But this is not so much a definition of consciousness as it is a description of the process of consciousness. It suggests that, in neurological terms, a number of processes are at work. First, the lower brain stem (RAS) must alert the cortex and provide a range of sensory information. Upon achieving alertness the frontal lobe acts in response to sensory information and a centralizing action occurs where information from the frontal and temporal lobes is activated germane to the present situation. A frame of comprehension integrating memory, time/space relationships, and imagery is processed in order to evaluate and develop reactions related to such factors as, cultural expectations, personal and social values, peer and present social responses, and all of this toward reestablishing a homeostatic state of personal control.

This is a highly simplified neurological overview of consciousness. It does not really describe consciousness but does suggest the complex interactions within a variety of cerebral and cerebellar areas which are required for a state of conscious response. Our point here is that should we attempt to view the processes of consciousness within the systems of the CNS, or attempt to describe it as a personal volition toward adaptive responses, there is often a great difference between reactive behavior from the child as opposed to responses created by a centralized conscious focus. In ADHD the fundamental basis for the disorder is the breakdown of the child's ability to control focused consciousness and behavioral responses due to a neurologic or biochemical deficit. In our belief, this is a rare occurance and results not only in a lack of focal ability but in random and uncontrolled redundant movement as well.

In the d/ADD child, as opposed to the ADHD child, it is our contention that the child is able to focus in a variety of functions and situations but cannot do so within certain and specific parameters such as a school task or activity. Further, this difficulty in certain functions is related to a deficiency in the "development of or management of situation specific skills" as opposed to the lack of general potentials to do so. Not only has the child failed in this particular area, the integrating systems have failed as well (parents, teachers, etc.) to assure that the tasks required of him were first determined after the authorities had assured he had learned the preliminary skills to do so. Thus, we as adults have failed on another and more significant level; we requested a behavioral skill for which we had not prepared the child. In this way then, all d/ADD cases represent a deficit in the developmental competencies of the child and a deficit in the instructional systems within which he responds. Neither are exempt from a need of responsibility in the errant behavior.

Summarizing our presentation in this chapter we must now recognize the overwhelming reality of working with and understanding the behavior of a d/ADD child. We should begin to understand the danger and the ineptness which invades the simpler concept that such children are merely in need of medication or behavioral modification. The ADHD child, with attendant physiological, neurological, and biological foundations for his or her inattentiveness and hyperactivity, may respond to these two interventions. But the d/ADD child needs a range of help which can only be given through considered and competent parent and teacher interventions designed to help the child "learn" new behaviors and strategies.

We first presented some general ideas about the genetic-temperament foundation of personality and behavior in the child. This interacts with not only parental and eventually school personnel, but more importantly with the environmental climate, including the socioeconomic and cultural environment of the child (to be discussed in more detail in a later chapter). As the child develops, sensory motor and spatial abilities provide a focus to physical expression of the child while developing language allows the child greater dimensions for understanding and learning about his world. Psychoneurological competencies develop in association with ever clearer differentiation and elaboration of personality and learning.

All of these systems interact within the child and with his world. There are an infinite number of problems which can develop as the child matures the first five years in one or several of the major developmental systems. All of these factors must be considered in understanding the child and how he is developing. The d/ADD child, with his difficulties in managing his behavior and attention, with rule-governed behavior, and with maintenance of sustained concentration and accomplishment, is always different to some degree than other d/ADD children. Each child, considering the multiple factors in development above, can have difficulties in different systems from other children and yet, they may all exhibit the same general problems. Is it not sensible to attempt to understand, in each child, the specific systems or processes which are a problem for him so that interventions can assist him in learning to overcome this difference? In essence, is it not possible to understand the child rather than merely describing his behavior and applying the same treatment for all?

One of the terrible consequences of the present fervor about the now defunct ADD classification is that in the main, it is only a classification which implies the child has a problem and must be given medication or behavioral modification as a primary treatment. This is a medical and "disease" or pathology viewpoint as we mentioned earlier. Our purpose here is to show that this approach, while helpful for the ADHD child in assisting him in control of a medical difficulty, is inappropriate for most children and does not attempt to learn of the child's actual developmental needs. The use of the d/ADD classification is primarily to encourage understanding of a child and his needs and providing developmental and educational intervention.

In the next chapter we want to look at specific case studies in order to clearly understand how these concepts can be utilized to develop effective programs for these children and how, parents and the schools must accept responsibility for the needs of these children.

REFERENCES

Annett, M. "A Model of Inheritance of Handedness and Cerebral Dominance." *Nature,* London, 204, 59–60, 1964.

Benson, D.F., & Geschwind, N. "Cerebral Dominance and Its Disturbances," *Pediatric Clinics of North America,* 15(3), 759–769, 1968.

Chess, S.; Thomas, A.; & Birch, H. *Temperament and Behavior Disorders in Children,* New York University Press, 1968.

Dimond, S., and Beaumont, J. G. *Hemisphere Function in the Human Brain,* (Ed.), Halstead Press, John Wiley and Sons, 1974.

Gaddes, W. H. *Learning Disabilities and Brain Function, A Neuropsychological Approach,* Springer-Verlag, New York, 1980.

Luria, A. D. *Higher Cortical Functions in Man,* New York, Basic Books, 1966.

Milner, B., Branch, C., & Rasmussen, T. "Evidence for Bilateral Speech Representation in Some Non-Right Handers, *Transactions of the American Neurological Association,* 91, 306–308, 1966

Subirana, A. "The Relationship Between Handedness and Cerebral Dominance, *International Journal of Neurology,* 4, 215–235, 1964

Zangwill, O. L. *Cerebral Dominance and Its Relation to Psychological Functions,* London: Oliver & Boyd, 1960.

Chapter Five

CASE STUDIES OF d/ADD CHILDREN

In this chapter we will describe several case studies of children who we classify as d/ADD in order to demonstrate the dynamics of their needs and differences. In the Appendix is listed a wide range of specific interventions which may be used with these children in the classroom. Our intent in this book is not to provide a classroom or instructional strategies manual but to demonstrate the underlying etiology of the syndrome. It seemed important though to provide samples of the various strategies which can be used relative to the behavioral and general learning difficulties of these children. General references will be made to intervention strategies in the discussion; however, most of the text will be committed to understanding the syndrome for school psychologists and medical professionals.

Before discussing the case studies, we need to clarify some of the terminology and methodology of the tests and strategies used to obtain the data which will be presented. This clarification will assist the reader as the case study proceeds. While much of the discussion and results in the case studies will be provided by the parents, school, and the processes involved in the testing, certain tests are common to analysis of the developmental abilities of the child. These tests are either individual psychological or standardized tests which school psychologists are specifically trained to administer to children.

Tests routinely used by school psychologists fall within categories such as fine motor skills, language and spatial skills, achievement skills, and personality skills. These tests are most often approved by schools or national and state education offices so that there is uniform data obtained for determination of special education or other individual services. Not only are these tests approved and required, they must be given according to clinical and standardized procedures by the school psychologist.

We do not want to involve ourselves in "testing procedures" or the ethics of diagnostic evaluation, but some brief discussion of this area is important as will be illustrated here. School psychologists in recent years have found themselves in a rather untenable position in regard to testing children. In the private clinical setting the practitioner is able to apply a wide range of approaches in diagnostics in order to assess and understand a child's needs and problems. In the public school setting, however, this latitude is generally not legally possible. For example, the private practicing psychologist is able to make inferences from his or her testing procedures and, in fact, it is the professional opinion which parents are seeking.

The school psychologist is more often required to provide objective and standardized testing in order to verify or classify a child for specific special education or other school services. By controlling the analysis and results of the school psychologist schools are less likely to be involved in litigation from parents at a later time because of an incorrect diagnosis or inference made following testing. For many school psychologists this is frustrating because while they may not be certified as clinical psychologists, they are capable of making inferences and so-called professional judgements but are severely limited in their ability to legally do so. This is, unfortunately, a necessary requirement in order to meet national law in regards to protection of the individual child. The laws designed to protect exceptional children from the abuses of the past, such as placement in inappropriate segregated classrooms or services, also has placed necessary restrictions on the process of evaluation in order to assure validity to results.

Hopefully, school psychologists reviewing the case studies presented here will be able to provide information to teachers concerning insights about child development which can be derived from the "process" of evaluation. While the school psychologist, to some degree is hampered in his legal responsibility to maintain specific test administration procedures, he can also point out potential needs of children directly to teachers without violating test ethics imposed by school regulations. In our program at the university we have, for several years, provided coursework for special education teachers in the developmental inferences provided by the school psychologist's test results. Specific tests and test data can allow the trained resource teacher with direct inferences concerning a child's needs while the school psychologist continues to maintain his work within defined parameters. Some of that sort of analysis will be provided in our discussions here.

In a process called "clinical teaching," some special education teachers are trained to initiate an on-going process of developmental analysis, applying teaching strategies, reevaluation, and subsequent redirection of teaching strategies. This process of continual reanalysis and alteration of intervention and teaching strategies allows for constant renewal of the intervention process to meet the child's changing needs. Unfortunately, special education teachers are not universally trained in this strategy and must wait for an annual or even bi-annual reassessment by the school psychologist in order to determine effectiveness of instruction and progress of the child.

In our discussions we will point out various diagnostic indicators which assist in determining the nature of a child's d/ADD difficulties. The first tests which are often used by diagnosticians are for the assessment of fine motor skills. These tests include asking a child to draw a person (DAP), the Beery Developmental Test of Sensory Motor Integration, and the Bender Gestalt. These tests involve having the child copy various forms and combinations of forms. In these tests the evaluator may learn about the child's sensory motor skills including fine motor coordination, spatial abilities, dexterity, directionality and spatial-directional orientation, and visual recall. Such tests tap into the function of the following areas of CNS organization discussed earlier:

a. The cerebellum
b. Sensory-motor strip in the cortex
c. Vestibular system
d. Visual and parietal lobes
e. Lateral dominance

Intelligence and language tests are varied both in form and structure but the WISC–R intelligence test or the Kaufman ABC are frequently used. Both of these tests yield so-called verbal and performance scores. In that the WISC–R is the older and perhaps continues to be the most widely used, we will use it as our model to discuss intelligence measurement.

The WISC–R (Wechsler Intelligence Scale for Children/Revised) is composed of two major categories of testing, verbal and performance subtests. Administered individually, the test provides several subtests in each category. The verbal subtests consist of the following areas:

1. *Information* — This subtest requires the child to respond to questions with specific information such as, "who is the president of the United States or, "How far is Cuba from the United States?" This is auditory recall and involves psychoneurological processing in the

left temporal lobe relative to auditory processing. Interestingly, while this is an auditory recall question, we find that difficulties in spatial-directional function and lateral dominance can affect the child's ability to recall specific information auditorially.

2. *Similarities* — This subtest involves asking the child to explain verbal relationships such as how two things are alike. The responses include both concrete and abstract responses. This subtest is perhaps one of the most critical as an indicator in relation to abstract verbal or linguistic reasoning. Here the psychoneurological processes fall within the temporal and frontal lobes particularly in the left hemisphere.

3. *Arithmetic* — Here students are asked to compute answers to arithmetic questions given verbally. This involves both spatial and temporal processing along with directional and spatial abilities.

4. *Vocabulary* — Questions involving vocabulary require the child to respond with both simple answers such as one word use or classifications such as tools, implements, and other elaborations. This involves auditory memory, auditory associations, and elaboration which can also involve creative imagery relative to right frontal and temporal lobe function.

5. *Comprehension* — This subtest looks at the child's social and practical learning and asks him to make conclusions in practical situations. This sort of processing involves both verbal and spatial abilities and nonverbal competencies. Thus, left temporal and frontal lobes are involved as is spatial imagery.

6. *Digit span* — In this subtest the child is asked to recall a series of numbers both forward and backward. This involves auditory recall and serialization which is related to the lateral dominance system.

These six subtests are typical of many tests which suggest that these particular functions are important competencies which professionals in child development, psychology, and psychoneurology feel represent underlying neurological abilities in linguistic intelligence. Yet deeper analysis of not only the responses children give to these questions but also of HOW they respond often tells more about underlying abilities than the responses themselves. Often, a child may score low on a particular subtest but it is more important to determine why rather than that his score was low. It is at this level of analysis that we begin to understand the child.

The second category of questions is within the nonverbal and spatial-frontal/temporal area of competencies. While the directions are given verbally, the operations involve nonverbal competencies.

1. *Picture completion* — This subtest involves the child finding missing parts or portions of a picture. The pictures begin simply and become more visually remote. This sort of spatial ability requires visual memory, so-called "gestalt" imagery (seeing the whole of something in one's mind), sequential visual scanning and search, and attention to detail. Much can be derived by the way a child searches, his attitude, persistence, and approach to the problem. Lateral dominance and cerebral dominance can both play a role.

2. *Picture arrangement* — Here the child must construct a series of individual pictures into a reasonable sequence of events. This involves visual sequencing, imagery of serialization of events, and visual gestalt.

3. *Block design* — Here colored blocks are used to construct patterns matching those displayed in samples. This task involves a kind of nonverbal and visual reasoning in constructing a pattern of spatial relationships. Problems in lateral dominance, visual imagery, attention, and dexterity can create difficulties.

4. *Object assembly* — This subtest involves the assemblage of a series of puzzles in which the finished product is unknown but familiar. This in involves a number of complex operations such as visualization, spatial relationships, visual gestalt, and transformation. These involve the right temporal and frontal lobes, parietal and occipital lobes, and lateral dominance.

5. *Coding* — This subtest involves copying a series of specific configurations within a time limit. This task involves lateral dominance, the cerebellum and vestibular system, the sensory/motor cortex, and manual dexterity.

There are additional subtests in this sort of analysis but we will limit our discussion to these. It should be remembered that subtests yield scores between 0–20. The average range is between 9–11. Scores of 7 and 8 are below average while those of 12 and 13 are above average. Scores 6 or below fall within the seriously delayed range while scores 14 and above will be within the upper 15–20 percent of the population. Specific understanding of these scores is not so important as merely understanding the general range in which they fall for this will assist us in our discussion of the case studies.

This brief overview of tests will allow us to present case studies within the following variables:

1. Family indicators and history
2. Present school and environment
3. Temperament and personality factors
4. School history and achievement
5. Perceived problem
6. Psychoneurological competencies and process
7. Achievement factors
8. Language and creative factors
9. Spatial-temporal abilities
10. Cerebral and lateral dominance

Before discussing the case studies, one additional theory concerning cerebral and lateral dominance needs to be presented as it will be significantly germane to our presentations. Annett (1964) proposed an interesting and perhaps significant theory concerning genetic determinants of cerebral and subsequently lateral dominance. Annett's theory is particularly interesting when added to the work of Benson and Geschwind (1968), concerning the fact that the larger pyramidal tract in the right cord might suggest increased innervation available to one side of the cord and lead to finer digital control on that side. It may be possible that how the left and right sensory motor fibers enter the spinal cord may determine dominance.

Annett proposed that handedness is genetically determined by the parents. She proposed a (D) gene pattern (right-handed) and a (r) recessive for left-handed. According to this theory dominant homozygotes (DD) from both parents resulted in right-handedness, recessive (rr) from both resulted in left-handedness. The heterozygotes, (Dr) one dominant gene from one parent and one recessive gene from the other, resulted in right-handedness and left hemisphere for language, but they may use either hand for skilled abilities and develop speech in either hemisphere. Referring back to our earlier discussion of the incidence of left and right dominance, Annett proposed this theory would predict that 64 percent would be pure right-handed, 32 percent would be (Dr) right- or left-handed, and 4 percent (rr) pure left-handed. This general percentage, seen again in a different theory, fits into our own observations of children with learning and attention difficulties. It is in this 32 percent that we will focus our attention in the case studies, for we feel that the relationship between cognitive abilities and dominance are poorly utilized in education and particularly in our concern for the d/ADD child.

Case Study 1
James T.
Chronological age (CA) 8.8

Referring conditions: James was referred by the family pediatrician following parent concerns over his reading failure and the teacher's desire to have him repeat second grade. The pediatrician felt that he might be ADHD.

Family environment: James lived with his paternal grandmother who had taken care of him much of his life prior to and after the parent's divorce. She provided day care for him and also assumed much responsibility for his overall care.

James' father had been left-handed and experienced much difficulty in early school years. He was overly active, often got into trouble at school and had been taken to his pediatrician several times for parent advise and assessment for hyperactivity. He remains, as an adult, somewhat nervous and assertive if not difficult to get along with.

General temperament and personality features: James, like his father, is an aggressive and assertive boy who loves physical activity. He apparently plays many little league sports and is relatively good. He becomes overly involved in these activities and may become angry if provoked. Additionally, he is spirited and warms to new situations and people easily. He is insightful and appears to be very capable in general social and interpersonal intelligence. He is alert and quick to pick up on innuendos and subtle forms of communication.

School background: James is in a suburban school district near a large city and though he lives near the edge of the city, the neighborhood is an older established middle-class, blue-collar area. Many people, including his grandmother, have lived there more than twenty-five years. The school is overcrowded and the teachers are often frustrated about the numbers of children in their classes. James is in a "middle group" class which is not significantly competitive and the teacher tends to be conservative. She has been teaching for twenty years and feels that too many children are passed forward when they should be retained until they are mature enough to handle the work required. She feels James' essential problem relates to his family situation and to a lack of maturity. The evaluation was completed in May at the end of the second grade.

Dominance, balance, and gross motor: James is right-handed and left-eyed but appears well balanced and adequate in gross motor skills.

Spatial-temporal skills: James, while right-handed and having good kinesthetic skills, appears to have some difficulties with temporal sequential imagery skills. He has difficulty remembering the sequence of letters in spelling, the months and days, and order of behavioral events.

WISC–R Intelligence Test

Verbal	*Nonverbal*
Information 10	Picture completion 14
Similarities 10	Picture arrangement 13
Arithmetic 7	Block Design 15
Vocabulary 9,	Object assembly 12
Comprehension 11	Coding 8
Digit span 7	
Overall verbal IQ 95–105	Overall performance IQ 110–120

The overall IQ obtained on the WISC–R displays generally average verbal and performance competencies with performance being somewhat higher. Yet, when we look at the specific subtests a very different and significant picture emerges. For example, in verbal abilities, arithmetic and digit span, both requiring internal spatial imagery, are very low suggesting some underlying mechanism which is dysfunctional. Interestingly, these two subtests involve the ability to organize in a left-right pattern and, based on his mixed dominance, this is suggestive of an internal confusion in directionality and potential for an internal orientation toward right-left patterning as seen in left-handed children. It is here that diagnostic activities often do not note this factor. This is a boy who we felt was primarily, in regards to Annett's theory, mixed dominant (Dr) with the father contributing the recessive gene (r) and the mother right-handed, the (D) gene. In cases such as this it is not imperative that we KNOW the (Dr) factor is genuine so much as it provides a means of developing an empirical understanding of the child's needs and a means of how to respond.

James displayed good performance skills but during the testing he experienced much difficulty with orientation of the various items into a whole. This is another characteristic in the "process" of working the problems often seen in mixed dominance children. They become frustrated with the directional-spatial orientation of working formal structures such as puzzles, block designs, and sequential pictures. During the process of working in all of these areas James lost points due to time limits. Yet, he did very well and would have done much better without time limits. This suggests that while his functional skills, i.e., working the problem, were only slightly above average, his actual ABILITY was higher. This would suggest at this time that his performance and subsequent visual spatial abilities may be somewhat higher than his verbal competencies.

At this point in the analysis we should be able to predict several probabilities. James will have trouble with sequential analysis, he will have difficulties writing and spelling due to reversals and difficulties structuring letters, and he will have frustration with school work.

Achievement skills: As we predicted James is having significant difficulties in phonetic skill training. He reversed many words during phonetic skill testing. For example, he read "kity for city", spilt for split." He had great difficulty integrating the sounds when he attempted to sound out the words. His overall reading recognition level is only 2.5 but drops to late first grade when he must comprehend words in sentences. This is an automation problem in reading/comprehension where confusion and attention is focused on recognition skills with no attention available for comprehension of the words. This is typical of cross-dominant children and is often seen as "dyslexia."

There are many forms and causes for the general classification of dyslexia just as there are for the ADHD syndrome. Here we see a psychoneurological but developmental syndrome which can result in problems in sequential organization, reversals, and attention and activity control. This is also a case which does not qualify for ADHD due to the lack of symptoms prior to the age of six years, pervasive hyperactivity, and in this case, rule-governed behavior. While James is distractible, has difficulties staying on task, and may be impulsive due to not "planning ahead or reflecting," he does not display pervasive hyperactivity.

Because James tends to be aggressive and may have some difficulties at school, the teacher essentially referred him for both failure in school and his general, though not critical, assertive behavior pattern.

We selected this case for it is a highly typical case pattern which we see in the clinic. Other cases, while displaying a similar dominance pattern, have other features which add to the problematic behavior in school.

James demonstrates these features:

1. Mixed dominance: probable (Dr) genetic syndrome resulting in poor directionality and spatial orientation.
2. Good kinesthetic skills which allows him to perform motorically

rather well and reduces any problems in directionality or spatial orientation in gross motor and athletic functions.

3. While adequate in self initiated motor activities, his mixed dominance creates a problem in sequential fine motor and language learning activities where decisions concerning orientation of letters and words is involved.

4. A general genetic temperament pattern of assertive/aggressive interaction.

5. Assertive behavior combined with poor linguistic sequential orientation results in poor impulse control. He will have difficulties planning and organizing his behavior and, due to his assertive behavior pattern will tend to respond in frustrating situations and threat environments with lower brain behaviors.

6. Overall behavioral attitudes toward school will be evasive and reactive.

James will need a number of key interventions requiring responses from both school and home. While he is reading within the late second grade in recognition, he needs a varying program in assisting comprehension. An alternate multisensory approach in reading will assist in continued progress in recognition and integrative phonetic skills. He needs a developmental approach in writing to overcome the reversal tendencies and to provide eventual skill in expressing his ideas. Strong behavioral limits must be provided, but he will need a highly nurturing teacher who can form a protective and supportive relationship. In the Appendix a number of strategies are listed for consideration in all of these areas.

In this book we do not intend to emphasize classroom instructional techniques but rather consider conceptual foundations for ADHD and d/ADD. However, we have collected and provided a range of intervention strategies in behavioral and general learning areas appropriate to the syndromes discussed in this book. Teachers and clinicians working directly with children should find these helpful. Further, an earlier book, *Learning Disabled Children Who Succeed,* by Hosler and Fadely (1989), includes somewhat detailed recommendations for instructional methods relative to children with many of the d/ADD syndrome characteristics.

Case Study 2
John
C.A. 7-2

(Evaluation completed in April of the first grade.)

Referring conditions: John was seen late in first grade late in the school year. The parents were concerned that he was having learning problems, i.e., completing his work, paying attention, staying on task particularly during seat work, and achieving as well as other children. The teacher felt that, while he appeared bright though small for his age, he might have attentional deficit problems and perhaps was immature.

Family environment and developmental history: John was an interesting child who displayed a severe developmental deficit. Due to his seeming intelligence and the teacher's lack of awareness of his early developmental history, and any sort of concept about special needs, John was not understood. As a consequence the notion of some sort of attention deficit along with immaturity was suspected. An extremely important characteristic in developmental history, one not reported to the school nor known by school officials, was that he had been an "early failure to thrive" child for his first year of life. The parents did not report this at this time for they also did not know the significance of such a problem for a seven year old.

General temperament and personality pattern: In general temperament John appeared typical. He was cooperative, alert, did not display an unusual activity level, displayed appropriate mood orientation, he was polite and seemed to get along well with other children. His general attitudes were positive except that he was beginning to show signs of uncertainty and a declining level of positive self concept.

Dominance, balance, and gross motor: John displayed typical right-handed, eyed, and foot preference, and generally no significant problems in basic cerebral/lateral dominance. But in gross motor balance and kinesthetic skills he displayed extremely poor competencies suggesting some pathology or lack of development in cerebellar, vestibular and sensory motor development. His overall level of competency in this area was typical for a child no older than three to four years of age.

Spatial-temporal developmental skills: As a consequence of John's extremely poor foundation in balance and gross motor development, he also exhibited very poor ability to organize sequentially, utilize fine motor skills, understand and use spatial recognition information, and apply such skills in time and sequence activities. Thus, while he did not have mixed dominance, he still had many of the same spatial temporal problems of a child with such difficulties. The spatial directional competencies of the cerebellar/temporal system are dependent on good kinesthetic competencies.

WISC–R Intelligence Test

Verbal	*Nonverbal*
Information 13	Picture completion 10
Similarities 16	Picture arrangement 7
Arithmetic 13	Block design 8
Vocabulary 17	Object assembly 6
Comprehension 17	Coding 5
Digit span-7	
Overall Verbal IQ 125–130	Overall Performance IQ 80–85

Here we see a significant pattern which often goes unrecognized in many school assessments. When these scores are combined into a full scale IQ, John will fall into the average range of 100–110. Often school psychologists are taught that a significant difference between verbal and performance scores can indicate a learning disability or possible neurological pathology. Such an assumption often involves the recognition that there is a significant difference, but few diagnostic inferences may be forthcoming.

In John's case, knowing of his early failure to thrive, we can infer much from this data. One basic theory which we have accepted when working with prematurity and early trauma in physical development is that, even though language may develop normally, there are often sensory motor and spatial effects well into elementary school if not into adolescence. It is not uncommon, pediatrically, for a physician to comfort parents during that first year with the belief that the child will "catch up" by the second or third year. We do see this in some children in language but often physical and sensory development are delayed by as much as two to three years by the age of six years. Size is often recognized as a consequence of these early problems and so are certain poor gross motor coordination effects, but the spatial-temporal relationships built on these foundations are not usually known or understood by parents or teachers.

In many ways John's case magnifies the difficulties in diagnosis in a dramatic way for two reasons, the spatial-temporal effects were not recognized and John was a superior child in language development. There is more than a three-year mental age difference between his level of language and spatial-temporal development. While he is able to relate well in language terms, he has significant difficulties in using language in sequential and time-related skills. This would not have been a problem until he had to deal with formal academic skills in first grade where much of the work dealt with sequential phonetic skills, and, most importantly, fine motor skills in writing. He would be unable to complete the written work in school and this would be particularly difficult if the teacher used a lot of individual worksheet activities as a major instructional strategy. She did! Thus, not only was John at risk for seeming like a bright child who should do well, but the instructional climate of the classroom was directly opposed to the manner in which he could most effectively learn. Subsequently, he was seen as distractible and unable to do his work, but the classroom instructional style was as instrumental in his failure as was his basic developmental deficits.

In Figure 7 we see a partial example of John's drawings which display problems in forming lines, working with diagonal lines and angles, cross lateral hand movements, and many other errors. In the included printing we see the result of this developmental deficit in poorly formed letters which are totally unautomated actions. He will not be developmentally ready for printing until he has had much work in fine motor skills on the blackboard in large movements.

Achievement skills: It is not surprising that John is unable to complete his written work for he is significantly unable developmentally at this time to produce effective automatic movements. He has to struggle to make letters and, with his poor fine motor skills, is unable to keep his attention on WHAT he is writing.

John is reading, more or less, in recognition skills within the late first grade but as we might expect he will have poor comprehension skills. Considering his verbal abilities he should be reading in the late second grade to early third grade even with little instruction. Conversely, considering his performance scores he would be only within the late preschool to early kindergarten level in fine motor and supportive skills needed to recognize letters and words.

We should be able now to see, developmentally, why John is so distractible, perhaps impulsive, and unable to complete his work. He is what we would call a d/ADD child. His problems are based in his developmental differences, the unrealistic expectations in this classroom, and his own frustrations over expecting himself to do well and yet being unable to do so. John IS a bright child but these other variables make it unlikely that this will be much help unless we, as educators, restructure his school program to intervene in his problems. He certainly does not qualify for ADHD and we can see why, should someone label him as ADD, medication and simple behavior modification will not work! John's problems are almost exclusively educational.

The regular education initiative where more and more exceptional

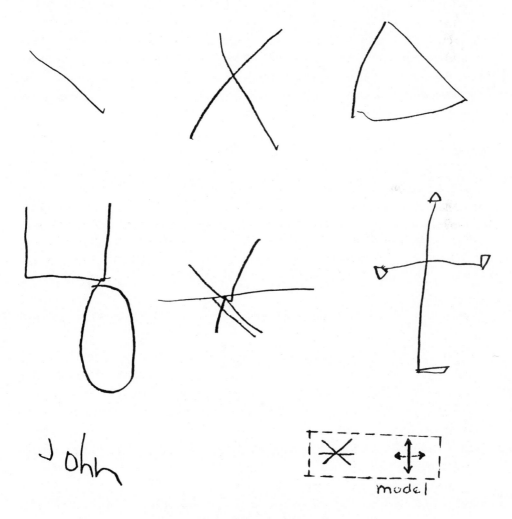

Figure 7. John/Portion of Beery Forms.

children are maintained in the regular classroom and where special services personnel spend more time with the children and teacher in this environment, will dramatically change the above conditions. Further, this problem highlights why most children labeled ADD or even ADHD should remain in the regular classroom. In John's case, due to his overall intellectual abilities and reading recognition skills, he would not qualify for most school programs in learning disabilities. Perhaps in a year or two following continued failure he will qualify but the emotional and social problems will have exacerbated the difficulties nearly to the point of no return. In a regular classroom initiative program, under the best of services, no label need be given and the teacher and school psychologist could focus their attention on the understanding of the child's needs and not on the legal classification of services. Parents today who are seeking to classify children as ADD in special education will, instead of assisting their children, more likely doom them to continued labelling and classi-fication conferences after which no one will know what the problem is or what to do for the child.

John, of course, will be recommended to repeat first grade. It is a solution in which hopefully time will do what we as parents and teachers cannot, resolve the child's problems. The problem with this approach is that too often the child is cured of the original problems, but emotional scars leave unseen injuries that may last a life time. In some children retention and maturation do work, but for a child like John, time may become a sentence instead of an opportunity. Further, it is unlikely that mere maturation will help him learn to write, to organize, or to compre-hend in reading. He will need supplementary work in these areas even if he is retained.

Case Study 3
Rene
C.A. 8-3

Evaluation done during summer months following first grade.

Referring conditions: Rene was brought to the clinic because of atten-tion difficulties at school, doing well one day and not the next, and forgetting what she learned.

The mother reported that as a young child, before the age of five, Rene had a serious difficulty with fluid build-up in her ears resulting in poor speech and language development. Apparently, she also had poor coordination in her preschool years as well as a general lack of interest in learning materials.

The mother was a professional welfare worker and therefore had a good background in many behavioral and learning problems exhibited by children. She had been alert to Rene's overall development patterns. Rene also occasionally was given allergy medication due to a number of inhalant responses.

In April, at the suggestion of the school, Rene had been put on a medication by the pediatrician for hyperactivity because school personnel felt she might be ADD. The drug appeared to have absolutely no effect on either her attention or her learning and was eventually discontinued as it was very expensive.

Family history and environment: Rene had a younger brother who was three years old and whom she appeared to love and enjoy being with. The father worked in a skilled labor position and participated well within the family. Overall, there were no unusual features in the family and other than Rene's difficulties in school there were no problems. The father was left-handed as was the mother.

General temperament and personality: Rene was a very quiet and unassuming child who appeared to be responsive to others. She was somewhat deliberate in her overall manner seeming to respond to requests and attention directed to her with some degree of structure. She tended to be a positive child and smiled often in response to attention. She answered the questions during the evaluation with a cooperative attitude and, we felt, rendered a good representation of her abilities. There was little if any indications in her general temperament that would suggest a lack of attentive potential. The parents did not feel this was a problem at home.

Dominance, balance, and gross motor: Rene, like her parents, is left-handed, left-eyed, and generally demonstrates much of the left-handed syndrome. However, during her kindergarten year she was attempting to write with her right hand and only recently switched to the left.

Rene demonstrated difficulties in left-right orientation and tended to reverse letters both when she was writing and during reading exercises. She had relatively poor balance in both static and kinetic assessments and appeared uncertain of directionality and the names for directions. In that she was eight years old at the time of the assessment, we could conclude that in both gross motor and spatial-temporal abilities she was more than two years delayed relative to age peers.

Spatial-temporal skills: Rene's poor spatial and temporal skills appear to be related to her lateral dominance problems and would preclude good organization of language. One question thus far in Rene's case is the possibility of some neurological involvement. Her overall spatial-motor development appeared to suggest a child who could also be suffering from poor language development and, with both the cerebral dominance uncertainty and the early speech and hearing difficulties, this would be expected.

WISC–R Intelligence Test

Verbal	*Nonverbal*
Information 5	Picture completion 10
Similarities 7	Picture arrangement 6
Arithmetic 7	Block design 6
Vocabulary 8	Object assembly 6
Comprehension 8	Coding 5
Digit span 3	
Overall Verbal IQ 75–85	Overall Performance IQ 75–80

Rene's results on the WISC–R demonstrated what the school, during the first two years of her schooling, had not really known. One could ask, "How could the school or the parents not realize how delayed Rene's overall development was?" Two factors are important here: schools do not have adequate kindergarten developmental screening programs, and teachers generally assume that a lack of early skill development relates to either a general immaturity or a specific learning or behavioral disability. Further, there is a greater concern for learning skills in education as opposed to understanding readiness or capability to learn.

Rene's verbal level falls one to two years below expectations for her age. There is a continuity in her specific subtest scores which suggests a general delay rather than a specific disability. Her performance scores also demonstrate this uniformity suggesting an overall general delay throughout all major language and sensory growth.

Rene's compliant and cooperative behavior tended to mask the seriousness of her problem. She is not mentally handicapped (retarded) by public school guidelines and, had she been tested by the school, would not have actually qualified for special services. The teacher's concern for her lack of ability to maintain attention in class, her wandering behavior, and her lack of follow-through in school work suggested the possibility, at least to the teacher, that perhaps she was ADD. Rene was not hyperactive, but her lack of attention and concentration seemed to fit what was felt to be the ADD syndrome. The failure of medication to improve her attention is now obvious, her needs are developmental and medication cannot alter those needs.

Rene's case is not uncommon! The teacher was a compassionate and capable person who, without the facility to understand Rene's needs, relied on what information was available to her. Most important here is that Rene can learn, there is little doubt that she needs additional time developmentally, and simply retaining her will not be adequate at this time.

Achievement skills: Rene, at this time, knows her letters though she still confused the usual "b-d" and so forth (see Fig. 8) and she is able to recognize whole words at the preprimer level. In essence, she is educationally within the late kindergarten to early first grade level. This is, in terms of her overall development and early learning problems, an adequate level of growth but certainly not for the end of first grade. The school appropriately has decided that she should be retained in first grade.

Rene's math, writing, and spelling skills are, as would be expected, only within the preprimer level as is the case with reading. She is, educationally, ready for first grade, or is she? Rene has had many developmental problems particularly in lateral coordination and speech. Her level of social comprehension and alertness suggest a child who is more competent than her actual verbal and performance scores would suggest. Though intellectually at the present she falls higher than mildly mentally handicapped and yet below average for the typical student, she is in what we call a "between the cracks" educational classification.

Rene's case, while somewhat clearly defined if one has the information, when viewed by a teacher, parent, principal, or a social worker within their particular environmental milieu, may be a number of things not really present in her make-up. The problems arising from an overuse of the ADD concept is not so much a problem in medical definition, as it is a growing need for educators to become more sophisticated in their craft. This is why every school and the field of education in general need to develop a greater understanding of child development and individual differences. Every child, upon entrance to school, should have a complete developmental assessment within the first few months. Assessment is a scary word to some parents and teachers, but we earlier mentioned the notion of "clinical teaching" in special education.

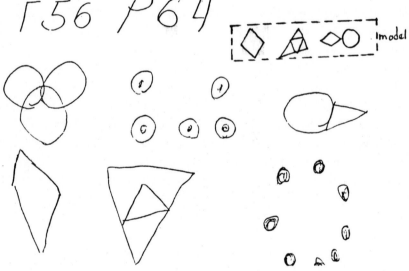

Figure 8. Rene's picture of person and Beery forms.

In a clinical teaching mode the classroom teacher works within a developmental assessment process whereby the child's progress and needs in sensory motor, language, cognitive, and academic skills are constantly monitored following an initial "status" profile. The profile is developed during the first few weeks of kindergarten following both testing and parental interviews so that a child's needs are understood and can be programmed within the curriculum. In Rene's case such an approach would have recognized her problems in lateral and cerebral dominance in conjunction with her language and speech needs. Special assistance could have been provided when she was five years old and not at the age of eight when psychoneurological maturity was less pliable and open to change. The problems at this time will be more intractable and require much more assistance than they might have.

Case Study 4
Ben
C.A. 5-2, 7-1, 8-1

Ben was seen in May for his first visit, two years later in May for a second visit, and a third visit in April of the following year.

Referring condition: Ben was first seen when he was five years of age prior to entering kindergarten. The parents wanted an assessment of his developmental level to see if he was ready for kindergarten. This case allows us a longitudinal view of a child's development where ADD was suspected. The parents reported that in preschool he was overly active and disorganized, had speech difficulties, became very frustrated and angry resulting in tantrums, and on two occasions had to be picked up from preschool due to impulsive and aggressive behavior. While the father felt he was academically ready for kindergarten (he knew his letters, colors, could print his name), he was uncertain as to his ability to maintain his behavior.

Family environment and conditions: Ben's family was an upper middle class family with two professional parents who are highly involved in their family. Ben had a sister three years old and a brother ten. There were no remarkable factors in the family that would indicate any significant problems.

Temperament and personality factors: Ben displayed an assertive and yet positive temperament with a very low threshold of responsiveness.

He was intuitive about others and highly sensitive to being accepted and of interactions with adults and children. One gained an impression of a very bright and exploratory child. He enjoyed playing games, responded to subtle humor and inferences, and was quick to point out his feelings and needs. He also indicated his frustrations in such areas as wetting the bed, disliking certain foods, and having problems in preschool.

Dominance, balance, and gross motor: Ben's parents were both right-handed but there was a left-handed uncle and grandfather on the paternal side of the family. Ben used his right hand for much of his work but also indicated that he could do things with his left hand (see Fig. 9). He was uncertain as to the days of the week, made some reversals when attempting to write his name, which he could not really do, and had great difficulty touching his right hand to his left ear doing so in reverse several times.

Spatial-temporal orientation: Ben was left-eyed and was attempting to use his left hand. The examiner was uncertain at this time if Ben wanted to use his right hand or, if as suspected, he had been encouraged to do so at his preschool. He was very frustrated in printing which was a very inappropriate task to expect of him during his fourth year in preschool. The preschool he had attended, according to the father, was an academic program where he had been placed to assist him in becoming ready for kindergarten. It was the impression of the examiner, though this was not communicated to the parents at the time as he was still in the preschool, that the program at the preschool was highly inappropriate in their management of Ben's early development and insensitive to his lack of sensory motor maturity and temperament in learning readiness.

WIPPSI (WISC–R for preschool age children)

Verbal	*Performance*
Information 9	Picture completion 10
Similarities 10	Animal house 7
Arithmetic 9	Block design 8
Vocabulary 13	Geometric forms 7
Comprehension 10	Sentences 9
Digit Span 8	
Overall Verbal IQ 95–100	Overall Performance IQ 85–95

The administration of the WIPPSI was helpful in exhibiting Ben's learning and expressive strategies though not particularly encouraging

Figure 9. Ben's circle and triangle at 5-2 years.

in actual performance levels. If one accepted the scores alone they would indicate a somewhat immature and less competent child than his overall personality and interactive competencies would suggest. There was a significant difference, though unsupported by objective measures, between his actual performance and his overall intuitive and responsive personality style.

Achievement skills: Ben was not achieving well at this time though at least as well as the average boy entering kindergarten. Yet, there were many reasons for concern here. Ben had significant variation in lateral dominance, uncertain hand dominance, tremendous frustration with his skills, and an ego centered and yet assertive personality style. These all combined to raise the issue, at the preschool, about his possibly being hyperactive and ADD.

Recommendations at this time: This is an interesting situation. Ben appears to be a bright and assertive child but his achievement in preschool and on the intelligence test does not support this. His choice, at this time, is to remain in preschool for another year or move into kindergarten. Ben wanted to go to kindergarten because many of his friends in the neighborhood were going, as well as some who attended the same preschool. Yet, from the foregoing data we can see why the parents decided to obtain an objective analysis to help them make this decision. The developmental data would tend to support the notion of remaining in preschool for another year particularly considering his speech and fine motor skill deficits along with the poor establishment of hand dominance.

It was recommended to the parents that he enter kindergarten. Why? Ben does not show a clinically defined ADHD syndrome. His activity level appears to be related to his inability to control motor and language skills as opposed to pervasive hyperactivity, impulsiveness, or even rule governed behavior. He has not shown significant behavioral problems to warrant concern about personality or social skills at this time. If he were to stay in preschool he would receive the same program as last year and it was felt that he needed to become involved in programming which would be supportive and progressive as opposed to merely waiting for maturity. The kindergarten program could provide needed assistance and stimulation in the organization of fine motor skills. It was suggested that he move into kindergarten and if that was successful move on to first grade where, if he needed to be retained he could be retained in a full-day program.

BEN'S SECOND EVALUATION: MAY, AFTER FIRST GRADE

This evaluation was two years following the first evaluation.

Referring conditions: Ben, after kindergarten and one year in first grade continued to have difficulties in fine motor skills and in organization of spatial-temporal abilities. The parents felt that he should be retained in first grade to allow for additional time for motor skill development and for emotional maturity.

Ben, during the later kindergarten year and into the early first grade had begun using his left hand and was now left-handed and left-eyed. While both parents were right handed, there were left handed relatives in the family. It was now suspected that he was (Dr) and that this mixed dominance most likely accounted for his poor fine motor skills. Further, Ben displayed continued poor gross motor balance negating the underlying basis for good spatial-temporal orientation.

WISC-R Intelligence Test

Verbal	Performance
Information 12	Picture Completion 10
Similarities 10	Picture arrangement 9
Arithmetic 7	Block design 12
Vocabulary 11	Object assembly 9
Comprehension 11	Coding 7
Digit span 7	
Overall Verbal IQ 95–105	Overall Performance IQ 95–105

Ben's general intellectual abilities remained within the same range as they had prior to kindergarten. This is very constant and, with a longitudinal view, it would appear that this was a fair estimate of his overall abilities. It is important to note though that he was having below average responses in arithmetic, digit span, and coding, all of which are related to temporal and fine motor skills.

Ben's drawings (Fig. 10) at 7-1 CA suggested a developmental level in fine motor and spatial skills not much better than middle kindergarten. His reading skills at this time were late first grade, suggesting that he had made real progress in this area in spite of his continued spatial difficulties.

While Ben had made progress in reading his writing, as might be expected, was very poor and he was unable to perform in an automatic way in this area. In the classroom he would often "daydream" and have difficulty completing his work. Yet, his general attention span in visual recognition of letters and letter sounds was coming well. There was real progress in this area and through the structure of a VAKT (Visual-Auditory-Kinesthetic-Tactile) approach he was able to compensate somewhat in reading for his poor organization and sequential abilities. This is consistent with approaches for children through multisensory learning methods and seemed to be working for Ben.

The parents were concerned that Ben might have some sort of learning disability and/or neurological problem. They had again been approached by the teacher concerning the possibility of ADD. We can see here how difficult it is for the teacher and in his case, as in many others, the teacher felt that medication might be of some assistance. The parents were encouraged to recognize that his lack of good cerebral and lateral dominance were playing a strong role in his ability to organize and learn. Much of the educational effort was apparently assisting him in reading, but the motor problems remained difficult. It was recommended that the parents might feel more comfortable if they were referred to a neurologist for a complete neurological to rule out ADHD or other complications. Further, it was suggested that he be retained and that during the year Ben receive special assistance in general gross motor and fine motor development including perhaps lessons in karate which might improve his concentration and gross motor balance.

Ben received an EGG, a CT scan, and a general neurological. That report suggested that there were no abnormalities and that the karate lessons appeared to be having a positive effect on his general gross motor organization. The only findings of note by the neurologist were that there was some increased intraorbital distance with moderate persistent epicanthal folds. There was some decreased eye coordination with the left slower than the right. He had marked hyper-extensibility in all the joints, worse on the left. He seemed to have some minimal spasticity of the left leg and some dysdiadochinesis.

The neurologist agreed that this problem was developmentally based and that there was nothing to suggest any specific neurological syndrome. Since there had been some localization the neurologist had recommended the CT and EGG but both were normal. The neurologist felt that time, patience, and an effective educational services program would be needed for the child to develop normally. He also felt that some medication might be in order but did not feel it was required at this time.

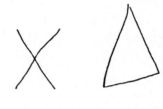

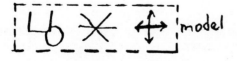

Figure 10. Ben's person and portion of Beery at 7-1 years.

THIRD EVALUATION: APRIL OF THE FOLLOWING YEAR

This was after a second time through the first grade.

Referring conditions: The parents were pleased with Ben's progress this year and felt that he had improved. He continued the Karate, the teacher had continued special assistance in reading and writing though writing continued to be a problem. The parents reported that while he still was prone to wandering off task, he was able to work effectively.

General temperament and personality: Ben was now a very enthusiastic child and full of talk and activity but within normal limits. He enjoyed school and felt that he was doing "pretty good" though he hated to write. He stated that he did like to draw though and was often doing so at home and school.

Spatial-temporal orientation: Ben's drawings (see Fig. 11) had improved and now showed relatively typical organization though his fine motor dexterity continued to be a problem. He would need special attention in writing.

WISC–R Intelligence Test

Verbal	*Performance*
Information 10	Picture completion 13
Similarities 11	Picture arrangement 11
Arithmetic 10	Block design 10
Vocabulary 12	Object assembly 11
Comprehension 12	Coding 11
Digit span 10	
Overall Verbal IQ 100–110	Overall Performance IQ 100–110

Ben's overall competencies remain within the middle of the average range and we can now suppose that this is the level typical for him.

Ben was now reading, at the end of his second year in first grade, within the early third grade with good comprehension. This is interesting for his progress in language arts was continuing consonant with his intellectual level though he had been retained. This now suggests that Ben was capable in language comprehension and in general was capable of understanding and using language at his chronological age level. His ability to organize himself and to work within fine motor skill areas such as writing and spelling continued to lag behind though they too were demonstrating progress.

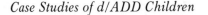

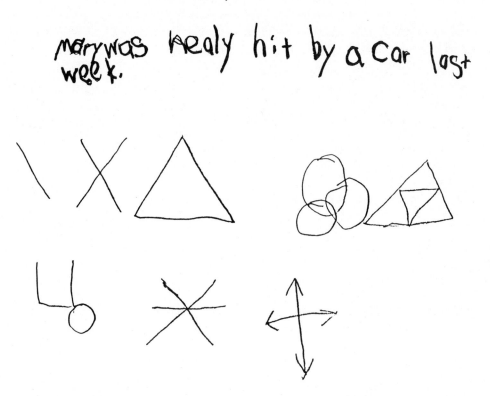

Figure 11. Portion of Ben's Beery forms at 8-1 years.

Reflections: Several important points need to be made in this case which had the benefit of psychological, neurological, and educational cooperation. The essential key in this case, was that of the consistent and professional assistance of his teacher in first grade. While she suspected ADD and hoped for medication, she was open to the realization that there needed to be some understanding of the cause for his wandering behavior which could have educational implications. She understood his significant difficulties in motor coordination, in spatial-temporal concepts, and in some wandering behavior due to difficulties in managing motor skills and time-space relationships. Her focus on phonetics with a multisensory approach allowed Ben to avoid many written assignments. Encouraging him to feel good and expect that he would improve, were also reasons that Ben eventually moved ahead successfully. There was little doubt that even his writing skills, which could be given more focus in second grade than reading, would continue to improve.

A second major factor here was to avoid the label and subsequent response of ADD and look instead for a developmental understanding of the basis for his behavior. As it turned out he was not ADHD in the clinical sense and though medication was available on the recommendation of the neurologist, neither the parents nor the teacher elected to follow this path. Medication MIGHT have improved his concentration and control but conditions of need were in developmental areas and not in neurological dysfunction. A label of ADD which might have encouraged the subsequent dependence on some sort of behavioral modification program to improve his organization and attention would also have failed because he had difficulties which needed special instructional and developmental responses.

A third factor which is highly significant is that the teacher and parents, working together along with his outside stimulation in motor development, allowed Ben to feel confident and encouraged a good self-concept while "everyone" worked to assist him.

In a different situation, with different peers, instructional philosophy, or cooperative environment, Ben could have been put on medication, no developmental or neurological assessment sought, and he could have been designated dyslexic, dysgraphic, or a number of other labels which would have done little to assist him. Here we see how such children can be managed and helped to success within the educational environment. Without the parents and teacher working as a team the progress could have been very different.

Case 5,
Matt
C.A. 11-11.

Evaluation done in November of 4th grade

Referring conditions: Matt's parents were highly frustrated with the school and felt that their son needed special attention which had been denied for more than two years. Matt had great difficulties in school. He did not complete his work, he didn't hand in many assignments, he tended to impulsively do things, i.e., got out of his seat and sharpened his pencil, talked out loud, called out to friends, and asked peers to help him with his work. He bothered other children with the constant movement and noises he sometimes made with his mouth, and he would infrequently laugh in class for no apparent reason. The parents had held him back in second grade because they felt he was immature.

Family environment: Matt was the youngest of four children, including 23- and 21-year-old sisters, and a 17-year-old brother. The father was a special technician in computers and his mother did not work. They lived in a rural area on a small farm. The older children had done relatively well in school and, as is often the case, everyone seemed to feel that Matt was the baby of the family and had been made overly dependent. The parents were caring individuals and in general the home was a good one. They felt that he needed a lot of encouragement and had to be made to follow through with his work.

General temperament and personality: Matt was a responsive and cooperative child who, though seemingly easy going and open to assistance, did not seem highly motivated and, as the teacher said, was somewhat disorganized, distractible, and impulsive in a good-natured way. There was no aggression and he seemed to get along with other children though they sometimes seemed to exclude him from activities.

School environment: Matt had difficulties in school for some time and prior to the work-up from private resources, had been seen by a school psychologist. The school psychologist had not given a complete psychological or an IQ test for the teacher and other school services personnel felt that, while he was having problems in school, he could do the work if he could focus himself. Due to the fact that he had been held back, they felt that the problem now might be more the possibility of ADD than any problem in intelligence or basic competencies. The school psychologist had administered several achievement tests and found that Matt had the following skills.

> Reading recognition..............................6.0 grade level.
> Reading comprehension........................ 3.6
> Mathematics..2.4
> Spelling..4.6

Some additional achievement tests were given which seemed to indicate the same basic levels of performance. In that Matt was in the fourth grade, by school standards he was generally less than a year below expectations for his grade level and, should he have some additional assistance in class and possibly some medication, he should be able to do adequate work. For these reasons an IQ test had not been administered. According to school formulas for learning disabilities, his achievement level was not sufficiently low to expect that even with some variation or deficit in IQ scores that he would have been eligible for any special services. Many recommendations were made to the teacher in management of his work, but other than these general findings nothing of note had been found and, more or less, his case was marked off as a lack of motivation, the possibility of an ADD syndrome, and immaturity.

This case highlights another major problem(s) we have in education, particularly special education and the analysis of children's needs. The first problem, as we will see shortly, was that the school had not, since Matt began school, taken a proactive role in understanding child development, learning theory, managing the individual needs of specific children who were not doing well, or initiated an on-going in classroom clinical teaching cycle.

The second problem is a common one for schools where a proactive developmental and clinical teaching approach is not in place. The attitude appears to be, if a child isn't doing well, retain him and let him mature into the ability to do his work. In essence, if a child fails the teacher feels it is most often due to immaturity. He had been retained and little benefit had been derived in terms of his ability to focus, complete his work, or manage his behavior. That having been done, the next assumption, supported supposedly by the test results, was that maybe he had ADD or was simply unmotivated. We will see how this concept of learning theory has had unfortunate results for Matt.

A third major problem in some school systems in smaller towns or rural areas is the large "special services cooperative" in which several school systems form a cooperative special services unit which each supports. In this case, for example, the school psychologist took five months, excluding the summer vacation which would have made it a total of eight months before the testing was done. Matt was simply one of several cases seen by the psychologist after which, since he did not qualify for any special services, there was no case conference and the parents were called to a conference with only the teacher and principal who reported the results. It was then that the parents sought an outside evaluation.

We are not devaluing the capabilities of the school staff or the psychologist in this case for it is not their problem so much as the administrative structure in this situation which resulted in a series of inappropriate responses to a child's special needs. It is a problem, after all, of money for services and administrative arrangements.

Dominance, balance, and gross motor: Matt is cross dominant, right-eyed and left-handed. He has a severe problem in spatial-temporal orientation and falls only within the early sixth year in spatial motor skills. His balance is fair but organizational skills are poor and would qualify him, in adequately designed programs, for a special education designation due to a spatial-motor disability. In Figure 12 we see a portion of his work on the Beery Test which evaluates fine motor and spatial motor abilities. This test or the Bender Gestalt for children would have been given by the school psychologist had a complete assessment been completed.

WISC–R Intelligence Test

Information-7	Picture completion 13
Similarities-7	Picture arrangement 10
Arithmetic-7	Block design 5
Vocabulary-12	Object assembly 5
Comprehension-11	Coding 6
Digit span-7	
Overall verbal IQ 90–95	Overall Performance IQ 82–85

The scores above reveal, for Matt, a very unfortunate pattern. While the overall scores suggest a child with low average verbal and performance abilities this picture is much more optimistic than the actual profile. The first three verbal subtests fall within a deficit pattern of more than two years below expectations for his age. In the performance subtests the block design, object assembly, and coding subtests are all more than two years below expectations and in fact reach nearly a level of three years.

Matt's parents revealed that when he was 36 months old he had severe seizures during a temperature of over 106 degrees and had been in the hospital for more than a week following the episode. Following that period he had speech and language problems and seemed to have to learn to talk again. Further, his fine motor skills had been affected and he always had problems with school work. None of this information had been shared with the school nor had the school sought it.

The WISC–R scores and the pattern of language and sensory motor deficits along with the speech and language problems, suggest the strong possibility of early neurological trauma in the left temporal and parietal lobes. While speech and language have improved there appear to still be problems in motor and spatial abilities which are illustrated in the three verbal and performance tests which, interestingly, are areas involved in this sort of neurological trauma.

We can see here that Matt is a child with severe developmental difficul-

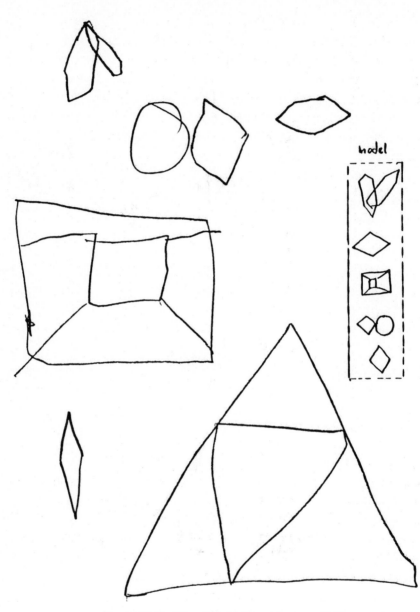

Figure 12. Portion of Matt's Beery forms at 11-11.

ties and contrary to the general notion that he is merely unmotivated, it is a marvel that he has been able to do as well as he has in school. The year's retention in second grade was helpful but is not enough. It was unfortunate that medically, following his seizures, the medical clinic had not followed up with the case. At three years of age there were no remarkable findings and he had been released. The problems which resulted from the trauma would not have become evident until the school years. It is likely that the trauma had forced an eventual switch to left-handedness even though he likely was to be a right-handed child. This is a possible case of "pathological left-handedness."

Matt was referred for a complete pediatric neurological workup and though there was evidence of the trauma, the problem at this time was essentially one of educational intervention. The school staff and the psychologist were brought together with the parents and eventually Matt was designated learning disabled and given resource teacher assistance.

There are many cases like Matt's that we could present, but these few cases illustrate the problem with the defunct ADD classification and the insistence of parents to obtain a separate category for ADD. Matt, as do many children, qualifies for the old ADD syndrome criterion checklists. To have labeled Matt ADD without additional clinical evidence would have continued to delegate him to an inappropriate and potentially damaging misdiagnosis which would have prevented appropriate intervention. It also demonstrates the errors in many school formulas which qualify children for learning disabilities.

In addition to the above problems in labeling a child as ADD without a complete psychological and medical analysis, often parents and even counselors focus on the behavioral aspects of the child's problems and, having satisfied themselves that the child meets the ADD criteria, proceed with medication, behavioral modification, and perhaps family counselling. But individual and group counselling, without the knowledge of how the child has developed in relation to sensory motor function, intellectual competencies, and language or creative abilities, means that critical aspects of the child's needs if not the more fundamental basis for his problems, can be missed altogether. Again, when one is applying what is essentially a medical diagnosis in a nonmedical environment without a full range assessment, there is a significant probability that an expert analysis of the child's problem will not be realized.

In summarizing this chapter several major points need to be reviewed:

1. An d/ADD syndrome represents a cluster of varied developmental differences which result in both learning and behavioral deficits which are particularly manifested in the school environment. Characteristics of this syndrome include over activity and poor attention to academic tasks, difficulties in spatial-temporal order,

reversibility, difficulties in writing, and impulsivity, and a lack of orientation to time.

2. These difficulties arise from a number of developmental differences and/or deficits which, within the school environment, create problems in learning and managing behavior within the expectations of the classroom.

3. In a large number of cases differences in lateral dominance and mixed dominance provide an underlying difficulty in organization in language and temporal abilities which preclude effective learning.

4. Due to ontogenetic differences in male and female spatial and language development, males tend to suffer more from lateral dominance difficulties related to learning.

5. Difficulties in lateral dominance and handedness appear to be frequently based in genetic clusters from parents in which dominant and recessive genes interact to present 25–35 percent of the general population with such differences.

6. Problems presented due to the mixed dominance factor also provide the basis for additional difficulties such as dyslexia, dysgraphia, and various learning disabilities related to reading and writing. In this way ADHD children and certainly d/ADD children fall directly into the learning disabilities realm.

7. In the majority of cases d/ADD children can be assisted through regular classroom intervention techniques as opposed to medication or behavioral modification strategies.

8. d/ADD children differ from ADHD children specifically in the etiology of the disorder, particularly in the absence of pervasive hyperactivity, rule-governed behavior, and early onset of these difficulties.

9. d/ADD children display improvement through maturation, but their basic differences do not change; rather, they must learn to compensate through special learning strategies and directed instructional accomplishments.

10. The combination of temperament/personality, general motor integrity, language intelligence, family structure, and many other factors, coalesce to create the specific salient characteristics of the d/ADD syndrome.

In the next chapter we will review the additional category of b/ADD which allows us to explore an additional range of potential effects of developmental differences which can create developmental differences resulting in learning and behavioral difficulties.

REFERENCES

1. Annett, M.A. Model of the Inheritance of Handedness and Cerebral Dominance. *Nature,* (London), 204, 59–60, 1964.
2. Benson, D.F., & Geschwind, N. Cerebral Dominance and its Disturbances. *Pediatric Clinics of North America,* 5(3), 756–769, 1968.
3. Hosler, V., & Fadely, J. *Learning Disabled Children Who Succeed.* Charles C Thomas, Springfield, Ill., 1989.

Chapter Six

BEHAVIORAL ATTENTION DEFICIT DISORDER

Personality has continued to elude us, even with the plethora of competent experts who have contributed to its definition throughout a history of investigation and theory. For the classroom teacher it is more often behavior than personal substance that is described. For the psychologist, personality describes a vague, though often seemingly definitive, body of theory and research that is seldom stable, and never measurable except in subjective terms. When one looks at the personality of a child, as we have mentioned earlier, what is seen is a transient phenomenon changing before we can establish its perimeters. Behavioral disorders of children, aside from outright psychotic episodes and lasting conditions, are more often behavioral descriptions rather than substantial investigations into the substance of behavior. In the DSM–IIIR conduct disorders have compounded the problem of identification of ADHD. Conduct disorders are often mixed into the ADHD formula and yet frustratingly separate from it. In the DSM–IIIR there is an attempt to separate conduct disorders from ADHD and yet the behavior of ADHD children often involves many of the problems of the conduct disorder.

We are not certain that the conduct disorder, as described in the DSM–IIIR category gives adequate efficacy as a distinct disorder and it seems to us in working with children who have behavioral disorders that one must recognize that there are two faces of attentional deficit disorders. One aspect is related to cognitive development while the second is related to personality and temperament, hence, our classification of d/ADD and b/ADD. The difference for us between ADHD and d/ADD was discussed in the preceding chapter. b/ADD represents, in our view, a category of children with attentional and organizational problems having the added feature of behavioral deficits as opposed to sensory and language cognitive problems associated with the d/ADD classification. The additional tendency of many professionals to view behavioral differences along with attentional deficits requires that, prior to our analysis of b/ADD, we concern ourselves with the notion of conduct disorders. We need to discuss the differences between conduct disorders and b/ADD. First, we will review briefly the notion of conduct disorders.

In the DSM–IIIR Conduct Disorder is described as follows:

A. A disturbance of conduct lasting at least six months, during which at least three of the following have been present.
   1. has stolen without confrontation of a victim on more than one occasion (including forgery.)
   2. has run away from home overnight at least twice while living in parental or parental surrogate home (at least once without returning).
   3. often lies (other than to avoid physical or sexual abuse).
   4. has deliberately engaged in fire-setting.
   5. is often truant from school (for older person absent from work).
   6. has broken into someone else's house, building, or car.
   7. has deliberately destroyed others' property (other than by fire-setting.)
   8. has been physically cruel to animals.
   9. has forced someone into sexual activity with him or her.
   10. has used a weapon in more than one fight.
   11. often initiates physical fights.
   12. has stolen with confrontation of a victim (e.g., mugging, purse snatching, extortion, armed robbery).
   13. has been physically cruel to people.

Note: The above items are listed in descending order of discriminating power based on data from a national field trial of the DSM–IIIR criterion for Disruptive Behavior Disorders.

B. If 18 or older does not meet criterion for Antisocial Personality Disorder.
   Criterion also includes mild, moderate, or severe.

Types include:

Group type—The essential feature is the predominance of conduct problems occurring mainly as a group activity with peers. Aggressive physical behavior may or may not be present.

Solitary aggressive type—The essential feature is the predominance of aggressive physical behavior usually toward both adults and peers, initiated by the person (not as a group activity).

Undifferentiated type—This is a subtype for children and adolescents with Conduct Disorder with a mixture of clinical features that cannot be classified as either Solitary Aggressive Type or Group Type.

An additional but related classification is that of Oppositional Defiant Disorder but this is less applicable to our discussion than Conduct Disorder.

It is important for parents and school services personnel to recognize that the foregoing criteria must be evaluated through the professional skills of a psychologist or other mental health professional. The reason this is so important is that many children, as in the organizational and attention problems of the ADHD criteria, exhibit conduct problems at various points in their developmental processes. Yet, in that the ADHD pattern includes many such behavioral descriptions, sometimes parents or even mental health professionals can ascribe more significance to the behavior than is warranted. Particularly the element of "rule-governed behavior" in the ADHD criteria can be easily broadened in one's view to imply stealing, lying, truancy, or using some sort of weapon in a fight with another child. These characteristics are part of the Conduct Disorder pattern and it is a simple leap of analysis to combine these elements into the ADHD syndrome and see a more severe condition than may exist. While a well-trained clinician may not make this mistake, the alarming number of nonprofessionals including parents and other school officials who are applying checklists as a means of diagnosis, may make such misdiagnosis.

Care has been taken in the DSM–IIIR to move away from the tendency to combine the ADHD and Conduct Disorder patterns and hopefully this will be accomplished in the field. Having stated this concern, we want to suggest that there are large numbers of children, perhaps greater than those in d/ADD patterns, who exhibit a combination of attentional disorders and behavioral difficulties. Where the d/ADD pattern concerns attention problems and cognitive difficulties, the b/ADD pattern involves attentional and behavioral problems. Obviously and unfortunately, a child may exhibit both cognitive and behavioral difficulties with attentional problems.

CHARACTERISTICS OF THE b/ADD CHILD

When we rule out the severity of conditions as seen in the ADHD syndrome and those of Conduct Disorders, there are a number of lessor behavioral problems which often are exhibited by children who also appear to have significant problems with attentional and organizational competencies. These characteristics are listed below.

1. A temperament of demanding, impulsive, disorganized behavior, along with aggressive tendencies which are, by their frequency, duration, and persistence, unusual in relation to age peers.
2. Appearance of the impulsive and demanding behavioral pattern prior to school age and often recognized in the preschool and/or family setting.
3. A behavioral pattern of disruptive behavior which is characteristic of either the family history of adults in the home, particularly the father, and which may be reinforced by either parent in early childhood.
4. A pattern of independence, opposite of the disruptive behavioral pattern in item (3), in which the child appears to play alone and enjoy isolation from peers and family members to a degree of significance in relation to age peers.
5. A tendency to identify with and engage in fantasy involving super-heros, war, sadistic or aggressive acts, science fiction, or archetypical creatures and situations.
6. Difficulties with value decisions, cooperative play and interactions, accepting blame, and making compromise in situations of conflict.
7. Poor self-image, personal uncertainty, or/and a lack of ego identity.
8. Tendencies toward physical destructiveness in response to per-ceived or real threats from peers or adults.
9. Tendencies of lying, deception, denial, and stealing in particular situations. Engages in fabrication and making up fantasies to explain infractions or behaviors which may be punished.
10. Difficulties maintaining attention in the classroom, completing work, or finding homework or assignments.
11. Impulsivity and difficulties in delaying gratification.
12. Significant language deficit or assets resulting in unusual polar cerebral competencies.
13. Poor goal-directed behavior and ability to see relationships between expectations of adults and personal actions.
14. Ambivalence in wanting to play with peers. Tendencies toward dominating peers and wanting to control play situations. Dislikes losing in game situations.

These fourteen characteristics are not, as in the case of conduct disor-der or ADHD, clinical criteria for identification so much as descriptions of behavioral potentials which exist for the b/ADD child. This means that, due to underlying developmental differences, these children tend to develop the foregoing difficulties. As can be seen the characteristics are very much like some of the criteria for conduct disorders and ADHD and yet, these characteristics are less severe and can be tied to specific developmental differences. Recognizing the child's behaviors and related developmental needs allows the parents and teachers to formulate strategies of assisting the child without the need to see his needs as a clinically deficit pattern. This will allow, hopefully, for intervention in a child's needs within the classroom and the school as part of the usual routine of classroom instruction.

If interventions are not successful and if the child meets the more severe criteria of ADHD or Conduct Disorder then that referral can be made. But this first stage of analysis of the child's behavior and attempted interventions may be successful and avoid outside analysis and further referral.

In our discussions to follow we want to demonstrate how these behavioral characteristics can emerge in children as part of normal though different developmental patterns. In that these behaviors exhibit such similarities to the Conduct Disorder it is easy to understand why many teachers and even clinicians sometimes assume the disorder when there may be more conventional and cultural reasons why the behaviors are exhibited. Again, this illustrates why it is important for teachers to be trained in child development and understand relationships between cultural and environmental factors and behavioral or attentional patterns.

We discussed temperament in the previous chapters and it appears again here in relation to b/ADD. It is in this category that temperament can play a significant role. The "temperamentally difficult" child who is from the outset of life intense, irregular, negative, and nonadaptable suggests the possibility that birth temperament can play a significant role in the developing behavior of the child. Temperament, in our work with parents over the last fifteen years, has played an ever greater role in our counseling with three-, four-, and five-year-old children. Twenty or twenty-five years ago mental health workers often sought to understand a child's behavioral and attention problems through investigation of the parent's strategies in managing the child's behavior. The mental health notions in the 1950s and 1960s too often laid the blame for behavioral difficulties of children primarily on poor parenting.

As we came to see how important birth temperament could be in the family, we realized that poor parenting might be less the problem than inappropriate or ineffective parenting strategies. This seemingly minor difference has had a tremendous effect on counseling, particularly on the maternal side of parenting. Suddenly, we could work with parents from the standpoint of education and understanding of child development and differences rather than parenting incompetence or even pathology. We could elicit the assistance of the parents in working out how to meet the needs of individual children rather than hours of attempting to place blame on marital or psychological problems; the parents became cooperative participants in successfully helping their child.

At birth children come to us as active participants in family dynamics rather than passive recipients of parental and environmental influences. Children, via their early temperament (personality), play an active role in shaping parent responses and, in the view of many developmentalists, actually shape and teach parents infant care. In the best of situations where the infant's early behavioral patterns are effective in gaining appropriate parent responses, all works out well. But few of us are perfect and neither are our children, and so in a significant number of cases situational and cultural deficits can create an early deficit pattern of material-infant interactions. At times these difficulties are resolved successfully or at least adequately, in others negative behavioral patterns are reinforced, and the infant learns not to trust or worse to perform an adversary role in the family as a means of survival.

Some clinicians, earnestly seeking solutions to family and child problems, may fail to investigate the dynamics of the early infant-parent interactions in order to gain a developmental picture of how the child came to be. We can be too quick to judge and miss important data that could transform not only how we view the family, but most importantly, how we move to assist them. Too often the treatment strategy or theory may induce the very problems we assume are inherent in the etiology of the behavioral disorder. Understanding the needs of the parents as individuals and how they adapt to their roles in relation to the early behavioral patterns of the child and his or her siblings, can give tremendous insight into how to respond. Teaching the parents more effective parenting skills or attempting to modify a child's behavior are often only temporarily successful for the true dynamics of the family may not be changed.

If understanding the early temperament of children is difficult for clinical personnel, it is even more remotely accessible to teachers when their attention must concern twenty or thirty children. Relating back to our earlier list of various systems of individual development, teachers are often frustrated in their efforts to learn about and understand the needs of children. Temperament, in that it is an area of development which is evident long before the child comes to school, is not usually a concern for the teacher. The teacher must deal with "personality" and not temperament. Our point here though is not one relating to the typical child who does not display any special needs. In cases of children with special needs, however, it is important that the teacher explore with the parents the early temperament of the child as a means of understanding the factors which may have contributed to the child's difficulty. We find that often the child's problems are consistent with the general temperament patterns exhibited by the child in infancy and during the first three years.

We refer the reader back to our earlier discussion for a review of the various aspects of temperament. It is important to establish a baseline of behavioral potentials in the young infant or child in order to understand behavior at a later point of problematic situations. This approach provides not only a more comprehensive picture of why the child is now behaving in the manner he is but also to understand the degree that such behavior is an integral part of his overall genetic/temperament pattern and how this may relate to present circumstances.

Once we understand the foundations of the child's natural behavioral patterns, we can assign importance or the lack of it to both his present deficits and the role parents may have or are playing. How the child resolves his difficulties will depend on our understanding of his behavioral patterns in relation to temperament and other areas we will explore shortly.

ENVIRONMENTAL SYSTEM

In the preceding chapter we presented seven systems which we suggested compose areas of concern in understanding children. We presented information about temperament, sensory motor development, spatial-temporal competencies, linguistic competencies, psychoneurological function, and the ego-consciousness executive system. We did not discuss the environmental system as we wanted to save it until this point in our discussion of development for it is intimately involved in the b/ADD syndrome.

As we discussed the various personal systems of the child in the preceding chapter, most functions involved internal development while the environmental system is exclusively external, it is the environment within which development of the child occurs. The environment includes all influences external to the child including the family, the cultural and economic status of the family, the community, schools, and geographic factors.

The temperament and general psychoneurological integrity of the child is, if we can use an impersonal analogy, a closed system of psychocybernetic growth designed for survival of the child as he matures toward independence. This is to say that the child has a complex biological program potential which can adapt to the environment in order to survive within it. We mentioned earlier how the care and nurturance, or lack of it, can propel an infant into the stance of trust versus mistrust, autonomy versus shame or initiative versus guilt as our discussion of Erickson's theory pointed out. The environmental influence, during these first few months and years of life can cause the child to adapt his developing responses and competencies to survive in what ever conditions he finds himself. This dynamic interaction between child and environment shapes the child and creates the various patterns of internal system processes. As the child matures during the first few years the adaptation of his abilities to the environment creates an ever-increasing intractable personality and behavioral structure.

To understand a child requires we recognize that maladaptive behavioral patterns may be transitional, i.e., a child facing a temporary crisis, after which he returns to his original pattern of behavior, or, it may be a learned and adaptive pattern which is now permanent such as a distrust of all adults. Transitional maladaptive behavior can be altered through nurturance and understanding, as well as support and assistance toward the focus of the crisis, or even maturation. Integrated and permanent patterns of adaptive behavior which become maladaptive in different environments can also be altered but only with extensive education, therapy, and effort over a long-sustained period. But one aspect of this thought needs to be explored further.

The notion of altering maladaptive behavior is an interesting one for this is, after all, the purpose and focus of therapy and rehabilitation. Yet, for those who have not inquired into maladaptive behavior it may be instructive to recognize that maladaptive behavior is by definition behavior which is not successful within a specific set of environmental conditions. Usually, we treat maladaptive behavior as a "disorder," "disturbance" or mental health problem of various descriptions; the individual "has a problem" which prevents him from adjusting to his environment. In many cases this medical concept of the child as a "sick" or disabled person is appropriate and requires "treatment" should it be therapy or behavioral modification.

But, as we will see, maladaptive behavior may not always have an etiology of personal dysfunction or even a biochemical basis so much as the presence of successful "adaptive" behavior which becomes maladaptive in a new environment within which the child has no experience. For example, a child who has developed within an abusive and threatening environment may learn to adapt through deception, avoidance, lying, or even stealing. In this case the child's survival depends on his ability to develop skills which allow him to obtain the ends of his needs. Upon entering school the child distrusts, avoids, feels inadequate, and becomes aggressive and, what has been adaptive behavioral skills now become maladaptive and the child may be at odds with not only the teacher but peers as well. He may be inattentive, aggressive, distractible, and impulsive all appearing much like the ADHD child.

It is easy to see how the abused or neglected child can develop early adaptive behaviors which become maladaptive upon entrance to school. But interestingly such a sequence can also occur in families where no abuse occurs, where socioeconomic conditions are positive, and where for all practical purposes the child seems normal to the parents until he enters school or a structured environment. For example, a classic situation involves the overindulged child who is quite able to exist in an overly nurturing, secure, and reinforcing environment of the overprotective home. The child may be quite manipulative and ego-centered which allows him success in the home and community environment but become severely maladaptive in the school environment. This is a somewhat common problem which, perhaps, most of us do not recognize is an adaptive-maladaptive pattern existing for many children other than those we usually think of such as the stereotypic deprived or delinquent.

The importance of this discussion is that when one focuses on an active and distressing behavioral pattern in a child we must realize that attempting to modify or reinforce appropriate behavioral patterns may be too simplistic even in counseling or therapy. This is why we see the b/ADD pattern as an additional way to look at children who have behavioral difficulties but who do not demonstrate severe conduct disorders or ADHD. Such children have a cluster of behavioral disorders which need some paradigm upon which we can truly understand them. Our point here is that in the present climate of schools there are distressing problems in the behavior and learning of children. We must not make the mistake, as we too often do, of assuming that this is some sort of clinical disorder such as Conduct Disorders or ADHD. Many of our contemporary problems may well relate to changes in family life, stresses of societal changes as a whole, or particular transitional problems of other sorts. But in order to make such a differentiation, between clinical disorders and changes in the nature of childcare and parenting, we have to look at developmental issues and sociological factors and for that we must improve the skills and training of our teachers.

Considering these dimensions of temperament and genetic-based behavioral potentials and the interactions of parents and their own personalities, we can see a complex matrix forming in which the behavior of the child is a manifestation of not only his behavior but the environmental climate in which he/she is embedded. Our experience tells us that there is though an internal striving in most children toward equilibrium cognitively in much the manner described by Piaget. Children will attempt, if at all possible, to develop adaptive skills in whatever environment they find themselves and they will attempt to seek love and positive relationships if possible. This is to suggest that while a particular child may exhibit a personality or temperament of aggression and chaos, we must accept that given the opportunity and assistance, he will attempt to adapt.

The fact that most children are successful from all environments good and bad, that is most adults are not psychotic nor criminal, suggests to us that even in the most adverse of environments there is a wonderful potential in all children for positive adaptation over time. From the time children enter school the classroom teacher becomes the master facilitator to create both natural and artificial environments in which the child learns adaptive behavior. For all of societies criticism of education today, the vast majority of children obtain a successful range of social and personal skills primarily within the cultural environment of the school. The teacher and her classroom, after the age of five years, are our most pervasive and consistent shapers of the behavior of children.

In the 1980s childcare and preschool programs in the United States became more important than they had been previously. By the middle 1980s more and more women had entered the workforce full time and 50 percent of these women were mothers. It is expected that by the year

2000 more than 80 percent of all women will be employed full time. In less than twenty years what was once thought of as the typical (and implied "best") model of the American family of a husband with a wife and two children with a mother who did not work or only did so part time, has become a minority. In fact, by the early 1990s only 5 percent of the population lived in homes that could be described this way. With this reality it can now be said that between temperament and school the other influences on the child are minimal including that of mother and father. Now the "teacher" and "school," if we include preschool and daycare as surrogate parents and teachers, become the major influence not only after five years but at birth!

The issue here is the suspicion that children who have an early temperament and behavioral pattern of aggression and impulsivity will respond best to the nurturing and understanding of the family constellation. To place such a child in an environment, particularly a family environment, where interaction is less available or not available at all, could place him at risk for later maladaptive behavior. Also at risk would be the high threshold, poor response, shy and withdrawing, and uncertain child. Such a child needs a highly secure and nurturing environment during the first three years to assist him in learning trust and risk taking in order to compensate for a poorly adaptive temperament. Perhaps, the general population of children will be able to adapt and fair well, but a significant number of poorly adaptive children will perhaps be placed at a higher level of risk than if they were at home.

Our intent here is not to enter in a review of the tremendous range of research today in the area of the effects of daycare on children. The reader may want to walk that path but our intent here and throughout the book is to raise issues which relate to the syndrome of behavioral disorders, activity levels, attentional disorders, rule-governed behavior problems, and inability to adapt successfully in varying environments. Certainly, the change in lifestyle in today's population, should it be in Japan, Europe, or America, may effect our children in ways never known, for in the coming internationalization of economies and culture we have no history to which to compare. Some researchers have investigated the notion that modern lifestyles may in some way be contributing to the syndrome of ADHD. This line of research, of course, is not of great interest in a field of science where variables must be controlled and limited parameters imposed. To study lifestyle as a contributor to impulsivity, hyperactivity, or other ADHD characteristics is not attractive to most researchers. Yet, it may be more easily studied from the concept of d/ADD and b/ADD as described here. We suggest that researchers in child development and early childhood education should explore this area.

The matter of culturally-deprived children has been studied in early childhood research and one of the early consequences of this has been the national Headstart program. It was known that children from deprived families, particularly when intact families did not exist, demonstrated a range of developmental deficits not experienced by their middle class peers. Such children often were language delayed, displayed lower overall intellectual competence and many behavioral difficulties. Conversely, with adequate early education, often dramatic increases in overall intellectual competence, improved language and behavior, and adaptive skills were obtained following educational intervention. The experience of Headstart suggests that in an effective environment children with varying problems in early development can display significant improvement. The question of a need for a good early childhood environment is not contested and the detrimental effects of deprivation and neglect are well-established. But what of the new deprived, the middle and upper class families who are now committing their children to a wide range of good and bad daycare from the early months of their lives?

If children with troublesome temperaments need the special care and management of a family during the first five years of life in order to adapt, what happens when they are in inadequate, daycare programs where individual adult supervision is at a minimum and trained educational professionals may be nonexistent? The robust and assertive infant may do well even in an inadequate environment but the at-risk infant may have to develop an early defense system in order to survive. For such infants long-term behavioral difficulties may be reinforced, ability to focus attention and manage impulses delayed, and social skills may be unlearned.

It is not then a question of can good daycare be found, though that is a serious question for all children, it is can infants and children who are at risk be identified early enough to save them from eventual failure and frustration? It is here that we feel another group of b/ADD children are presently being literally "trained" toward behavioral disorders. Such children may be coming in ever increasing numbers as more and more parents must work and the development of adequate early care programs either do not exist or are beyond the means of most families. The

latchkey child has already become the focus of many studies and promises to be an increasing problem. If poor care in a daycare center is
unacceptable, what of no care at all?!

VALUES AND SELF

The development of a metacognitive self-awareness is a critical process
in all children if they are to become independent and capable human
beings. Metacognitive, objective awareness, implies that an individual
can look at information or even himself or herself in a somewhat removed
or objective manner. To be self-reflective, for example, to have feelings
of self-worth and identity, and to be able to place one's self in a role in
play situations in relation to others, to see one's effect on others, and to
recognize a sense of control and responsibility all are dependent upon
differentiation of self or ego consciousness. The developmental routes
one may take toward establishing a concept of positive self-image are
many and are entwined both within the emergence of self from the
original temperament and reflex cluster and in response to the environmental factors of parenting, siblings, culture, economics, and school.

Children from dysfunctional families where the abrasive difficulties of
divorce, drugs, and deprivation are prevalent, often are unable to develop
positive and clear identities. Without the development of this sense of
self the R–Complex behavioral system remains in control and the child
is to a degree captured within his own basic instincts and energy for
survival. Such children learn to survive in whatever way they can and
it needs to be expected that metacognitive self-awareness is seldom
achieved. These children will be impulsive, evasive, and disruptive in
their environment. Attention span, concentration to tasks that have little
meaning, or difficulties in rule governed behavior become characteristics that prevail.

We also see these sorts of problems in the middle class family where
severe dysfunctional family characteristics are not evident. Drugs, divorce,
alcohol, and deprivation are not the issues; rather, overly aggressive and
achievement-oriented families can produce dysfunctional children if
you will, children who are unable to adapt in a positive way to their
environment for they are overly aggressive, competitive, and demanding.
There are many paths to maladaptive behavior which result in behavioral
disorders.

Involved with the issue of self-concept, though it is most often viewed separately, is that of values or moral behavior. Values are no less a complex issue than self-concept but, in the process of successful adaptive behavior, values play a more critical role than most people realize. Based on Piaget's concepts of cognitive and value development, Kohlberg hypothesized stages in moral development that elaborated on Piaget's theories (1976).

Kohlberg organized six stages of moral development into three levels or moral progress, the preconventional level in which morality is externally governed, the conventional level in which the child responds to expectations for conformity on the basis of social norms, and finally the postconventional or principal level in which morality is perceived in terms of abstract principles. At the first level infants begin their world where external forces control and shape their behavior from a hedonistic and opportunist ego orientation. In the second level, armed with ever expanding cognitive elaboration, children eventually adopt the social norms of society as their own. In the higher levels, the adolescent and adult finally "reason" out a general construct of moral behavior and values as their own.

When we reflect on the myriad of internal and external forces which affect the developing values and attitudes of the child, we can be overwhelmed with the task of assisting children in eventual adjustment. The complexity of how a child accepts responsibility for his behavior and is able to maintain attention to task, adaptation to the environment and culture, and development of a healthy and successful self-concept and personality, requires a highly sophisticated educational environment. The notion then, of ADHD and its etiology must take into account all seven levels of child development we have mentioned here.

In this work we are not attempting to manage all of these seven levels of development in detail and particularly not the entire environmental constellation for that has been done and is available from a range of professional research. There is not room here to explore all of these areas, nor would the authors attempt to do so. We are attempting to suggest to the teacher and to the school psychologist that the notion of providing an effective educational environment in today's society requires far greater competence than we have brought to the task in the history of education. No longer are we merely communicating the information of society to children, nor are we responsible for limited socialization as part of our task; we are becoming more and more responsible for a major portion of the job of understanding and intervening in the needs of the child toward becoming a fully functioning human being. It is our dire prediction that with the family changing and the care of children falling more and more to outside influences, our educational institutions are faced with increasing inability to serve children in ways society needs.

The arguments in education about which is the better philosophy of instruction pale in the light of the demands now placed on teachers and schools by the community and parents. We are not now ready for the task. The ADD fiasco is but one symptom of our failure in schools to provide a developmental environment in which the child can successfully find the nurturance and climate in which both his deficits and assets can be accounted for.

Our concept of b/ADD is an attempt to force us as educators to begin to look at the needs of children in personality and behavior just as the d/ADD concept embodies much of the notion about cognitive and intellectual development. In the range of behavior and needs of children inherent in these two classifications we see beyond the more clinical concept of ADHD and into an expanding range of problems facing our children which are educationally- and family-based. To skirt this issue by attempting to label all such children as ADHD will not resolve the problem. We have to recognize that many of the children now falling under the defunct category of ADD or Conduct Disorders are not children with a clinical or neurological problem but rather with broader problems and issues which should be recognized as needs in intellectual, cognitive, and behavioral areas.

This all brings us back to our point that focuses on disorders, including the research on ADHD, or the general label such as ADD, is distracting educational professionals from the potential presence of a real breakdown in the current capacity of our schools to meet the needs of children. Curriculum in our schools today, realizing even the minimal areas of developmental concerns listed here, must extend itself beyond the simple notions that a new instructional technique, reading series, or certainly medication or behavioral modification will solve our problem in meeting the needs of children.

We should begin to realize that for all of the "clinical and research parameters" inherent in effective research concerning ADHD, it is missing the point! In the case of either Pavlov's conditioning theory or Skinner's operant behavior theory which spawned the entire behavioral modification era, we are finally prostate in terms of meeting the real needs of changing behavior or learning. We modify behavior through shaping it with rewards and various social reinforcements, but it is the action of the child in cognitive terms and a change in the cerebral processing which will make the difference. Children must "learn" new behaviors which are often the result of cognitive processes and "gestalt" which, after all, are no less accessible to behavior modification than is behavioral research. Medication, in terms of ADHD resolution, appears to be the only legitimate medical treatment for ADHD. But, importantly, this is only because it, in cases where it is appropriate, acts to bring the child into a state of cognitive readiness and process interaction, conscious, and self-activated learning. The real change, subsequently, is within the expertise and skill of the teacher to help the child.

Now let's look at three cases of b/ADD, our classification of children with behavioral difficulties accompanied by inattention, overactivity, impulsivity, and in many cases aggressive or assertive reactions to authority or rules. We use only three cases for our intent here is to make several points about the notion of behavioral problems of children which are founded in development and learning. It is important that we understand that these problems do not qualify these children for either ADHD or Conduct Disorders as defined in the DSM–IIIR though in most cases parents or teachers felt that the children were ADD.

Case Study 1
William
C.A. 4.9

William was seen in April prior to his fifth birthday in July.

Referring conditions: The preschool teacher where William attended recommended to the parents that he was hyperactive, disregarded rules and directions of teachers, was sometimes argumentive and did not wish to participate in planned activities but wanted to create his own. ADD was suspected.

Family history and environment: William's parents were a concerned couple who were also highly frustrated with William's behavior at home as well as at school. The family was a middle class rural family and though the mother worked part-time, she was home each afternoon with William who was their only child. The couple was in their early thirties and had been married in their late twenties. Both came from families which had more than three children and had experienced a range of behavior of siblings. At home he was argumentive, often refused to go to bed at the set time, was constantly demanding attention, and was very picky about eating.

The parents were anxious to understand and help William but felt both incapable and uncertain as to how to do so. In general, other than their frustration, they were caring individuals who displayed no significant family pathology.

Temperament and personality pattern: William was assertive and yet positive and cooperative during testing and the parents verified that for all of the chaos he caused he was a very happy and enthusiastic child. He had been an active baby and seemed to need little sleep. He began asking questions about things the parents felt were unusual when he was two years old and had not stopped. He learned quickly and seemed to have insights about people and the way they acted. But he was also demanding and would periodically have tantrums if he didn't get his way.

Dominance, balance, and gross motor: William displayed good general coordination, loved to draw and generally displayed excellent gross motor skills. William displayed typical right-handedness, right eye, and general spatial organization.

Spatial-temporal skills: William had good general organization to time and sequence, an understanding of behavior and sequence in language, and general cognitive competencies.

WIPPSI Intelligence Test

Verbal		Nonverbal	
Information	15	Geometric Designs	15
Similarities	15	Animal house	12
Math	17	Block design	13
Vocabulary	17	Coding	14
Sentences	15	Mazes	13

William's intellectual scores demonstrated a gifted child who is falling within the three-year range of developmental advantage in language over age peers and also well above average in nonverbal or performance scores.

Achievement skills: William was highly interested in reading and was already reading within the late first to early second grade level in recognition and comprehension. He had, more or less, learned early reading without any formal instruction other than the plentiful time which his mother spent reading with him. At this time he had not attempted writing but enjoyed playing with a small computer which had been given to him for his birthday. The preschool in which he participated was primarily a social environment and no academic skills, unlike many urban preschools, were emphasized.

William was small for his age but "wiry," active, and appeared to enjoy the testing session often "quipping" and making jokes. When asked why he was so aggressive and active, he stated, "I like doing stuff." When asked what he would do with a boy who said and did things that upset adults, he said, "I'd beat his butt!"

William's responses were interesting for, though he could not really appreciate it, he revealed a very astute concept in child development and one that often gives parents of gifted children one of their many early challenges. We see many parents with four- to six-year-old children who find their assertiveness and aggression overwhelming. Freud spoke of the problems when a child identifies with the same sex parent and a period of development where there is competition between the child and one parent with the other parent. But this is not so much a Freudian complex in sexual growth as another issue which often occurs at this age. For the professional interested in the psychodynamic theory these problems at this age are easily identified as a period of personality growth. We tend to see another and perhaps more realistic factor in this period of turmoil.

Between the age of approximately four and a half and five and a half years many children, particularly boys, experience a surge in seeking independence. We see this as a period not unlike that of the adolescent crisis and struggle for independence. Often, the five-year-old boy, beginning to enter kindergarten and having reached a significant level of cognitive and sensory development, enters a period of desire for independence. Many times the young five year old can become quite assertive and demanding for a period of time. Interestingly, this transitional period requires from parents an increased strength in providing limits to behavior while at the same time giving more independence and support for the child. The child is psychologically ambivalent during this period, on one hand seeking independence, and on the other desiring the strength and limits of the parent. It can be a frightening time and parents must be able to impose the security of limit setting without being overly restrictive. It is difficult at best and totally frustrating at worst.

The child needs security that parents can provide and yet he rebels against such limits. This produces, in some children highly out-of-bounds behavior and yet anger when parents are not able to control his behavior. In a sense, the child needs limits to reassure him for he sometimes is overwhelmed and fearful of his own omnipotence.

William, in his childish perception stated it very clearly, "I would beat his butt!" He felt out of control and angry at his parents and needed reassurance. Yet, in William's case, because he was so gifted, he actually had intimidated the parents with his intellect and they felt inadequate to manage his behavior. Once, the mother said, "When we tried to spank him, he told us we could do it but it wouldn't work." We have heard this from many parents of gifted children. Parents and teachers, though they do not understand it, are often intimidated by gifted children and often they feel inadequate in their care and instruction. In such a situation parents have to be given support and advice on how to manage these children for they are often more demanding and capable not only in learning but in interpersonal areas as well.

To a lessor extent this period of development can be just as difficult for parents of normal children as well and in families who are actually inadequate in parenting skills this phase can launch an extended period of behavioral difficulties for the child which extends into school and is worsened by the teacher's inability to manage the behavior. Inadvertently, many teachers see the child's behavior as some sort of severe emotional problem if not ADHD or Conduct Disorder. When the problem is identified as basically the behavior without understanding the underlying issues, as in the case of William, it is easy if not even a bit expedient, to attempt to deal with the behavior rather than the underlying issues. How do we manage the behavior? Can some sort of modification be used? How can rewards and punishment help?

The problem for the counselor and the parents is the same as in the case of medication for the ADHD child, while the "situation" may be managed, what are the long-term effects. In William's case, as with many children, this efficient and basically "behavioralist approach" misses the point. The point is that it is fundamentally significant in the development of the child that they, within their level of comprehension, resolve the disequilibrium of this stage of cognitive development. The child himself must work through and "act on" the situation mentally in order to understand and resolve the issues. Again, we see why the use of external manipulation to manage the child's behavior is unlikely, in the welfare of the child, and his or her real growth, to having a lasting effect.

There are real and substantial issues in this case which too often are not well understood in the crisis of the situation where a teacher and parents are experiencing the transition of any child from preschool to elementary age development. Imagine what consequences can be wrought for those children who do not have intact families, where one parent alone must juggle the responsibilities and demands of work and parenting. Does the kindergarten teacher have the training and background to help this child and parent? Should she be expected to? Once, when we were teaching emotionally disturbed children in a public school program, it became apparent that many parents would not become involved in counselling within the program. In fact, many would not even come for parent teacher conferences. The program eventually required participation and the warning was issued that without such participation children might not be allowed to continue. We really couldn't make such a rule, it was a bluff. It didn't matter for the parents still didn't come.

We realized at that point that while parent counseling and participation were clinically significant, if we did not try to assist the child before us with or without parents, nothing would be done. It is the same for all teachers. There will be many children who have behavioral disorders because of the family environment, but if we are not trained to assist in any case then we too will fail the child. Are our teachers well enough trained? Should they be required to accept such responsibility? It really doesn't matter for though we must continue to attempt parent involvement, either way, the child is with us! The same is true with the b/ADD child, the ADHD and Conduct Disordered child, regardless of our attempt to label the child or to medicate him, our skills must be up to the task of understanding him and helping him developmentally as well as academically. Actually, one cannot truly be effective in teaching if we do not understand the needs of young children. William's case was eventually resolved through counseling with the parents, an understanding and capable kindergarten teacher, and supplementary educational programming to challenge him.

Case Study 2
Dan
C.A. 7-11

Dan was seen in October in the second grade.

Referring conditions: Dan was referred because of poor achievement, hyperactive behavior, impulsiveness in the classroom, negative and aggressive behavior, frustration and anxiety, and seemingly poor self concept. The parents wanted to determine if he was ADD or had other problems. While he had problems in classroom learning, the teacher and parents were primarily concerned about his behavior.

Family environment: Dan's parents were concerned and capable individuals who were highly involved in their children's school. Dan had two sisters, one six and one ten years old. The family lived in a small town where the father owned a service-oriented store and the mother stayed at home. They were active in the community and the children participated in many activities. The family would be considered upper economic though within the average range for national income.

General temperament and personality factors: Dan was a very enthusiastic and active boy who was assertive, distractible, had difficulty maintaining attention, and was impulsive. He talked loudly and incessantly in situations where he felt comfortable.

Dan was also somewhat anxious and insecure responding to others which resulted in poor social comprehension. His difficulties in interacting with peers was often the consequence of his poor recognition of the feelings and purposes of the behavior of others about him. Dan had a low threshold of responsiveness and though disorganized was very receptive to information.

Dominance, balance, and gross motor: Dan was right-handed but left-eyed. Both parents were right-handed, but there was a history of left-handedness on the mother's side of the family. Dan had significant difficulties in general balance of organization related to spatial motor skills.

Spatial-temporal organization: Dan's difficulties in basic lateral dominance and motor competencies resulted in poor temporal orientation. This affected his ability to deal with time and sequence and doubtlessly contributed to his problems in behavioral organization. It was difficult for him to work with multiple information relationships in an integrative way.

WISC–R Intelligence Test

Verbal		*Nonverbal*	
Information	13	Picture completion	17
Similarities	13	Picture arrangement	10
Math	10	Block design	9
Vocabulary	15	Object assembly	9
Comprehension	13	Coding	8
Digit span	7		
Verbal range	118–125	Performance range	100–110

Dan's results on the WISC–R reflect a highly unstable developmental pattern. The first feature occurs in the general pattern of scaled scores. In the verbal area are indicators, i.e., information-13, similarities-13, comprehension-13, and vocabulary-15. These scores indicate an above average level of verbal abilities.

In nonverbal areas picture completion is significantly high while in general the others are below average as is digit span in the verbal areas. Taken at the extremes, the high verbal abilities are within the 120 range while the lower areas in performance fall with the 85 range for a general difference of more than 35 points. This profile, significant in its range of difference, presents a peculiar and highly conflicting cognitive cluster.

The higher level of verbal competencies here suggests a boy who will, consciously, have excellent informational processing skills with a high level of verbal association and awareness. Conversely, the "drive system," i.e., the vestibular, cerebellar, and cerebral parietal-temporal interface, will not support organization of these verbal abilities. Dan has many intricate verbal perceptions and efficiency in processing verbal information without the underlying frame of organization needed to control those perceptions into meaningful responses. In essence, we see here a clinical case of ADHD where frontal lobe function, though having superior verbal processing available, does not have the associated spatial temporal competencies to organize it. This results in a neurological verbal "machine" which will take in and respond to verbal information in an almost endless loop of disorganization.

Because of the frustration caused by his own inability to organize and yet a high level of verbal comprehension, Dan feels incapable. He is unable to perform academically in written work but as we will see is able to perform on objective tests. His frustration makes him defensive and aggressive along with reacting at random to social situations and peers.

Achievement skills: With the interesting mix of developmental difficulties seen above one would be highly interested in how such a child might do in the classroom. The answer may be surprising for a moment.

Vocabulary... 80th percentile
Comprehension.. 93rd percentile
Total reading...89th percentile
Language expression.. 92nd percentile
Math computation.. 85th percentile
Math concepts and appl..93rd percentile
Total mathematics.. 93rd percentile
Word analysis..68th percentile

These scores are from a statewide testing service completed in March of the previous year or, about seven months before the current assessment. They are, perhaps surprising because they suggest a boy that is doing very well academically.

At the time of this testing, conversely, Dan is doing poorly in the second grade. He doesn't complete his work, he does not finish written assignments, and he tends to disregard the teachers threats and demands. Here, as in the previous case studies on d/ADD cognitive problems, we see a boy who is unable to organize his motor and spatial abilities to successfully PRODUCE work but, looking at the above scores on state norms, he is within the upper 10 to 15 percent of the population in achievement. The difference is that in a testing situation he does not have to write much, the tasks are more interesting because a greater variety are presented in less time, and finally, he doesn't have to organize himself because his work is so highly structured and controlled. Thus, on the achievement test we see his learning or achievement level while in the classroom we see his skill and ability to apply that level of achievement toward work production. But we know that his production will be low both because of poor writing skills and poor organization and attentional maintenance ability.

The primary referral in Dan's case was behavior and a lack of accomplishment, but without the foregoing information little would be understood about his problem or what to do with it. His is a complicated situation in that there is an interaction between a highly active temperament, a significant verbal/performance abilities pattern, and spatial-temporal delay and difficulties. The way in which all of these factors have come together produce the conflicting factors in his overall behavior. He is, to coin a new use for a contemporary phrase, dysfunctional.

Dan is then a combination of ADHD and b/ADD and will require a rather extensive plan of action both at school and home in order for him to be successful. The following notes concerning his condition and needs will summarize this case.

1. Dan has a temperament of high activity and low threshold who is sensitive and quick to pick up on information from the environment. This makes him an inquisitive child who will seek out stimulation from about him and respond to it through investigation, inquiry, and observational responses. Such children seek activity, can become bored easily, and want responses from people about him. Such a child can be challenging to parents in that they are constantly seeking something to do, someone to do it with, and frequently changing activities.

2. Dan is a highly verbal child who often comments on what he is doing or experiencing, asking questions, and wanting help or involvement. He is able to learn information easily and this stimulates verbal interaction.

3. Due to Dan's highly verbal and active temperament and personality, he has difficulties focusing on one activity and often will engage in several activities in a short period of time.

4. Dan has poor spatial motor organization and, with his high level of activity and interest in novelty and involvement, is very disorganized resulting in not following through with a particular activity well. Further, though he is highly verbal he will often talk and ask questions before actually following through himself. In the classroom this means that he may not attend to a task well and constantly seeks teacher support or direction in activities which he should be able to do himself. Yet, his poor spatial motor skills result in a lack of ability to write and perform fine motor skills adequately. This results in frustration and increased dependence on an adult or teacher who becomes frustrated with his need for assistance.

When Dan requires attention from adults he can tirelessly demand such assistance even though he could perform it himself with patience and follow-through. When he is rebuffed by adults he becomes angry and at times may do something he is not supposed to in order to vent his anger which then results in more rejection from the adult and a circle of frustration and rejection instigates more frustration. This cycle must be broken but at school many inadvertent responses from adults result in frustration unknown to the teacher.

5. Socially this pattern of behavior results in seeking attention and play from peers without regard for their needs or interests. This demanding but nonreciprocal interaction with peers results in peers rejecting him also and this again creates anger with peers. His own needs are so strong he is unable to recognize the needs of others.

6. Eventually, failure in school and rejection from peers and adults develops into an ever increasing difficulty in all aspects of the classroom and school environment. This then prevents the development of success in social and educational learning strategies and a declining level of self confidence and self concept strength.

A case like Dan's is a combination of ADHD and behavioral difficulties which present a number of problems for himself and those about him. Simply labelling him or approaching one aspect of his needs will be unsuccessful for we have to recognize the interrelatedness of all of his needs.

Dan's problems could not be resolved through a single approach and therefore the school and parents had to develop consistent strategies and work cooperatively in a number of areas at the same time and for an extended period in order to assist Dan. Maturation will resolve many of his difficulties and will require time.

Dan was placed on medication and this had an overall calming effect on much of his over-activity. He was started in an individual program of word processing skills on the computer in order to bypass the on-going fine motor and writing skills and allow him some way to express his ideas in a structured and controlled manner in the future. He needed much individual attention and structure and this was accomplished at school through both peer tutoring and some adult volunteer assistance. He was placed in a part-time learning disabilities resource program in order to allow him more freedom of movement during learning activities and several sessions a week in a peer facilitation program where he could, in a structured learning situation, role play and interact with other students in "social skillstreaming."

The parents formalized much of his time at home and developed daily routines which did not vary from day to day relative to study times, household chores, bedtime and eating, and his diet was carefully monitored. Some behavioral modification was used as a supplementary approach both at school and home.

Case Study 3
Mark
C.A. 9-7

Testing was done in March of the third grade. Mark had been retained in the first grade.

Referring conditions: Mark had been in the same school since kindergarten and his learning difficulties had been consistent. He tends to be impulsive and aggressive sometimes hurting other children seemingly without provocation. He was inattentive in class and had great difficulties understanding and following directions. He had some minor speech difficulties and stammered when he attempted to explain himself. He was defensive and felt that others often picked on him.

Family environment: Mark's father was a truck driver with a relatively adequate and stable income. He was a strong disciplinarian and used physical punishment often when he became involved with Mark and his two brothers aged 5 and 14. His brothers also had difficulties in school and the older boy had been in a juvenile detention facility on two occasions for stealing and a minor house break-in. The mother was a secretary in the firm where the father worked and the kids were latchkey children in that they were home each day for an hour before the mother came home from work. There was some evidence that the father and mother both had difficulties with alcohol though neither were identified as an alcoholic nor received any sort of treatment.

The parents, though strict, appeared to be loving toward their children and expected them to go to school and to do well. However, the parents were seldom able to come to school or attend parent conferences. The father had quit school in the ninth grade but the mother had finished high school. They both attended church along with their children regularly.

General temperament and personality: Mark, as far as could be determined, had always been an active and aggressive boy. There was some question relative to difficulties during the birth and in the first three or four weeks when apparently he had milk allergy reactions which were quite serious. Mark was a large baby and continued to be large for his age. Having been retained a year he was by far the largest boy in his class.

Verbal communication was difficult for Mark who had trouble with not only some minor speech defects but syntax and sequential organization of time-space orientation. His behavior more often gave the impression of a moderately contained rain storm and a degree of chaos accompanied him throughout the day.

School environment: Mark attended an inner city school where conditions were not positive. There were several gangs evident and at the present he was not involved but it seemed likely that he would be. Mark lived in a lower economic neighborhood but not in the sense of a high crime area, rather, it was an older blue collar area where most families had been long-term residents. However, bordering this area were several low income housing projects which had been allowed to deteriorate over the years.

The classes were large at the school and the school was generally in poor repair.

Dominance, balance, and gross motor: Mark was right handed and right eyed but seemed to have difficulties in fine motor skills and working in a consistent left to right pattern. His general coordination was minimal but did not present a general problem for him. His overall balance and coordination though were marginal.

Spatial temporal orientation: Mark had poor orientation in spatial temporal abilities. Even at nine years of age he had some difficulties saying the names of the days in order and definitely could not consistently recall the sequence of months in a year. He could not remember verbal directions and often did not know what was expected of him.

WISC–R Intelligence Test

Verbal		*Performance*	
Information	9	Picture completion	15
Similarities	7	Picture arrangement	9
Arithmetic	8	Block design	10
Vocabulary	9	Object assembly	9
Comprehension	11	Coding	7
Digit span	6		
Verbal range	90–95	Performance range	100–105

Achievement skills: Mark was reading within the early third grade in recognition but his comprehension, when he actually spent some time reading, was perhaps no better than late first grade. His writing skills were nonexistent and were therefore not functional as a learning skill. Mark had great difficulties in math and only recently mastered the addition and subtraction facts which were not very helpful since he often did not attend to the problems and made many copying errors.

Mark is a stereotype. The teacher did not recommend Mark for any special assistance nor did she suggest to the parents that Mark might benefit from medication. The reason she made no suggestions or referrals was that Mark was only one of many boys she had in her class who were very similar. Interestingly, the teacher's own son was on medication for ADHD but at no time in our interaction with her in information gathering did she suggest that Mark might be ADHD.

Mark is an inner city child who is culturally deprived and as the teacher stated, "You know he is from one of the families near the housing project." This statement carried all of the trappings of outright stereotyping and prejudice but one also had to recognize that this was not a new teacher, she had been teaching in this school for more than twenty years. Mark, in her view, represented a culturally deprived child who was from a family that did not value education and were poorly educated themselves. The obvious implications were all the expected ones: such children will never do well; without effective parenting they don't stand a chance; they will end up on welfare or in jail anyhow; or, they will be into drug sales and will quit school by the time they are sixteen.

Mark was not only large for his age and grade placement, he was "bad" in the old sense of the word. He had come to learn that power and size rendered respect and fear from peers. Having no other significant attributes, he developed these as best he could and became known more or less as a bully in his class.

While we dislike the teacher's attitudes and the implications they imply about her willingness to help Mark, there are numbers of deprived children who have certain types of difficulties which are often predictable. The sociological research is overwhelming in its focus on such children and families and much is known about the effects of poverty on poor or subpoor groups in this country. We also are aware of the few significant special programs and grant driven projects which have yielded impressive results . . . until the money ran out. Headstart is a good example of a program that worked, then failed for many because politics changed and the advantage of special programs for the disadvantaged had no advantage for the politically advantaged. Headstart continues but as a wounded soldier, still full of fight with lots of courage, but poor prognosis without reinforcements.

Culturally deprived children represent a large cross-section of ethnic, racial, religious, and economic groups. Often culturally deprived and "poor" are used synonymously, yet, in terms of education and developmental differences the economic status of the family is most likely the least of the problems in terms of cultural deprivation. Mark is an example of a culturally deprived child and though his family is not poor, they are in the lower socioeconomic strata. But Mark's difficulties stem from a number of conditions common to what we refer to as cultural deprivation and which, in too many cases, result in a cluster of behavioral and developmental features which lead to long term failure in many individuals.

It is interesting to us how much confusion and stereotyping there is within this group of children by teachers and other professionals. Conversely, there are features of this group which make them difficult to assist over the long term. We need to explore this area here because this is a group of children who, if the ADHD definition had not been changed, and, if it had become a category of special education, would have been segregated into a separate program. Once segregated in disproportionate numbers from other economic and cultural groups, they well could have suffered even worse than failing in the regular classroom.

In our viewpoint culturally deprived children coming to our clinic and those with whom we work in the schools, represent a special category of developmental and educational need. Mark is a good example. Our own classification and characterization of this group is as follows:

1. The first and foremost characteristic of the culturally deprived child is information and education deprivation.

To be deprived of culture essentially indicates in this case that a child has not been exposed to nor had the advantages of cultural opportunities which would allow them the foundation of knowledge and social skills to interact effectively in the larger society.

Television, for all of its bad effects, has provided an opportunity for enculturalization in ways not possible a century ago. For children today programs like *Sesame Street* are a way of providing some equalization in enculturation for those who are deprived. Still most remain in disadvantaged positions in school.

Children who are culturally deprived live in homes where books, magazines, and other literature are not available nor do parents obviously read to their children when they are young. This has the effect of denying them early experiences in values, knowledge, and the interest in reading so important for early learning. Further, such homes do not encourage nor provide information about the larger culture outside their home.

2. Deprived of early learning and informational experiences including trips and involvement in community activities, these children come to school without the same level of knowledge and zest for formal learning which their peers exhibit. Being thrust into an environment in which language and learning are the primary activities and basis for interaction, they are often bewildered by the nature and substance of the environment.

Social learning, communicated through an interaction and appreciation of community culture, is poorly developed in these children. They have not established a foundation for the basic social skills required to be successful in a learning environment and therefore often are unable to assimilate or accommodate new experiences and cooperative learning skills.

3. Because these children are not spoken to and engaged in communication skills through language activities, they do not develop early skills in time-space relationships, in using language to mediate in social interactions, nor appreciate the use of language to share information and feelings.

The lack of early stimulation in language development is perhaps the most damaging for such children for it affects their ability to "think," reason, and develop metacognitive skills. This all affects the child's general verbal intelligence and, unless the school can eventually compensate and remediate this problem, will result in long term mental deficits which become more and more intractable as they mature.

4. The foregoing problems then form the basis for a lack of effective moral development and adoption of the cultural rules and expectations prevalent in school and the larger society. For these children "being good" means avoiding punishment until the threat is past, stealing is when you get caught, and aggression and dominance are the values of success.

Impulsive behavior occurs in these children because they do not have the intellectual and moral basis to predict future consequences, to see their role in behavioral events, and develop trust for others.

Upon reviewing the foregoing conditions of cultural deprivation we can see that the R–Complex and basic instinct system continues to rein over the child's behavior. One author once stated that culturally deprived children live lives in which boredom, conflict, and threat occupy much of their conscious attention. Within this sort of environment, without the advantage of language and cognitive skills, these children come to school exhibiting classic symptoms of ADHD including behavioral deficits, attentional problems, impulsivity, and difficulties with rule governed behaviors. Yet, in the main they are less identified as ADHD than emotionally disturbed, delinquent, Conduct Disorder, or socially maladjusted children.

The culturally deprived are also often excluded from the ADHD classification by the notion of "lower intelligence." We touched briefly upon this factor earlier and found it curious. The exclusionary criterion of lower intelligence, while prevalent in several studies, was included in Barkley's definition as long as the mental age factor was accounted for. But while these children do poorly on intelligence tests, this does not mean that they are mentally handicapped nor that they would qualify for this category.

These children offer an important look into the defunct notion of ADD in which they would have been included because in general they do meet most of the 14 criteria. They still represent a very close qualification for ADHD but in general are excluded. Within the group we will find a higher level of activity and impulsive behavior than in the typical population of children. We will find more impulsivity and problems with rule governed behavior, and we will see many other major ADHD characteristics. But we have another label which has most often been given, that of disadvantaged, culturally deprived, and educationally deprived. Here, though, when we look at developmental deficits we see that these labels do little to school us on the underlying needs of these children.

The culturally deprived child needs "real" instruction for he or she is unable to meet the generally "middle class" concepts of behavior and culture typical of our educational system. We talk a great deal of equality and equal opportunity for an education in our schools but history and present-day problems demonstrate that there are large numbers of children for which the typical school environment is not only ineffective, it is a hostile and rejecting environment. Accepting this, what then is our point in all of this discussion?

We began our discussions with some history of MBD and hyperactivity, we reviewed large numbers of major research studies, we explored developmental aspects of the CNS and theories about learning, and then proposed that there are large numbers of children who meet criteria for special assistance in public schools due to deficits in development and behavior. We have suggested that the "clinical" viewpoint about ADHD results in a significantly small number of children who may be ethically given this label. Further, we have suggested that the ADD phenomenon and present radical views held by many teachers and parents were about to perpetuate an inaccurate presumed need for special services in our schools not unlike that of learning disabilities in the 1960s.

Our concern is that ADHD is a special classification which, for all of the rhetoric, is most likely a disorder related primarily to CNS dysfunction, genetic foundations, endocrinological dysfunction, dietary difficulties, or other organic and physiological problems. Further, even if a child does have this disorder it remains one generally reserved for the economically advantaged in that obtaining the diagnosis and medication is beyond the means of most poor and disadvantaged families. Thus, interestingly, while many minority and special cultural groups are fearful that public school classification would discriminate disproportionately against them, by the same token such children who do have ADHD are less likely to have treatment available to them.

Reflecting on the substance of our discussions here, we hope the reader recognizes that many children have learning and behavioral difficulties which are founded in developmental differences and defects. Secondly, we want to make clear that in our opinion, most children who demonstrate a pattern of behavior and learning which is similar to the ADHD pattern, usually do not have a distinct disorder but rather are children in need of more understanding and change in the educational environment in which they attend.

We have suggested a number of developmental areas which need to be understood and incorporated into the main stream of instruction in our schools. On one hand, there are a number of children who meet the criteria of ADHD, but as we have suggested in several guidelines, schools must use the skills of external community medical and neurological professionals to clearly establish the nature and needs of such children. Research in the cause and etiology of ADHD will and should continue, but it is a field somewhat aside from the critical need in education. Conversely, the major population of children presently being identified as ADHD by nonprofessionals and teachers are children with special developmental needs. It is our contention that this larger group of children is the responsibility of our schools and parents for their needs are primarily cultural and educational.

The central issue appears to be one of change in curriculum and structure of our educational systems and the way in which parents participate in schools. We are not blaming school professionals for the problem nor are we pointing the finger at parents. The issues will require a changing structure in the very philosophy of education and the responsibility of our educational system. Schools are under attack as if they, as a separate institution from society, are somehow the singular cause of our dilemma. Schools are society just as are parents.

Business is the major consumer of educations product, skilled and capable citizens who can enter the workforce. Therefore, the business community across the country is taking a major role in becoming involved in change in our schools. Schools across the country are suffering in the most severe way from a lack of funds and in general parents in this country still are not willing, apparently, to accept the cost of schooling their children. School psychologists, resource teachers in special education, speech therapists, and other specialists in schools need to be freed to apply the skills they have within the regular curriculum instead of performing administrative services.

We are optimistic. ADHD represents an old and ineffective solution to the needs of children. Simply identifying a problem, providing a label, and attempting to provide a short-term treatment, will no longer work. The regular curriculum initiative which serves to bring all children within the general structure of education, must be allowed to work. But the skill and technologies required to train teachers, to allow them to apply their skills, and give them the responsibility to make decisions at the level they are applied, all remain barriers to effective change. In conclusion, other than medical intervention such as medication or neurological treatment, schools must accept responsibility for children who have special needs. We believe that education has the potential for change and can develop a more enlightened cadre of future teachers. We trust that they will!

REFERENCES

Kohlberg, L. (1976) Moral stages and moralization: The cognitive-developmental approach (pp 31–53). In T. Lickone. (Ed), Moral development and behavior: Theory, research, and social issues (pp 31–43). New York: Holt, Rinehart & Winston.

APPENDICES

Appendix One

INTERVENTION STRATEGIES

In the appendix that follows we have included examples of how teachers can develop a range of intervention strategies based on the needs of the ADHD child. Should the child be a true ADHD child or a d/ADD and b/ADD the following strategies are a good example of how far beyond the notion of mere behavioral modification or cognitive strategies teachers are able to go.

One of the problems consistently observed in clinical research studies concerning ADHD is the lack of understanding that most researchers demonstrate in learning theory or the realistic aspects of how children are taught. These examples, developed by teachers, are not intended to be a complete program of intervention strategies. The following examples should be helpful to teachers in understanding the sorts of behavioral management approaches which they as professionals can and should develop in their own program. We hope that the work of these teachers will stimulate interest in special cooperative teacher study programs to develop an increased knowledge base of information and instructional strategies.

Materials in this section are taken in part from a special needs project grant from the Michigan Department of Education. We wish to express our appreciation to Dan Livingston and Jan Vogel for sharing these materials with our readers. Special thanks to Sandra Dupuis who served as the project writer and coordinator.

DIFFICULTIES WITH AUTHORITY
AND ACCEPTING CRITICISM

1. Compare classroom and teacher to a sports team. Involve group in a discussion of team behavior, including practicing skills, respect for others and appropriate responses to coaches. Relate present behavior in the classroom to a position in a future career. Have the group do a skit of specific game situations to make these issues relevant.
2. Develop a class atmosphere of acceptance so that criticism can be constructive and free of ridicule — Model this as an instructor.
3. Avoid cornering a student — offer options for the student to escape embarrassment while complying with your authority.
4. Work directly with the student to develop tolerance for authority by:
   a) relating problem to a real life or home situation
   b) running through a few mock-up situations

    c) agreeing ahead of time on a nonverbal cue as a reminder when student begins to act negatively

    d) reinforcing student for reacting appropriately

5. Once student makes gains, gradually increase direct orders and/or criticism to prepare student for actual situations.

6. Have students differentiate between critical and neutral statements.

7. Have students differentiate between constructive and destructive statements.

8. Use role playing techniques in which students react to critical statements in an appropriate way.

9. Direct critical statements to students in a non-threatening time and place— Avoid condemning a student in front of the group.

10. Have the students evaluate one another with the rule that a positive statement must be made before a critical statement is made.

11. Frequently provide POSITIVE feedback to the student.

12. After criticism is provided, allow the student to correct the project or assignment and then discuss the final product.

13. In the appropriate situation, allow the student to express his/her opinion about the program and the instructor.

FREQUENTLY INTERRUPTS CLASS

1. Establish rules for class participation and conduct. Explain rationale for the rules and consequences for violation.

2. Insist that the students listen to the complete explanation before asking questions, commenting, or beginning work.

3. Establish and maintain eye contact.

4. Establish a nonverbal cue with the student to remind him/her that he is interrupting.

5. Set aside a specific time for discussion and questions. Structure lectures to allow time for feedback.

6. Provide a prompt or cue indicating a time for questions or to signal for participation.

7. Shorten instruction times between question and comment periods.

8. To prevent interruption, have student record items needing instructor attention and share at an appropriate time.

9. Ask student to write down comments he feels are important—frequently ask for his input.

10. Establish a student contract offering several realistic options (numbers 5, 6, 8 and 9 above) to avoid interruptions.

11. Refer the student for counseling, if warranted.

DIFFICULTIES IN MEETING ASSIGNMENT COMPLETION REQUIREMENTS

1. Develop a purpose for time limits. Give student reason for limits or eliminate them and change limits.
2. Begin with a time frame in which the student can achieve success. Gradually shorten time length, with student monitoring his/her improved time — Provide reinforcement.
3. Eliminate unnecessary time-consuming behaviors (time off task, poor organization, errors that require correction). Analyze the reasons behind student's slow production rate (lack of ability, need for pre-requisite skills, poor strategies, etc.) and then work with the student to develop strategies that will improve assignment completion time.
4. Insure that student has materials organized for task completion before beginning. If all materials are present, student may need assistance in organizing them most efficiently (i.e., right-to-left orientation, sequentially, etc.).
5. Provide time cues so student begins pacing himself/herself, a manual timer is helpful.
6. Provide written schedules or checklists, possibly broken down by task. Have the student cross off items when completed to promote a sense of accomplishment.
7. Ask for parent reinforcement, such as practice at home.
8. Begin with a reduced workload, gradually increasing amount to be accomplished. Provide reinforcement for improvement.
9. Reduce distractions.
10. Use buddy system by pairing student with a peer who meets time standards.
11. Utilize specific diary for student to keep records.
12. Establish a set time for individual skills or tasks as a goal for the student.
13. Provide practice time in class.
14. Evaluate student more often in order to determine level or amount of improvement.
15. Provide good role model.

TENDENCIES TOWARD OVERLY DEPENDENT BEHAVIORS

1. Attempt to reduce the desirability of teacher attention by stressing the value of independent working habits.
2. Make an agreement with the student that the teacher will check with him, rather than the student approaching the teacher. Gradually lengthen period of time between contacts.
3. Remember to reinforce student for NOT seeking attention, by providing it when it is not demanded. This is easy to forget when the student is working alone, but very effective.

4. Ignore demands for attention that are dependency-related, explaining that you will get back to the student after work is completed.
5. Establish a nonverbal cue with the student to tell him that you recognize him; nod, smile, provide eye-contact, walk towards or near the student. Reduce nonverbal cues as need decreases.
6. Provide personal attention unexpectedly, before student requests it and when student is working.
7. Move around the room frequently and touch base with the student.
8. Provide the student with a buddy or partner.
9. Involve parents in planning to reduce this behavior. It is probably happening at home and parent involvement in the plan will help you and the family.
10. Encourage all students to reinforce each other. Establish an atmosphere for mutual support in the classroom.
11. Arrange out-of-class time for personal attention.

UNACCEPTABLE WORK

1. At the beginning of each project, clearly establish specifications or standards which are acceptable. Provide a list of the criteria. Do not lower standards for handicapped student.
2. Provide examples of the ranges of quality which are acceptable.
3. Establish a level of quality at which the task must be redone or corrected.
4. Provide the opportunity for repetition and practice before the student begins a task.
5. Provide the opportunity for correction of work or improvement of skill. Reinforce the student's attempt to improve or correct work.
6. Encourage student to compare his completed task with predetermined standard or example. Provide time at the end of each work period for student to evaluate his own product.
7. Check back with the student frequently and review completed work.
8. Allow student to visit other classes and see similar projects.
9. Discuss reasons for minimum quality expectations.
10. Have the class set standards as a group, and evaluate each others work.
11. Involve the student in the work and performance evaluations.
12. Provide review of or instruction in entry level skills of the task (math processes, terminology, vocabulary).

ENCOURAGING INDEPENDENCE

1. Make sure the task is at the student's level. Break task down into sequential steps. Give clear directions.
2. Make sure activities are realistic for the student. Know the student's strengths and weaknesses.
3. Be sure the student is aware of the end and purpose of the task.

4. Seat student near teacher for more frequent checks, attempting to gradually lengthen the period of time between contacts.
5. Be sure student understands directions. Have student repeat the directions back to you. Develop a checklist of sequential steps for student to check off.
6. Reinforce correct completion of task by assigning high interest activities for those who finish their work independently.
7. Have student work through a task once with a peer or a buddy, and then redo it independently.
8. Set up learning centers or work stations so that each student can progress at his own pace.
9. Demonstrate importance of independent work habits—bring in guest speaker from the community to demonstrate this.
10. Assign individual projects that relate to student's high interest area.
11. Give small assignments that can be accomplished successfully, gradually increasing amount of work to be done independently. Task analyze all areas.
12. Tell the student that he is capable of working independently, reinforce him when individual tasks are completed.
13. Give the student leadership responsibilities occasionally.
14. Help the students develop a sense of pride and accomplishment in doing their own work. Ask the student to express how she feels about the accomplishment of tasks.
15. Provide an atmosphere where the student sees individual work as a sign of personal responsibility and growth.
16. Isolate the students' work areas, if distraction is a problem.
17. Make direct contact with the student often (eye contact, verbal, physical, etc.).

DEVELOPING ORGANIZATIONAL AND PLANNING SKILLS

1. Help the student get organized by requiring a notebook or folder. Label and index it for the student if necessary.
2. Write due dates on chalkboards and on handouts.
3. Assign projects within specified time frames. The first tasks are those which can be completed in short amounts of time and gradually assign tasks requiring more time for completion.
4. Supply time sheets for the student to complete for each assignment, project, etc.
5. Monitor student on a regular basis to prevent falling behind.
6. List the class assignments and the dates they are due somewhere in the classroom. Remind the student to refer to the list.
7. Provide assignment sheets to other support personnel who are involved with the student.
8. Provide written schedules of daily or weekly events that will occur. Provide an extra copy to other staff members working with the student as well as the student.

9. Keep extra supplies and copies of materials on hand.
10. Review with the student the amount of time required to complete tasks. Encourage him to develop a checklist.
11. Have the student keep a daily log of activities.

DEALING WITH A SHORT ATTENTION SPAN

1. Provide physical clues during instruction (writing on board, using charts, etc.) to direct student's attention back on task.
2. Provide personal cues such as maintaining eye contact, touching the student's shoulder, pointing, writing on the chalkboard, etc. to keep the student's attention.
3. Provide an outline for the student and don't deviate from it during presentations of lectures.
4. Give short presentations rather than a long instruction period and interject hands-on activities between instructional sequences.
5. Vary instructional techniques: presentations, assignments with buddy, cooperative educational groups, puppetry, experiments, visual aides.
6. Have students repeat sequence of steps and main ideas. Avoid yes and no questions during discussions.
7. Encourage the student to mentally visualize each step of spoken and written instruction. Have him repeat steps back to you.
8. Don't deviate from the subject matter; reword the main concepts frequently.

STAYING IN SEAT OR STUDY AREA

1. Specifically outline the study area, verbally or with chalk or masking tape if necessary.
2. Make sure the student knows the teacher expectations for time spent in study area and appropriate reasons for leaving.
3. If possible, place student in a study area free of distractions.
4. Move around the room to be physically close to student and answer questions as they arise.
5. Build in appropriate opportunities for movement. Provide structured breaks.
6. Determine reasons why the student is leaving study area. Discuss the reasons why he is leaving.
7. Develop a baseline to help identify the number of times the student leaves the work station and develop approaches and strategies for increasing time at study station.
8. Develop a nonverbal cue to let the student know he has left his study area too often.
9. Restructure tasks that are beyond the student's independent work level.

STAYING ON TASK

1. Make sure student is able to do task—begin with less difficult tasks and gradually increase level of difficulty.
2. Limit (as much as possible) noise level in the classroom. Reduce distractions. Isolate student if necessary.
3. Use rewards (bonus points, free time, valued assignments) for students who stay on task.
4. Develop a reason for the task, make it relevant to the student so it fits into a larger picture.
5. Develop a buddy system so students can monitor each others progress.
6. Provide short breaks during a tedious task or reinforce a percentage of completed study with a break.
7. With the student, separate the tasks into subtasks and provide a checklist and time schedule so the student can monitor his task completion. Consider the use of a timer.
8. Identify student's individual study area or study station.
9. Check back with student frequently and provide positive reinforcement.
10. For the student's personal awareness, identify the frequency of distracting behaviors. Work with him to decrease the amount of off-task behavior.
11. Have the student develop a daily log of tasks to be completed.
12. Review the previous days assignments and tasks completed.
13. Make sure each task has a stopping place or ending point.
14. Give the student a cue, either verbally or nonverbally, to return to task.

DISPLAYS EMOTIONAL PROBLEMS

1. Provide an isolation booth or "office."
2. Give assigned tasks in small units followed quickly with an immediate assignment of the next unit of work.
3. Give opportunity for tension release through light muscle activity between periods of study and work.
4. Establish a cue with the students that directs his attention back on task.
5. Provide a progress chart.
6. Provide an award for student successfully staying on task.

FABRICATION OR CHEATING

1. Avoid accusing the student in front of the class. Do not allow other students to publicly accuse the student.
2. Clearly identify consequences for cheating and be consistent with follow through.
3. Prevent the need or the opportunity for cheating by requiring original work only under circumstances you can control.

4. Give alternative type of tests which are less competitive or stressful, such as open book, take home or project completion.
5. Explain the use of student evaluation and testing to the student so that he understands its purpose.
6. Look objectively at the criteria for success and failure in your program, to assure that they are fair and reasonable.
7. Allow the students to correct their own work, or have students correct each others work.
8. Be available to answer questions. Set aside a specific time and/or place for this.
9. Isolate the offending student's work area.
10. Move the student closer to the instructor.
11. Provide additional time for the completion of assignments or tests, if this appears to be the reason the student is cheating.

DISRUPTS CLASS AND OVERLY ASSERTIVE

1. Establish base rules and consequences and consistently enforce them for all students. Clearly define classroom behavior limits and consequences for violation of limits.
2. As the instructor, provide a model for the verbal respect and self-control. Avoid using sarcasm or harassment with students.
3. Set the tone you want in your classroom. Encourage students to treat each other with respect, both verbally and with actions.
4. Do role-playing situations where the student is verbally disrespectful, with consequences. Use brainstorming to identify appropriate alternatives for handling the situation.
5. Discuss privately with the student those behaviors that are disruptive and unacceptable. Ask the student for an explanation of the behaviors and the source of frustration.
6. Remove the student from the situation causing him to be disrespectful. Point out to the student what is a constructive conversation or action and what is disrespectful.
7. Establish a nonverbal cue to let the student know his behavior is getting out-of-hand.
8. Help the student identify alternative words or actions to use in times of stress.
9. Don't encourage this behavior by tolerating it, address the problem immediately.
10. Draw up a behavior contract with the student who is having difficulty. Establish amounts of time, starting small and gradually increasing, where the student controls the behavior. Be sure to follow through on this, both with rewards and punishments.
11. Isolate the student who is having repeated difficulty.
12. Initiate a meeting with the counselor, special education contact person, student, and parent to identify strategies.

13. Reward the student for showing respect.
14. If the behavior or language is being used to get attention, ignore the language or behavior which appears to be inflammatory. The behavior may increase initially but should gradually decrease. Give the student the attention he seeks as a result of positive behaviors.

WORKING WITH SELF CONCEPT

1. Find out the student's strengths and build on those; ask questions, attend an activity in which he is participating, demonstrate some level of interest in the student. Relate the strengths to classroom work.
2. Find tasks the student can do efficiently, such as writing schedules or assignments on the chalkboard, locating materials, taking attendance, cleaning, managing computer supplies or materials. Use these activities as starters, being careful not to eliminate other class activities, or set the student apart.
3. Voice your approval of good working habits, positive growth in any area, and work well done. Recognize small changes.
4. Encourage student to talk about himself, make note of comments you can turn to positive actions in the classroom.
5. Recognize student regularly by greeting him daily, ask about weekends, holidays, events, etc.
6. Do not use student's problems as a basis for negative examples to other students.
7. Give small attainable assignments, gradually increasing amounts as student progresses.
8. Working with the student, identify specific goals for a two- to four-week period and develop a progress chart. Check off goals as they are met.
9. Provide a student or adult aide to assist with critical components. Be cautious that the aide doesn't DO the work for the student.
10. Communicate concern and understanding of all student's abilities.
11. Establish a climate of fairness and support to the student.
12. Time attention and positive reinforcement helps to change negative feelings, but must be given honestly and sincerely.
13. When possible reduce classroom pressures; such as competition for your attention, timed-tasks.

ROLE IN AND SEQUENCE OF BEHAVIORAL EVENTS

1. Specifically identify classroom rules and regulations. Make a chart or some kind of visual display.
2. List in the same order as the rules, the consequences of breaking rules, carried out to the letter. Don't include anything that can't be followed through.
3. Provide instruction and practice on identifying consequences of behavior,

such as using safety films, employers as guest speakers, or having students role-play related situations.

4. Relate circumstances where an accident or near catastrophe took place due to someone's lack of awareness.
5. Ask that the exceptional student be observed by special needs coordinator for suggestions for developing these abilities.
6. Demonstrate basic precautions to be taken to avoid accidents in the classroom.
7. Reinforce critical safety rules as often as possible.
8. Explain direct and indirect consequences of behavior (such as establishing a bad reputation, invoking limited privileges, developing poor peer relations, getting poor grades, or having problems getting and holding a job).

PERSONAL PROBLEM SOLVING

1. Arrange time outside of class period for personal attention.
2. Assist the student in identifying and listing problem areas. Work to solve one at a time, and reinforce positive changes, however small.
3. Encourage students to provide support and reinforcement for each other.
4. Move around the room often and touch base with the student. Be available to help with problem areas in a friendly and supportive way.
5. Be objective. Try not to prejudge student in light of their special education label or previous experiences.
6. Encourage the students to talk with you at an appropriate time, and then carefully listen to what is being said.
7. Share with counselor, support personnel, and the student, the problems which have surfaced. Refer the student for counseling if necessary.
8. Mutually decide on a plan of action, establish time lines, provide reinforcement and follow up.
9. Encourage the student to make her own decisions. Provide reinforcement as the student tries and gains confidence in decision-making skills.

DIFFICULTIES IN PERSONAL ROLE AND BEHAVIOR

1. Identify the appropriate behaviors which are expected from all students.
2. Use role playing exercises to outline and demonstrate appropriate values and behaviors.
3. In a private meeting with the student, identify the specific inappropriate behavior, how often it occurs, and in what situations. Target one or two behaviors to work on and a time line for checking back. Reinforce changes.
4. Establish a nonverbal cue with the student to let her know that behaviors are getting out-of-hand (shaking of the head, touch on the shoulder, etc.).
5. Provide some personal contact time for the student.
6. Videotape all students during work time to initiate class discussion on appropriate work and interpersonal behaviors.

7. Identify societal values and how they relate to the work process.
8. Encourage the student to express motives and values on a one-to-one basis and to each other.
9. Separate student from those peers who have a bad influence and assign each to a different task.
10. Ask the students to discriminate between the views and opinions of different friends.
11. Discourage student from identifying with peers who exhibit extreme behaviors.
12. Identify what terms the student uses when labeling himself; stupid, dumb, retarded, delinquent, etc. Reclassify self-labeling terms with more mature, more definite descriptive terms, such as speech impairment, short temper, aggressive behavior, etc.
13. Provide direct instruction in group processes.
14. Provide the student with a specific responsibility or position of leadership.
15. Utilize a partner in the classroom to help the student monitor his own behavior.
16. Portray a good role model.
17. Identify and reinforce all appropriate behavior in the classroom.
18. Refer to special education or other resource person for counseling.

COMPLETING READING ASSIGNMENTS

1. Make sure that reading materials are clearly printed or copied, that there is adequate light, and the area is free from distraction, if possible.
2. Introduce reading activities with a related filmstrip or movie.
3. Teach techniques for skimming and scanning materials.
4. Shorten reading assignments by having students read only first, last, and key sentences within the paragraphs.
5. Deemphasize the amount of time it takes to finish a reading assignment, emphasize completion and accuracy.
6. Provide reading materials and assignments to special education personnel or other resource for additional instruction.
7. Provide additional time for reading assignments for the slower reader. Encourage her to schedule the extra time needed for studying. Allow student to have reading material at home or during study hour to complete assignments.
8. Provide an outline of the required reading assignments ahead of time, with due dates.
9. Provide worksheets with important vocabulary, key facts, major concepts defined and summaries of critical material.
10. Schedule time for group discussions regarding content of reading related assignments.
11. Provide demonstrations that relate to the reading materials.
12. Provide student with a reader if material must be covered in a specific time frame.

13. Highlight key concepts in reading materials. If possible, mark book sections you want student to concentrate on.
14. Teach strategies for good reading comprehension (emphasizing introductions, initial paragraph sentences, titles and summaries).
15. Arrange to have materials recorded on cassette tape.
16. Break down reading assignments into small sections (small reading assignments each day rather than one large assignment at the end of the week).
17. Have a daily or weekly time set aside for free reading in which the student can choose whatever he wants to read.
18. Read aloud to the students each day to develop an interest in reading for fun.
19. If available, use reading consultant, tutor, or aide.
20. Reward the student for staying on task even when it's hard.
21. Let the student know that you understand and can allow, within reason, extra time.

DIFFICULTIES IN INFORMATION SEARCH

1. Teach student where information is available (textbooks, occupational directories, manuals, etc.) and show them how to use resources. Provide students with opportunities to practice with and become proficient in the use of resources. Model the use of resources by frequently referring to them yourself.
2. Equip your classroom with a variety of informational resources.
3. Spend time teaching the class how to use manuals, charts and other materials. Review the use of the index, topic headings, etc.
4. Make a reference manual specifically designed for your classroom. Include common problems, vocabulary, and where to find specific information, etc. In the classroom, label all reference materials, and organize the materials available in the class by subject area.
5. Teach or review how to find information located in a point, bar and line graph. Provide instruction and practice in identifying units of measure.
6. Review texts for usefulness. Ask your curriculum resource consultant or reading specialist for assistance.
7. Teach skimming and scanning techniques.
8. Plan time to review texts, manuals, and resources with students. Explain the purpose and procedure for using the table of contents, index, glossary, appendices, and supplemental charts, diagrams, and materials.
9. Review and explain all alphabetical and numerical cataloging systems. Provide practice in using these systems.
10. Color code materials if possible, or catalog and structure material storage for easy student access.
11. Verbally emphasize key points to be stresses in text.
12. Have the students practice outlining the key text areas.
13. During class discussions have other students tell the class on what page, section, etc. . . . the information is contained.

14. Check with librarian or media specialist or other resource person to see if the students have had instruction in the use of reference materials.
15. As the student reads the material, have him highlight or mark the key areas. Explain how to select the materials or areas to be highlighted, first and last sentences, key words, summaries, etc.

PROBLEMS ORGANIZATIONALLY AND SEQUENTIALLY

1. Condense information, using basic terms, so student isn't overwhelmed with information to sequence.
2. Teach the student to identify or highlight key action verbs within written directions.
3. Outline the purpose of assignments or tasks. Provide examples of the finished product when possible or appropriate.
4. Insure that directions are written at the reading level of the student.
5. Provide information or written directions, well in advance. If directions relate to a procedure to be followed later, provide an organizational system for easy access.
6. Demonstrate how each event is dependent on the preceding event, so the students can see the logic of the sequence.
7. Sequence your own instruction so you establish a pattern for the student. Highlight by outlining or diagramming the desired sequence of events.
8. Provide memory hooks. For example, you might teach a word in which each letter sequentially stands for an event. (Acronyms)
9. If directions contain several steps listed in a paragraph, place a symbol (colored mark or stop sign) at the end of each step or number the steps.
10. Develop symbols for key action words found in written directions. Provide in listed format.
11. Provide pictures of the different tasks. Have students put them in order.
12. Have student repeat information or events orally in order or in written form before proceeding with assignment.
13. Provide hands-on experience starting with simple sequential activities, moving to more complex.
14. Preteach information, telling the student what he will learn.
15. Type worksheets, tests, etc., rather than hand writing them.
16. Provide a checklist of job tasks for students to follow.
17. Have students develop a calendar for completion of specific assignments. Provide a master calendar for classroom events and activities for students to follow.
18. Sequence work by providing easiest problems first to build up confidence.
19. Check students progress frequently to insure they have followed proper sequence or procedure.

DIFFICULTIES IN WRITTEN ASSIGNMENT SPELLING

1. Develop a classroom dictionary in which the students put in new words that they learn. Also include terms and definitions that are commonly used in the classroom.
2. Post unit-related terms on the board or on hand-outs. Insist on correct spelling of all posted terms.
3. Have available reference materials; dictionaries, pocket dictionaries, lists of the most commonly spelled words, The Bad Speller's Dictionary, and phonetic dictionaries.
4. Pair students to proofread each other's work before handing in assignments. This may not catch all errors, but will develop an awareness of spelling.
5. Provide a four to five minute period at the end of a written assignment specifically for proofing work. Have a number of dictionaries and other resources available.
6. Provide a related spelling list of critical terms (share with special education teacher). Point out clues that will help with memory (i.e., smaller words within a larger word).
7. Provide written backup (overhead projector, chalkboard, etc.) during lecture.
8. Label materials, objects, and equipment in the classroom.
9. Set a standard regarding appropriate spelling.
10. Have the student compose original sentences using spelling words.
11. Evaluate written work with two grades; one for content and one for spelling and grammar.
12. Present jumbled letters of spelling words and have the students unscramble them. You can also use crossword puzzles as a fun way to practice spelling.

READING TEXTBOOKS, CHARTS, GRAPHS, TESTS, ETC.

1. Minimize words, keeping instructions clear and concise.
2. Use an outline of directions, or illustrate with simple drawings. Use a rebus, incorporating pictures with key terms.
3. Arrange to have critical material taped for the student.
4. Arrange for a volunteer to read the material to the student, preferably a student from another class or an adult volunteer.
5. Request materials from special education which have a lower reading level than the text, but the same basic content.
6. Verbalize the necessary information, demonstrate, and use cue cards.
7. Outline important facts or points on the board or in a hand-out. Condense the materials to include only the important information.
8. Provide tactile representation of the charted material.
9. Avoid cluttered graphs, encourage spacing and clear labels.
10. Ask special education personnel to teach the student the specific skills necessary to see correlation between tangible and graphic representations.

11. Give tests orally or ask support personnel to do so for you.
12. Use typed rather than handwritten tests or worksheets.
13. Have students alternate in reading material out loud, preferably in small groups or situations that wouldn't embarrass the poor reader.
14. Ask the student to demonstrate the skill you are evaluating and test him on his performance.
15. Allow student to complete unfinished reading assignment in special education classroom. Do not automatically send student there when the rest of the class is reading, rather support his attempts and encourage improvement.
16. Establish a schedule outside of class time when the student may receive specialized instruction.

DIFFICULTIES IN READING COMPREHENSION

1. Discuss and teach techniques for utilizing a textbook effectively:
   a. Key in on all titles and headings first, to get an outline idea of the book or chapter's concept.
   b. Read introductory paragraphs and summary paragraphs.
   c. Attend to any highlighted vocabulary. If possible, highlight text with yellow marker to key the student in on main ideas.
2. Teach new vocabulary before assigning any regular reading. This is a good preview activity for the whole class and creates a mind set for the material to be covered.
3. Have the student listen to a taped edition of the text.
4. Pair student with a partner who reads well. Have the better reader read each section aloud and then have both students take turns discussing the material with each other. You can also have the students take turns reading aloud to each other, page by page, paragraph by paragraph . . . etc.
5. Provide alternative information sources to the text, for example, easier reading material, filmstrips, films, tapes, lecture, demonstration.
6. Relate reading passages to teacher demonstrations, related audio visual materials, equipment, and other materials.
7. Utilize filmstrips, movies, videotapes whenever possible in place of reading materials.
8. Utilize method where students first survey titles, headings and subheads, then formulate questions out of them. Then they read the passages to answer the questions, recite the answers out loud, and review them at a later time.
9. Develop questions related to the materials at different levels, considering the following factors; the student's ability to recall concrete facts and information, analyze, evaluate and apply information. Contact resource personnel for assistance.
10. When purchasing new reading materials consider materials appropriate to lower reading levels.
11. Provide adaptive or supportive materials, such as charts, graphs, movies,

filmstrips or materials written at a lower grade level, but with the same major concept.

12. Highlight key areas in textbook, drawing attention to specific and critical areas in the book.

13. Outline the key concepts to be found in written materials.

14. Use worksheets which ask for information you want and provide page numbers on which it will be found. Provide study questions which direct the student to key concepts.

15. Provide study time when the teacher is available to assist.

16. Arrange with special education or other resources to have written material recorded.

PROBLEMS IN MATH COMPUTATION AND PROBLEM SOLVING

1. Identify minimal math requirements for the course (mastery of addition, subtraction and multiplication facts one through ten). Request resource teacher, student and parents to make fact mastery a priority, practicing at home and school with flashcards, worksheets, computer software, etc.

2. Provide calculators and other support equipment such as manipulative rods, blocks or other available hands-on materials. Work with special education personnel to assure that the student is taught the skills needed to use a calculator.

3. Student may need practice in math skills and application. Provide additional practice for those skills a student understands through reasonable homework assignments. Correct that work and require all incorrect problems to be redone.

4. Encourage students to use reasoning. Have students TALK THROUGH a problem with you. Utilize class BRAINSTORM sessions to analyze a problem and explore possible solutions. Aim for an atmosphere where suggestions are accepted without ridicule. MODEL PROBLEM SOLVING IN YOUR CLASSROOM.

5. Provide time and examples to the student. Review the entire mathematical or problem-solving procedure. Explain where information for the math calculation came from, why the specific function was used, and whether or not the answer seems reasonable.

6. For problem solving, require the student to first identify the information given and the outcome or questions under consideration. Provide practice in this process.

7. As a teacher, be aware of the math skills necessary for real world situations (making change, figuring tax ...). Set up stations in which the students can practice various skills.

8. Visually display common formulae with examples on charts, graphs, or flash cards.

9. Provide hand-outs or worksheets on a regular basis using the necessary calculations for completion of all math processes.
10. Provide concrete examples to help the student transfer the skill from the class situation to an on-the-job situation.
11. Use role-play to demonstrate consequences of math errors in a job situation (over-charging customers, providing too much change, etc.) so that improving math skills becomes a priority to the student.
12. Have each student make a booklet of all handouts and assignments to use as a reference book for mathematical processes.
13. Allow student pencil and paper to make calculations.
14. Use practical situations as they come up in the classroom to reinforce the learning of math concepts.
15. Provide a chart of formulas, common measurements, etc. which the student can place in his folder for referencing. Do not include basic skills that are critical for task completion, such as multiplication tables, unless it will be a reasonable accommodation in the work environment.

COMPLETING WRITTEN ASSIGNMENTS OR TESTS

1. Provide examples of what kind of written work is expected (set standards).
2. Allow printing, writing, or typing whenever possible.
3. Provide the use of lined paper, graph paper or other structured format.
4. When possible, use formats low on writing for assignments and tests; multiple choice, fill-in the blank.
5. Explain the importance of good writing and the consequences of poor writing in job situations.
6. Allow the use of a tape recorder for assignments, tests, etc.
7. Allow the student to take tests orally.
8. When giving a choice of assignments, include nonwritten choices such as oral reports, demonstrations, construction of models, exhibits, etc.
9. Have student dictate the work to someone else and then have him copy the information himself.
10. Collect examples of student's written work and establish a personal standard. Don't accept less than her best work.
11. Keep written statements short to allow slow writing students to keep up with what is being written and what is being said.
12. Print information on one side of the board at a time (organized and neat). Walk to the other side and continue, then erase the first side and continue.
13. Require proper writing style, body position, and provide the appropriate size tables and chairs.
14. Use an overhead projector, visual aides, or structural overviews for lectures and demonstrations.
15. Supply printed outlines; write main ideas on board. Cue verbally and physically the important points to be recorded.

16. Xerox prepared overheads for students.
17. When using prepared overheads, expose only one item at a time.

TAKING WRITTEN NOTES

1. Have another student take notes for the student. Provide carbon paper, sensitized or NCR paper for the note taker.
2. Allow the use of a tape recorder for classroom notes.
3. Provide an outline in handout form for class discussion topics, lectures, key concepts for each unit.
4. Provide written material (texts, pamphlets, lecture notes) to be highlighted by the student during lectures or discussions.
5. When using an overhead projector, use the roll-up acetate which can be given to the student after the lecture for copying.
6. Xerox any prepared overheads which you use as handouts.
7. Outline main ideas on board while lecturing. REQUIRE students to copy the outline for study purposes.
8. Instead of written assignments, allow demonstrations, oral presentations, construction of models, etc.

DIFFICULTIES IN VARIOUS MEMORY FORMS

1. Present information in a manner that focuses the student's attention on the information you wish for them to recall. This may include outlining main ideas at the chalkboard, stressing and repeating key concepts in your lecture, or illustrating main ideas with pictures, models, etc. Begin all instruction with a brief description of what you want them to learn that day—refer back to each key concept as you elaborate on them—and summarize those concepts again at the end of your presentation.
2. Highlight what you wish them to remember by changing your voice pitch or loudness. Let students know, with some consistent key term (important) what you want them to attend to.
3. Repeat key terms and ideas throughout your lesson.
   a. Begin by explaining briefly what you are going to teach
   b. Provide instruction, again stressing main points
   c. Summarize main points at the end of instruction
   d. Allow students to feed ideas and questions back to you
4. Build on basic memory skills—start simple, remembering one or two items with support devices, or aids and gradually increase amount to be remembered and decrease supportive aids or devices.
5. Develop checklists with the student to assist her in remembering important activities, information, assignments or events.
6. Provide structural study time specifically for memory training.

7. Identify to the student those items, lists, or information that needs to be memorized.
8. Provide eye contact during conversation. Reinforce auditory recall by visual cues.
9. Provide regularity and structure of classroom activities. Try to do instructional activities, lab work, take breaks, skill training, etc. in the same sequence or at the same time daily or weekly.
10. Have the student take notes and keep them in a folder or binder.
11. Frequently review required information.
12. Each day have the student repeat the necessary activities, information, or events which will take place.
13. Refer to parallel situations in which students were involved; remember when we did this last week.
14. Relate the events to something that is important to the student. Associate an important event with what is expected of them (the assignment must be finished before recess).
15. Make sure events are taught in logical sequences. When an instructor wanders in the lecture, the students have more difficulty retaining the information.
16. Task analyze and break down tasks into easy to follow and understand steps.
17. Provide a syllabus with key ideas and information.
18. Provide time and opportunities for students to explain the ideas back to you.
19. Force students to become active learners. Ask frequent questions—make student response a priority in your instruction.
20. Develop a sequence to be used for task completion and class activities. Follow the same sequence in all tasks, if possible.
21. Try to reward for remembering instead of punishing for forgetting.
22. Use short quizzes instead of long tests.

DIFFICULTIES WITH FOLLOWING ORAL INSTRUCTIONS

1. Sequence directions in a logical order.
2. Limit length and difficulty of directions. For example, say "First put your name on the paper" as opposed to "The first thing I want you to do is take out a pencil and write your name on the paper."
3. Repeat sequence of directions and accompany them with illustrations and checklists.
4. Use visual demonstrations in addition to oral instruction.
5. Begin simply and gradually increase amount and complexity of directions. Provide adequate time for following directions; give one instruction and when student masters it give two, etc.
6. Make sure student is paying attention before instructions are given. Provide a cue that you are about to give directions or provide instructions; flash lights so student knows it is time to watch, or call name of student prior to giving instruction.

7. Provide a checklist, outlining steps of instruction.
8. Look directly at student when giving instruction.
9. Have student repeat given steps or instruction.
10. Establish a consistent or sequence or events so the student can anticipate when directions will be given. Give examples of what will be expected from the student. Teach the meaning of action words used in directions, such as rotate, grind, blend, fasten, etc.

Appendix Two

TEMPERAMENT CHARACTERISTICS
AND INTERVENTION

Materials in this section were developed for the authors as part of a project at Butler University. Special thanks to Gretchen Sullivan.

Activity Level: The motor component present in a given child's functioning and the daily proportion of active and inactive periods. This temperamental quality is not likely to be a factor in school adaptation for the child with average or low level of mobility.]

CHARACTERISTICS of the child who has a high activity level:
1. He wiggles and squirms in his seat.
2. He drops things.
3. He plays with things.
4. He gets involved in activities with a nearby classmate.
5. He gets out of his seat often.
6. He usually hears only part of the teachers directions and then gets involved trying to find out the remainder of them from a classmate.
7. He usually does not have his place when reading.

CAUSES of high activity level:
1. A child who is just not physically and mentally mature enough for school.
2. Child has unstable home.
3. Child has had too many failures at home or at school.
4. Child wants teacher's attention.

SUGGESTED activities for the child with a high activity level:
1. Make a checklist to see if the child really has a high activity level, to see what time of day is most difficult for him, and to see what objects bother him.
2. Once the problem of behavior has been established, explain to the child what you are going to do, determine a reward for him, decide what time of day you are trying to eliminate the behavior, and continue to keep records. (Gradually decrease the reward as the child improves.)
3. Teacher must be patient—repeat directions pleasantly—make directions simple— avoid expressions of annoyance.
4. Teacher could have a signal (ring a bell) to get the children's attention and to slow them down. They must stop and listen to the directions when they hear the signal.

5. Structure this child's activities so that he has just certain things to do during a specific time. The teacher could use a timer.
6. Mark his papers immediately after he finishes.
7. Break the child's day into short segments until he is able to handle longer periods of working at his desk.
8. Make arrangements for this child to get short periods of motor activity throughout the day. This could be done by allowing him to go to other gym classes, by assigning an older student to do exercises with him or by having the whole class do exercises at timed intervals.
9. Make the child a helper in class to run errands, pass papers, etc.
10. A small section of the room could be divided off by using screens. large pieces of cardboard, etc. to give the child some place to go and do some exercises without disturbing the others in the class.
11. The teacher might even ignore the child to see if this would slow the child down.
12. The teacher could do the reverse and give the child all her attention and as the child improves the teacher could give her attention to the other children.

APPROACH OR WITHDRAWAL: The nature of the child's responses to a new food, object, person, method, or academic subject. The child with high approach ability responds positively to new stimuli, new people, places, toys, and learning demands. Other children may initially withdraw from new situations, but be able to deal with them later after many exposures. This is the child that "warms up slowly."

CHARACTERISTICS of the child's withdrawal/approach to things:
1. He may adjust to new people but not to new situations.
2. He may be able to adjust to new situations, people, objects, food, and methods only after many exposures to them.
3. He is insecure.
4. He may seem to lack self-confidence.
5. He may refuse to try new equipment, food, books, methods, etc.
6. He may look to others for protection in a new situation.
7. He may lag behind the rest of the class appearing to have difficulty mastering the material.
8. He may be unable to do things when the teacher is near.
9. He may have a temper tantrum or cry because he is unable to cope with the new things.

CAUSES of the child with withdrawal approach:
1. A very structured, protected life at home.
2. Child may have been deprived to the point of not knowing what to do with the new information.
3. Child may use this to get the things he wants. In effect he may be saying, "Play it my way, or I won't participate."

4. Maybe a defense mechanism used against people for frustration from a loved adult.
5. Child just has not had the experience of interacting with others.
6. Child may use this to get the teacher's attention because he has not had enough "tender loving care" at home.

SUGGESTED activities for the child with a withdrawal approach:
1. Use a checklist to determine if the behavior is detrimental and to see when it occurs so that a behavior modification program can be established.
2. Once the problem of behavior has been established, explain to the child what you are going to do, at a level that he will understand. Then determine a reward for this child and determine the time of day or period of time that the improvement of behavior is expected. Continue to keep records so that you may determine if this is improving the behavior or not.
3. Give this child more time to get his work done by assigning less for him to do. Do not confront him with a kind of "shock treatment" based on threats, punishments, etc. Use the careful setting of minutes limits and achievement goals.
4. The teacher must find ways to get the child to participate even if she uses trickery. Place the withdrawing child in a group of nonaggressive children, but somewhat ascendant. This will help him see that participation is fun.
5. New methods and materials can be presented more slowly for this child.
6. New methods and materials can be worked in with the older more familiar things so that the child will feel more secure with it.
7. Be sure to find the child's level of success and present new material from this level, not the level of the class.
8. Find the child's interest and build on it. Introduce new things around this interest.
9. Give this child a duty in the room that he may do for several weeks and become proficient at it. Then have him show the class how to do this task so that he will gain some self-confidence, and it will help his classmates to count on him as part of the "group."
10. Do not draw attention to the child who "warms up" slowly. Find an area that the child performs better in such as art, music, gym, etc. and draw attention to these.
11. If this child appears to use this behavior to get the teacher's attention, ignore the child and observe him. Keep a chart to determine if his behavior gets better or gets worse. If this seems to be working and the child improves, the teacher may gradually give him attention.

ADAPTABILITY: The speed and ease with which current behavior can be modified in response to altered environmental structuring. The highly adaptable child may not engage in new learning procedures, but it may only take him a few exposures to master its meaning. The child with slow adaptability coupled with a negative first reaction to a new scholastic demand will have difficulty.

CHARACTERISTICS of the child with slow adaptability coupled with a negative first reaction:

1. May be last to approach things in a group.
2. He will appear not to try.
3. May appear to lack motivation.
4. Will withdraw from learning situations, especially new situations.
5. He will look to leaders within his peers, teachers, or parents for their reactions to these things.
6. He may refuse to accept help or try. Refusal may be in a form of a tantrum or crying.

CAUSES of slow adaptability:

1. Child has been sheltered or overprotected from new situations. Perhaps his parents have made all the decisions and manipulated his environment for him.
2. Perhaps he has been deprived from environmental situations.
3. His first tries at adjusting to and manipulating new situations were failures and attention was brought upon this by the parents, sisters or brothers, or a teacher.
4. General acceptance from peers, parents, or teachers have not been good.

SUGGESTED activities for the child with slow adaptability:

1. The teacher may use behavior modification techniques.
2. Present new situations and materials whenever possible through familiar situation.
3. Reassurance and acceptance by the teachers, parents, and peers as he goes through a new situation or handles new materials.
4. The teacher may structure the new situation so that he has to go through it just certain steps at a time, very slowly.
5. The teacher may verbally prepare the child, in advance, by having several class discussions or by having several individual discussions with the child.
6. Use very high interest level material for the child to present new things.
7. Have others in the class involve him in group activity. First at something he can do and then by bringing in new materials.
8. The teacher should not discourage the child if he is trying to adapt but not exactly as she wanted him to.
9. Try to counsel the parents in understanding the child's problems and to see their part in the situation.

INTENSITY OF REACTION: The energy level of response irrespective of its quality or direction. These children express their attitudes to stimuli in an intense manner.

CHARACTERISTICS of the child with a high intensity of reaction:

1. If happy, they are exuberant.
2. If friends have a negative reaction to them, they hate them.
3. If teacher does something wrong in "their" eyes, she's a creep.

4. Their acceptance or rejections of things will go from one extreme to another, "love to hate," there is never an in-between.
5. They attempt to influence friends, teachers, parents, etc. but they are seldom successful.
6. He wants to be the center of attention.

CAUSES of high intensity reaction:
1. Child lacks love and attention at home.
2. Child feels that sister or brother receives more attention than he.
3. Child may be getting all the attention at home but not at school.
4. A family member may have the same characteristics and the child is imitating them.
5. This may be his way of resisting to a change.
6. Parents may have a poor attitude towards school and the child may have developed this characteristic to gain favor of parents.
7. Child may be trying to get the teacher's attention.

SUGGESTED activities for the child with high intensity of reaction:
1. The behavior modification technique could be used.
2. Give this child specific things to do in the classroom so that he will get recognition from others.
3. Have him work on special projects as a reward for his good behavior.
4. Have a quiet work area in the room where he may go to be away when you see the negative actions starting and when he begins to feel this come on.
5. Physically placing your hand on the child's arm as he begins to get "wound up" may be enough of a reminder to help change his behavior.
6. The teacher could give the child something to do or change the subject when she begins to realize that the child is getting "wound up."
7. Help the parents to have a better attitude towards school by inviting them to school or by making a phone call to the home just to tell them something positive about their child, or you could make a home visit.
8. Try to guide the parents in their understanding of what they are doing to the child by giving him all the attention. Do this by telling the parents the positive side of their child first.
9. The teacher should be patient with the child—never let him see how upset" she may get from his intense reactions.
10. Instead of giving the child attention when he is wound up, perhaps the teacher should give her attention to another child to see if this will stop the intense reaction.
11. Have another teacher take an interest in the child and his progress of learning to control his reactions.

THRESHOLD OF RESPONSIVENESS: The intensity level of stimulation required to evoke a discernable response to stimuli, environmental objects, and social contacts.

CHARACTERISTICS of the child with a high threshold of responsiveness:

1. Child feels and reacts as if fate is against him. He knows "the teacher isn't going to ask that".
2. Child spends most of his time studying what he considers important only to find this is just one-fifth of the total examination.
3. High threshold to visual stimulation.
4. High threshold to auditory stimulation.
5. High threshold to tactile stimulation.
6. He is destructive in the normal classroom, but high thresholds may help in music or art.
7. He needs things repeated to him often.
8. He may give up easily.
9. He may often center his attention around things that have very little to do with what is going on in the room.

CAUSES of high threshold of responsiveness:
1. Culturally deprived child.
2. A home situation where a parent or parents are very dominant and the child has lived in turmoil.
3. The child may be very immature due to the fact that he is the only child, or the only boy or girl, and has been allowed to do anything that he wants to do.
4. Child may lack development in the areas of vision, auditory, or tactile because he is shutting the outside world off to dominate brothers or sisters, parents, teachers; or because a traumatic shock like the death of a parent.

SUGGESTED activities for the child with a high threshold of responsiveness:
1. Find a quiet part of the room to study in.
2. Present the material to the child in several ways and several times whenever possible; use concrete, semiconcrete, and abstract methods.
3. Be patient, repeat material, give more visual and more tactile cues when needed.
4. Divide the class to work in teams or groups whenever possible. Be sure this child has a teammate that will be patient and has a low threshold response.
5. Give the child a specific list of things to study. The list may be verbal, visual or both.
6. A tape recorder and tapes could be made of the assignments so that the child could use this in a less destructible place with an earphone whenever he wanted.
7. Use many pictures, filmstrips, and films to help the child. He may be able to go to the library or another room to see these if it is not necessary for the whole class.
8. Help him verbalize his understanding of things by giving leading questions or words.
9. Channel his attention to other things such as projects for class activities.
10. Make all directions simple.

QUALITY OF MOOD: The amount of pleasant, joyful, or friendly behavior as contrasted with unpleasant, unfriendly behavior or crying.

CHARACTERISTICS of a child with a poor quality of mood:
1. Unfriendly.
2. Unpleasant.
3. Unhappy.
4. Usually not accepted by individuals or the "group."
5. A negative attitude toward most everything.
6. Disagrees with the teacher.
7. Child may verbalize that he is being picked on.

CAUSES for the poor quality of mood:
1. Not enough early approval or attention as growing up.
2. Lacks self-confidence due to much failure.
3. Parents have the defeatist attitude and the child associates with this.
4. Teacher may have a defeatist attitude for the child to associate with.
5. Child has not been accepted by others or himself.
6. Child may be spoiled by the parents.
7. Child may come from a very deprived environment.

SUGGESTED activities for the child with poor quality mood:
1. Don't try to put this child in his place, he may have something to give.
2. Explore the child's disagreements and try to pick out something that the class can learn from him.
3. Compliment the child on something that he has done to build up his acceptance of you. Be sure that this compliment is sincere.
4. Give him projects to do in the class or outside the class and have him present it to the class. This will help the class to accept him.
5. Divide the class into small groups giving this child a project to do in the group. Manipulate arrangements of the groups so that he will get in a group that will be more likely to accept him.
6. Ask this child to help another child in the class that may be having difficulty with something he can do.
7. The teacher may need to take a good look at the child. He or she may be having problems and is taking it out on the class.
8. A class discussion on the deprived child may be conducted on a day that this child is not in the class in order to help the other classmates understand.
9. For the child that has been spoiled, the behavior modification technique may be one of the best methods to handle this characteristic.

DISTRACTIBILITY: The effectiveness of extraneous environmental stimuli in interfering with, or in altering the direction of on-going behavior.

CHARACTERISTICS of a destractable child:
1. Any extraneous stimuli going on influences the child. (A child drops a pencil, the principal passing the door, a friend with his fancy new watch.)
2. He usually is thinking about things that have very little to do with class.
3. More often than not he will have difficulty sitting still and will move around the room freely.
4. Doesn't hear all the instructions given for an assignment.

5. Can't keep his place when reading or when someone else is reading.
6. Becomes frustrated when he does not understand what is going on.

CAUSES for the highly distractible child:
1. Child comes from a home that has very little stimulation in it.
2. Or the reverse, the child comes from a home where there is a constant "turmoil."
3. A very nervous or unstable mother during early development of the child.
4. The teacher may be presenting the lesson in a "slow" methodical manner.
5. The teacher may be very distractible person herself.

SUGGESTED activities for the child with high distractibility:
1. Find a quiet place in the room for this child to work.
2. Use moveable screens, cardboard or dividers to shield the child from extraneous stimuli.
3. Give the child only the necessities to work with.
4. Use the behavior modification technique.
5. Make a page cover so that the child will not be distracted by other pictures or problems on the page.
6. Structure the material presented to the child:
   a. Material at his level.
   b. Limited amount of material.
   c. Immediate scoring of the material.
   d. Directions clear and simple—one step at a time.
7. Teacher needs to reduce her verbalization.
8. Try blindfolding the child for a short period of time so that he will hear only class recitation. A tape recorder could be used in place of a true situation.
9. The tactile stimulation of the teacher's hand on the child's arm or shoulder will sometimes be enough of a reminder to return to the task.

ATTENTION SPAN AND PERSISTENCE: These two categories are related. Attention span concerns the length of time a particular activity is pursued by the child. Persistence refers to the continuation of an activity in the face of the obstacles to maintenance of the activity.

CHARACTERISTICS of a child with short attention span and low persistence:
1. Child withdraws attention from a topic before the teacher has finished.
2. Child doesn't know what he is to do on the assignments.
3. Child may be moving around the room going from one thing to another.
4. Child prefers fantasy to reality.
5. Child engages in repetitive behavior which interferes with learning.

CAUSES of a child with short attention span and low persistence:
1. Child has been spoiled at home and has not had any expectations placed upon him and thus has not matured.
2. The teacher is presenting the material at the wrong level for the child.
3. There has been no structuring in the home for the child.

4. The parents have the same problem as the child thus setting a poor example for the child to imitate.
5. Child may have continuously failed at things as he was developing.
6. Child may be trying to get the teacher's attention.

SUGGESTED activities for the child with short attention span and low persistence:

1. Use the behavior modification techniques:
    a. Point-out the behavior
    b. Record the behavior
    c. Consequate the behavior
2. Try switching the mode or channel the material is presented on until you find the one he learns best by.
3. Heighten the vividness and the impact of the stimuli.
4. Use a timer when giving him the material to work on. At first make the time short and as he begins to improve, lengthen the time.
5. Break up the child's day so that he does not have great lengths of time to sit at his desk.
6. Find the child's areas of interest and present new material around this or give special projects to help lengthen the low persistence.
7. Present material with which the child will have success. Be sure to mark his papers immediately after they are finished.
8. Programmed instructional material should be tried.
9. If teaching machines are available, try these.
10. Use various games to increase interest: (Flashlight Game—Lights off, the teacher flashes the light around the room, stopping at various words or objects and the child is asked to identify them.
11. Try ignoring the lack of attention for a period of time. Keep a record and see if the child's attention improves when he isn't getting the attention from you that he expected.

Appendix Three

SOCIAL SKILL DEVELOPMENT

These materials were, in part provided by the Special Education Division of the Department of Education in the State of Indiana.

Social Skill: AGGRESSIVENESS causing physical harm to others.

Definition: Inability of the child to control overt activity, and to repress hostile feelings.

Illustration: Pupil has self-control around others and is willing to respond to discipline for overt acts.

Anxiety States Contributing to Behavior:
1. Aggressiveness may be a result of overindulgence or overprotection associated with parental rejection.
2. It may be symptomatic of inconsistent and unfair disciplinary measures.
3. It may be a result of some inhibition or intimidation within his environment.

SUGGESTED APPROACHES:
1. Seek and eliminate the cause of aggressiveness. Discipline should not be physical use of the same force which the child is being taught not to use.
2. Create ways to work with others in a well-monitored situation. Praise group efforts. Encourage class recognition for successes.
3. Do not allow aggressive behavior to serve as a bid for attention. The adult must set the attitude for the remainder of the class conduct and must insure that the aggressiveness does not serve attention-getting needs.
4. Provide opportunities for aggressive play activities that give some unrestricted physical activity without hostility.
5. Establish clear-cut expectations and consistent routines.
6. Assign a mature child as a monitor, who has the respect of the aggressive child, to help the pupil who cannot handle it in a nonpunitive fashion and who sees this as a means to gain aggressive control.
7. Use behavior modification procedures by reinforcing nonaggressive behaviors.

Social Skill: BAD LANGUAGE

Definition: Use of inappropriate or unacceptable language, obscene language or swearing.

Illustration: Pupil has a sense of being able to refrain from use of generally accepted vulgar communication and swear words.

Anxiety States Contributing to Behavior:
1. Bad language may be a defense against forces opposing student.
2. It may be an expression of hostility.
3. It may be appropriate to a certain value system and be culturally determined.
4. It may be a temporary emotional release, a reaction to frustration.
5. It may be an emulation of an adult status symbol.

SUGGESTED APPROACHES:
1. Carefully define limits of acceptance. Discuss importance of appropriate language choice. Delineate clearly that it is the language that is not acceptable, not the individual.
2. Avoid excessive punishment; it may make the child resentful. Bad language may be used as a weapon to get even when he needs a deep desire for retaliation.
3. Avoid conveying shock or abhorrence; this makes the act more attractive. If the language is used for eliciting a reaction from authority, the reaction must not add to the pleasure.
4. Determine if the language use is imitation or modeling a terminology common to the child's family. If this is so, assist the child to make judgments on the appropriateness of bad language in a school or public setting. Help him to substitute more socially appropriate language.
5. Assist the child to resolve frustration in a more acceptable fashion. If the behavior is the result of emotional tension, find other means if dissipating the tension. Help to raise frustration tolerance by encouraging appropriate effort and by offering help to solve difficult problems. Reinforce situations where emotions have been controlled. Provide a satisfactory substitute for releasing tensions and resolving frustrations such as discussion sessions, or physical activity. Provide opportunity for varied activity and time-out periods before tension builds up.

Social Skill: BACK–TALK

Definition: Use of impertinent language, or acts suggesting defiance of authority and regulations.

Illustration: Pupil has developed an ability to accept correction, to refrain from impertinence or deliberate disregard of regulations and authority figures.

Anxiety States Contributing to Behavior:
1. Disrespectful back-talk may imply feeling that individual is not worthy of regard.
2. It may imply that a learned appropriate response has never been required, and that an offensive manner is the expected manner of behavior.
3. It may be the result of being "tricked into" conformity so that the pupil has lost respect for adult authority.
4. It may be the result of excessive and inappropriate use of physical force as a means of discipline. A disrespect for all forms of discipline has developed.
5. It may be the result of inconsistent discipline; too much rigidity alternated with too much leniency so that expectations are not established.

6. It may be the result of insufficient limits placed on behavior so that the pupil has never learned to respect control.
7. It may represent a message from the pupil for a desire for someone to establish needed power over him.

SUGGESTED APPROACHES:
1. Use a controlled discussion period to help verbalize what he admires, what he sees as a basis for power and achievement. Others can be enlisted in this discussion if group is carefully selected and kept small. Guide discussion to note how admired qualities are seen in action.
2. Help the pupil to distinguish feelings and actions that are unacceptable and help him to see the futility of certain disrespectful actions.
3. Do not ignore the individual's feelings. Try to make a sincere attempt to understand attitudes even if they are contrary to accepted attitudes.
4. Set consistent rules for use of impertinent language and certain definable disrespectful acts. Be certain there are no unreasonable expectations. Do not be too rigid on insignificant behaviors, but be firm and consistent in disciplining behaviors that have been mutually agreed upon as acceptable.
5. Reinforce acceptable behaviors by giving leadership activities.

Social Skill: BOISTEROUSNESS IN ENTERING CLASSROOM AND IN HALL]

Definition: Inability to control self so that class entry and exit and general school behavior is quiet and orderly.

Illustration: Pupil is able to move about in class and school in a quiet and restrained manner.

Anxiety States Contributing to Behavior:
1. Boisterousness, bragging and bossiness may be a way to establish identity among peers.
2. It may be a result of anger or frustration.
3. It may be a symptom of a neurosis based on over-dependency.
4. It may serve as a need for attention.

SUGGESTED APPROACHES:
1. Provide a well-structured environment and delineate expectations for orderliness and noise. Discuss appropriate behavior for certain typical and frequently repeated situations in the school. Involve the class in establishing rules of conduct.
2. Establish an opportunity for some individual and one-to-one experience for this pupil in order to identify attention needs.
3. Redirect and rechannel need for attention into more accepted forms. Give opportunity for leadership but be sure it is well-directed and appropriately monitored.
4. Reinforce immediately when controlled actions are shown and when improvement in noise level and boisterousness is apparent.

Social Skill: CRYING

Definition: Inability to control crying spells, to adapt well to new environments.

Illustration: Pupil has ability to adapt to new situations without undue stress, has become mature in independence.

Anxiety States Contributing to Behavior:
1. Crying spells may be symptomatic of overprotection, unmet dependency needs of the parents, possessiveness, over-solicitousness.
2. It may be related to over-sensitivity.
3. It may be a result or related to poor physical health.
4. It may be an adaptation of a manipulating personality.

SUGGESTED APPROACHES:
1. Try to establish rapport with the pupil without over-emphasizing the giving of special attention.
2. Be firm, keep self-control, but avoid harshness and punitive approaches.
3. Attempt to ignore the crying by focusing on another child. Reinforce the control of crying. Do not reinforce the crying behavior by giving a great deal of attention to the child when he is having a crying spell.

Social Skill: DECEIT: CHEATING, LYING, STEALING

Definition: Inability to give accurate representation of a situation, taking other's possessions, or other deceitful measures.

Illustration: Pupil refrains from falsehoods, stealing, and cheating. General trust is established.

Anxiety States Contributing to Behavior:
1. Deceit in its various forms may be due to an overstress of a certain achievement.
2. It may serve as a defense mechanism to give status.
3. It may be a means of ego enhancement.
4. It may be serving a need to retaliate against authority or to outwit an authority figure.
5. It may be related to an environmental insufficiency.

SUGGESTED APPROACHES:
1. The premium for the behavior must be removed. It will continue if it is a successful behavior. It will discontinue when the rewards are gone.
2. In general, do not be indifferent to all three manifestations of deceit: cheating, lying, stealing. However, do not use excessive punishment or this may enhance the behavior. If stealing is the problem, the stolen goods must be returned. Temptation must be minimized in every way by insuring adequate supervision and by leaving no valuables for easy access.
3. Do not accuse unless you have facts. Do not give pupil a chance to deny. Present with incontrovertible evidence. Unsubstantiated accusations will only reinforce child's self-image as a liar or a thief; it may generate self-righteous indignation.
4. Do not degrade the pupil; recognize the ego-building factors in the behavior.

Sometimes these can be undermined by simple commenting that you know something is untrue.

5. Cheating can be controlled by removing the need for it as well as the opportunity: Make expectations meet with abilities. Require original work and control this by monitoring many writing assignments. Also give opportunity for shared work by assigning group projects. Arrange classroom seating to minimize opportunity for copying.
6. Lying may be a symptom of a deeper unsatisfied need. Try to determine the need for changing the facts.

Social Skill: DESTRUCTIVENESS

Definition: Destroying public and school property, defiling or spoiling it and failing to care for own possessions.

Illustration: Pupil is able to care for school materials and personal possessions in appropriate fashion.

Anxiety States Contributing to Behavior:
1. Destructiveness may be symptomatic of some unmet dependency need, frustration due to unrealistic expectations or some emotional disturbance, leading to violent hostile impulses.
2. It may be a result of displaced anger and anxiety.
3. It may also be a result of failure to develop appropriate respect for other's property. Respect for property is a learned behavior.

SUGGESTED APPROACHES:
1. Provide opportunity for pupil to talk about antagonisms and hatreds. The hostile feelings must be accepted even though the appropriate behavior must be changed.
2. Avoid conveying amusement, tolerance or extraordinary reactions to discussion about actions. In no way should the actions of the child be reinforced.
3. Through one to one situation attempt to discern the emotional needs that lead to destructiveness.
4. Be firm, consistent, but supporting in constructive suggestions to curb such actions. Provide alternate activity. Teach respect through group discussion, role playing, and filmed lessons.

Social Skill: EXCESSIVE CLASSROOM MOVEMENT, HYPERACTIVITY

Definition: Inability to contain oneself, distractibility, excessive psychomotor activity.

Illustration: Pupil has established some control over actions.

SUGGESTED APPROACHES:
1. Do not scold or administer physical punishment for excessive activity.
2. Plan purposeful movement activities.
3. Be less rigid and restricted about expectations.
4. Shorten school assignments so that they can be easily completed.
5. Explore drug therapy through team assessment of ADHD.
6. Try to provide a center of reduced stimuli.

Social Skill: INSOLENCE, EXHIBITIONISM, COCKINESS FAILURE TO GIVE
    OTHER STUDENTS A CHANCE TO PARTICIPATE

Definition: Inability to restrain from participating constantly, and to exhibit precocity;
    will not take turns in acceptable fashion; a nonconformist.

Illustration: Pupil is able to give others opportunity to participate and to respond
    and can control himself when he knows the answer but is not asked.

SUGGESTED APPROACHES:
1. Do not use this pupil as an example even if he accomplishes an unusual task.
2. Give the pupil acceptance and importance on a personal one to one basis but
   avoid giving him whole class prominence.
3. Give him class leadership assignments only when he has earned the privilege
   by being socially acceptable (i.e., when he has learned to take turns and give
   opportunities to present ideas).
4. Do not assign this student any more unusual or spectacular projects than are
   given to the other students. Challenge him with special projects that he can
   do well but give him his recognition personally. Have him report in writing
   or a brief interview until he has learned restraint and control.
5. Develop peer acceptance through his ability to control his spontaneous out-
   bursts and his cockiness.
6. Avoid either/or situations. Do not back him into an emotional or physical
   corner; you may make him defy you to avoid embarrassment. Don't use
   ridicule, sarcasm, or confrontation. Use a firm voice but do not suggest
   coercion.
7. Keep word at all costs. Do not trade bribery for behavior. Be strict but be fair.

Social Skill: ISOLATION

Definition: Inability or refusal of the pupil to mingle with peers in acceptable social
    interchange.

Illustration: Pupil has ability to be involved in group activities in a satisfactory
    manner.

Anxiety States Contributing to Behavior:
1. Isolation may be a withdrawal from reality.
2. It may be the result of underachievement and frustration.

SUGGESTED APPROACHES:
1. Be sure that school work is appropriate for ability so that the child is not
   discouraged, or unchallenged because it is too simple.
2. Do not allow peer ridicule.
3. Find opportunities to give praise to help the pupil know his own worthy
   contributions.
4. Use personal interests of the pupil as cues to involve his enthusiasm and
   attention. When he becomes socially involved, reinforce immediately.
5. If isolation is severe, arrange a one to one situation with a carefully chosen
   class member in order to build confidence in his own ability to interrelate.

6. Do not force group activities until the child shows some ability to do some interrelating. However, plan group activities so that child is not left in the fringe areas consistently. Arrange some inadvertent and casual involvement. If he can handle some limited leadership in some activity, give this opportunity but handle it carefully so that there is no chance for failure.

Social Skill: OVER–DEPENDENCE

Definition: Failure to make independent decisions, to develop habits of responsibility.

Illustration: Development of self-confidence and independence from adults with the ability to make mature decisions.

Anxiety States Contributing to Behavior:
1. Anxiety and dependence may be the result of overprotection in the home environment.
2. It may be a manifestation of a low self-concept.
3. It may be the result of a lack of decision making opportunity.
4. Emotional needs of parents may be satisfied through child's dependency.

SUGGESTED APPROACHES:
1. Encourage friendship with an independent self-propelling pupil; however do this with monitoring. Avoid overwhelming.
2. Involve pupil in a special activity that has a special responsibility insuring that expectations are appropriate and can be met and that instructions are well understood. Let another child assist until confidence is gained; when confidence is established, put the pupil on his own.
3. Provide many opportunities for good ideas to be put into action. Give opportunity to be game leader, activity captain, etc.
4. Develop responsibility for independent action by giving pupil a chance to verbalize how he would solve certain problems. Then give him a chance to do this. Let him choose a team of helpers to carry out an idea that has been well-planned and monitor it well to avoid failure.
5. Encourage group recognition and approval of asserting behaviors.
6. Build confidence with affection and patience; enlist support of the group but do not let this child become the focus of envy because of the special attention he is getting.

Social Skill: POKING, SHOVING, HITTING, STRIKING OTHER CHILDREN]

Definition: Inability to control overt hostility in the school or on the playground.

Illustration: Pupil is able to stand in line and maneuver in the school without showing aggression to other students; and is not absorbed with violence in an unusual manner.

Anxiety States Contributing to Behavior:
1. Absorption with violence and overt activity at school may be a realistic pantomiming of pupil's hostile feelings.
2. It may be a reflection of his social environment where every conflict is met by fighting.

3. Bullying, cruelty to animals, interest in violent drawings and stories may be a representation of serious emotional disturbance.

SUGGESTED APPROACHES:
1. Give child many opportunities to resolve hostile feelings through discussion. This may be done on a one to one basis with a counselor or teacher or in small groups if this group is well-monitored and participants are carefully chosen.
2. Channel pupil's interest toward physical but non-hostile activities—football, wrestling, boxing; with younger pupils, many active running games provide an outlet for aggressive feelings.
3. Through role playing, wide use of appropriate literature, films and filmstrips encourage feelings of sympathy for underdog, animals, etc. Discuss cruelty, violence in a nonpunitive manner to develop understandings of protectiveness.
4. Use behavior modification techniques for specific acts of shoving, hitting, and poking.

Social Skill: REFUSAL TO PARTICIPATE BECAUSE OF UNVERBALIZED FEARS

Definition: Apprehension, tension, anxiety are preventing the child from active involvement in class activities.

Illustration: Pupil willingly participates in all academic and social activities involved in the school curriculum.

Anxiety States Contributing to Behavior:
1. Worry and fear may be related to a neurotic depression caused by loss of emotional support in the home.
2. A change of environment may precipitate concerns of popularity and acceptance.
3. It may be accompanied by crying, unusual sensitivity, moodiness, depression and irritability.

SUGGESTED APPROACHES:
1. Where possible remove peer pressure or pressure to participate until the situation is completely understood.
2. Give reassurance for each new event, or experience.
3. Be consistent in language and methods of approach.
4. Avoid unpredictability by making most events routine.
5. Eliminate apprehension by being certain pupil understands expectations and methods of procedure.
6. Familiarize child with new procedures by discussing them without building apprehension before he is exposed to them.
7. Involve child or pupil in discussion on cause for concern and anxiety.
8. Evaluate well after each new assignment or experience to insure that confidence has been built through the experience. Involve pupil in new experiences gradually.
9. Encourage spectator activities before complete participation.

10. If possible, provide a choice of assignments and be sure the choice is one that can provide a reasonable amount of success.
11. Intense participation should be alternated with free choice in order to dissipate tension.

Social Skill: REFUSAL TO FOLLOW DIRECTIONS

Definition: Stubborn rejection to do assignments or to follow directions.

Illustration: Pupil willingly completes assignments and follows instructions in doing classwork.

Anxiety States Contributing to Behavior:
1. Stubbornness may be a withdrawal or retreat from another problem.
2. It may be the result of low achievement and inappropriate expectations.
3. It can be compensatory or adaptive reaction.
4. It may be accompanied by some rebelliousness and overt hostility.

SUGGESTED APPROACHES:
1. Be sure expectations are reasonable. Do not ask pupil to do anything that would be demeaning or cause embarrassment.
2. If the problem is a result of low achievement be sure that remedial help is given. Find resources for individual help, tutorial aid, then work into a small group where achievement and expectations are appropriate.
3. If the child appears to reject instructions because he has not developed independent work habits appropriate for his level, he must be given responsibility gradually with well-outlined programming and his work must be well-monitored until he can take the responsibility himself. Demands must be adjusted to his rate of growth.
4. Be consistent and firm and give structure until pupil has developed mature habits. Inconsistency adds to confusion.
5. Present frequent opportunities to do something well that his peers can recognize.
6. When responsibility is given that is commensurate with his ability to handle it, then limit amount of adult interference so that he can judge his own independent decisions.

Social Skill: TANTRUMS

Definition: Inability to control temper, outbursting, irrational talk, and aggressiveness.

Illustration: Pupil can control frustrations and handle tensions in a controlled manner.

Anxiety States Contributing to Behavior:
1. Temper tantrums may result from inconsistent methods of control; or from conflicting standards among authority figures.
2. They may result from undue attention being given because of some physical disability or prolonged illness.
3. They may be related to over-critical nagging parents.
4. They may be symptomatic of apprehension or anger.

SUGGESTED APPROACHES:
1. Ignore the tantrum; convey to the pupil that the tantrum does not result in a victory. Do not reason during outburst.
2. Attempt to determine the cause or contributing factor and help to correct. Discussion should be made when the tantrum has subsided. If it is an expression of fear, give necessary comfort and reassurance. If expectations are unrealistic attempt to adjust the situation to make achievement and expectations more congruent.
3. The tantrum should not bring attention; if it is necessary to remove the pupil from the class because of a tantrum it should be done calmly without comment. It usually subsides without an audience.
4. Adults should model calm, considerate behavior; praise and reinforce during the absence of tantrums.
5. Try to prevent by laying groundwork for an activity that will give group support. Enlist support of group for efforts for this child.

Social Skill: TRUANCY

Definition: Purposeful school absence or tardiness.

Illustration: Regular and punctual attendance at class.

Anxiety States Contributing to Behavior:
1. Truancy may be a withdrawal approach to school related problems.
2. It may reflect an inadequacy in meeting demands of school.
3. It may be a result of environmental conditions that prevent adequate school achievement or school attendance.
4. It may reflect a poor self-image.
5. It may be the result of an overprotective, over-solicitous home.
6. It may be a manifestation of a school phobia.

SUGGESTED APPROACHES:
1. If necessary, adapt the school curriculum to meet the needs of the child so that school achievement is possible.
2. Plan a daily activity in which this pupil can find at least one measure of success and pleasure.
3. Devise a special project individualized for this pupil that is dependent on his presence for completion. He may have to feed the turtle, clean the bird cage, or change the aquarium water. He may be in charge of the tape recorder, or the filmstrip projector, or supervise opening exercises so that school does not function without his presence.
4. Find frequent opportunity for oral and written encouragement for satisfactory behaviors.
5. Develop positive and mature communication lines with the home to assist in decreasing dependency needs with the mother.

Social Skill: WHINING, RESISTANCE TO ROUTINE IN A NEGATIVISTIC MANNER

Definition: Inability to accept correction for unacceptable behavior without annoyance and refusal to show willingness to participate in class expectations.

Illustration: Child willingly accepts correction and class involvement.

Anxiety States Contributing to Behavior:

1. Whining may be a form of negativism, a resistance to routine that may be an avoidance of reality.
2. It may be an immature behavior manifestation.
3. It may be a kind of withdrawal from group participation.

SUGGESTED APPROACHES:

1. This pupil needs help in developing more satisfactory ways of meeting his needs. Through discussion, attempt to discover the basis for negativism. Set aside a definite time each day, 5–10 minutes, and give him undivided attention. Work towards terminating this gradually as time progresses.
2. Do not confront this pupil with a rigid order. Attempt to give a choice of activities, but be firm and consistent about expectations. Do not say "Will you please . . .".
3. Avoid negative attitudes among peers and insure a positive classroom climate to make negative feelings less prominent.
4. Urge parents to avoid confrontation but to use positive, reassuring manner.
5. Use behavior modification to eliminate specific whining incidents. Keep a list of complaints and help the pupil to eliminate these from his repertoire.

AUTHOR INDEX

267

SUBJECT INDEX